Making the African Continental Free Trade Agreement a Success

In 2019, African heads of state and governments launched in fanfare the African Continental Free Trade Agreement (AfCFTA), a historic agreement for economic transformation across the continent. But now comes the hard bit: how to make the agreement a success.

In this book, senior experts from across the world come together to provide a comprehensive analysis of the conditions needed for the AfCFTA to successfully spur economic development in Africa. It puts forward three foundations for success: demography dividend, digital economy, and economic diversification. In addition to trade policy, the book recommends that African policymakers should strengthen fiscal and monetary policy coordination, adopt and implement the appropriate regulatory environment, and build suitable connectivity infrastructure. The stakes are high. If implemented correctly, the book argues that the AfCFTA could speed up trade within Africa, which could double every five years. Success would mean growth, investment, changing trade patterns, jobs, economic transformation, poverty reduction, and a continental market for services.

Driven by concrete, evidence-based strategies for long-term growth, this book is an essential read for policymakers, development practitioners, economics researchers, and everyone with an interest in the future of Africa.

Albert G. Zeufack is the World Bank's Country Director for DRC, Angola, Burundi, and Sao Tome et Principe. Prior to his appointment he was Chief Economist for Africa from May 2016 to June 2022. He was also Practice Manager in the Macroeconomics and Fiscal Management Global Practice and leader of the World Bank-wide Community of Practice for the Management of Natural Resources Rents. His main research interest is in the micro-foundations of macroeconomics.

Fulbert Tchana Tchana is a World Bank Lead Country Economist. Since joining the Bank in 2013, he has worked on analytical, advisory, capacity-building, and lending operations in the Middle East and Africa. He supported these countries in the areas of economic modeling, growth and productivity analytics, economic and trade diversification, oil revenue management, subsidy reform, and regional integration. Before joining the Bank, his previous positions included Economist for Cameroon's Ministry of Finances and Assistant Professor of Economics at the University of Cape Town, South Africa.

Aly Sanoh is Senior Economist in the Poverty and Equity Global Practice of the World Bank. His work focuses on understanding the drivers of poverty and inequality reduction in the Sahel countries. He has held positions in the Office of the Chief Economist of the Africa Region, where he conducted macroeconomic and microeconomic analyses for Africa's Pulse.

Making the African Continental Free Trade Agreement a Success

Pathways and a Call for Action

**Edited by
Albert Zeufack,
Fulbert Tchana Tchana,
and Aly Sanoh**

Routledge
Taylor & Francis Group

LONDON AND NEW YORK

Designed cover image: Ketut Agus Suardika © Getty

First published 2024
by Routledge
4 Park Square, Milton Park, Abingdon, Oxon OX14 4RN

and by Routledge
605 Third Avenue, New York, NY 10158

Routledge is an imprint of the Taylor & Francis Group, an informa business

British Library Cataloguing-in-Publication Data
A catalogue record for this book is available from the British Library

ISBN: 978-1-032-59851-2 (hbk)
ISBN: 978-1-032-59847-5 (pbk)
ISBN: 978-1-003-45656-8 (ebk)

DOI: 10.4324/9781003456568

Typeset in Times New Roman
by Newgen Publishing UK

To the youth of the African continent and the diaspora, we hope this book inspires and guides you in building a resilient and thriving Africa.

Contents

Figures

Tables

Boxes

About the editors and contributors

Editors

Albert G. Zeufack, Country Director for DRC, Angola, Burundi, and Sao Tome et Principe, the World Bank

Aly Sanoh, Senior Economist in the Poverty and Equity Global Practice, the World Bank

Fulbert Tchana Tchana, Lead Country Economist, the World Bank

Contributors

Vincent Belinga, Sr. Economist, the World Bank

Souleymane Coulibaly, Lead Economist, the World Bank

Théophile Bougna, Economist, the World Bank

Amal Nagah Elbeshbishi, Professor Mansoura University, Egypt; Sr. Economist, UNECA

Mohamed Coulibaly, HEC Montréal, Canada

Tendai Gwatidzo, Associate Professor at the University of The Witwatersrand's School of Economics and Finance, Johannesburg, South Africa

Woubet Kassa, Economist, the World Bank

Constant Lonkeng Ngouana, Deputy Division Chief, the IMF

Mama Keita, Regional Director, UNECA

Angella Faith Montfaucon, Economist, the World Bank

Kolobadia Ada Nayihouba, Université de Montréal, Canada and consultant at the World Bank

Pegdéwendé Nestor Sawadogo, Consultant the World Bank & Lecturer at the Université Clermont Auvergne

Natnael Simachew Nigatu, Consultant at the World Bank and visiting scholar at Purdue University, USA

Witness Simbanegavi, Lead Economist, South African Reserve Bank

Clarence Tsimpo, Sr. Economist, the World Bank

Komi Tsowou, Regional Advisor—AfCFTA, UNDP Regional Service Centre for Africa

Foreword

I am thrilled to present *Making the African Continental Free Trade Agreement a Success: Pathway and Call for Action,* a book supporting the successful implementation of the AfCFTA to benefit the development of the African continent.

The book argues that the successful implementation of AfCFTA will have a far-reaching impact beyond its economic and distributional consequences. Successful integration will lead to structural change stemming from regional integration within Africa and changing trade patterns.

The book states that the AfCFTA success is about growth and redistribution; most importantly, it is about the free movement of people and the structural transformation stemming from deeper trade integration within Africa. Hence, it requires assessing critically and renegotiating existing trade agreements between Africa as a bloc and the rest of the world. Success means the AfCFTA has a positive impact on economic transformation, jobs, and poverty reduction. It also means that the AfCFTA creates a continental market for services. It is an agenda the Secretariat under my leadership is championing.

The authors highlight three foundations to achieve success: demography, digital, and diversification. First, Africa's demographic dividend may start to pay off soon. Today, the median age in Africa is 18 years, compared to more than 30 in other continents. By 2050, Africa will make up almost twice the young population of South Asia, East Asia, and Oceania combined. Africa could leverage its young population and global demand for natural resources to spur economic growth. Second, Digital trade is the next most significant opportunity for Africa. It offers opportunities for people at the bottom of the pyramid who can sell their products locally or across borders. This cross-border trade in Africa has great potential, given the AfCFTA prospects for harmonized low tariffs. Third, Africa exports less than it imports from other countries. This large imbalanced trade relationship must be addressed, and the AfCFTA is a step in the right direction. Rebalancing trade towards emerging markets over time, increasing intra-Africa trade, and improving trade export sophistication is needed. Success in economic and further trade diversification will lie in the ability of African countries to integrate regional and global value chains.

I commend the authors' call for action to achieve success. The book calls on African policymakers to take action to strengthen fiscal and monetary policy coordination, adopt and implement the appropriate regulatory environment, and build suitable connectivity infrastructure. Regarding fiscal and monetary policy coordination and harmonization, the focus should be on tax and exchange rate policies within the continent to avoid competitive tax breaks or devaluation/depreciation, leading to a race to the bottom. Efforts should be made to reduce within-continent financial transaction fees. Regarding the regulatory framework, the AfCFTA will depend on African policymakers developing and implementing industrial, competition, and trade policies that support manufacturing value-addition in the continent and intra-Africa trade and developing appropriately empowered institutions to develop and implement supra-national policies. Also, a successful AfCFTA will lead to the construction of relevant continental transport infrastructure (roads, ports, airways, waterways, and other intermodal connectors) and IT infrastructure (optic fiber). Continental policy to optimize the installation of optical fiber across the country or coordination to acquire satellites will be critical.

This book, written by world-class experts with deep knowledge of the intricacies of African economies, will be instrumental as the AfCFTA becomes a reality with a tangible impact on the well-being of the African population.

Wamkele Keabetswe Mene
Secretary-General of the African Continental Free Trade Area

1 Making the AfCFTA a success

Potential, pathways, and call for action[1]

Albert G. Zeufack, Fulbert Tchana Tchana, and Aly Sanoh

1.1 Introduction

In June 2019, African heads of state and governments launched in fanfare the African Continental Free Trade Agreement (AfCFTA), a "historic" initiative. The Agreement is already in force among many African Union members, and works are currently going on to support its implementation. They are focused on defining the set of rules that each participant's country will use at customs and on which goods trade should be based.

How can Africa leverage the AfCFTA for economic transformation by 2063? Transformation means moving from subsistence agriculture to higher productivity in manufacturing and services. To make the AfCFTA a success, there needs to be a clear understanding that it is not only about trade and poverty reduction but also about investment, job creation, and economic transformation.

Covid-19 has brought back the issue of African economic transformation to center stage. The need for Africa to be able to manufacture its vaccine shows how critical is the success of the AfCFTA. The countries involved in the AfCFTA need to produce vaccines for themselves. Developing countries with few resources cannot tolerate losing market share, especially when generating less revenue. Covid-19 is just one example of shock that has illustrated the lack of capacity on the continent to manage its destiny in the face of frequent shocks.

Climate change is an opportunity for economic transformation. Value addition to green minerals and industrialization can go hand in hand. It can solve the problem of over-reliance on raw material exports. The AfCFTA can be a driver for creating technological innovations. Africa needs the resources to discern the best technologies while at the same time producing its own. It is essential to have technological autonomy to determine the future course of development. Trade policy can be used as a tool to achieve sustainable development.

"Making the AfCFTA a Success" is a contribution to support the AfCFTA with new findings and proposals on how to successfully implement the AfCFTA to the benefit of the development of the continent. It argues that the successful implementation of the AfCFTA will have a far-reaching impact beyond economic and distributional consequences. Successful integration will lead to structural change stemming from regional integration within Africa and changing trade patterns.

DOI: 10.4324/9781003456568-1

The book documents that historically Africa's intracontinental trade is larger than the share of intraregional trade (see Lonkeng in Chapter 2 of the book). Hence, trade patterns suggest that intra-African trade is greater than the sum of its parts as official trade statistics tend to underestimate it given the informality of cross-border exchanges (see Bouet et al. 2018). Therefore, it establishes that the AfCFTA can speed up trade within Africa, which could double every five years. It also documents that i) greater economic and social benefits from participating in the global value chain (GVCs) are achieved when investments in skills are in line with comparative advantages; ii) greater gaps in the supply of critical technical and advanced skills, including STEM and ICT-related skills and skills requirements for backward participation in GVCs in agribusiness, manufacturing, digital economy, and logistics (see Belinga and Nayihouba in Chapter 11 of the book).

The remainder of this chapter defines what should be considered a success for the treaty, then on what the potential success will be based, and finally makes a call for reform and action to achieve the needed success.

1.2 What would success look like?

Ultimately, success is about growth and redistribution; most importantly, it is about the free movement of people and the structural transformation stemming from deeper trade integration within Africa and changing trade patterns. This would require revamping established trade agreements between Africa as a bloc and the rest of the world. Therefore, the African Growth and Opportunity Act (AGOA) and Everything But Arms (EBA) will have to be revisited while considering a free trade agreement with Asia. The AU should engage the US, the EU, China, and other major emerging markets for a better trade agreement that will leverage economies of scale provided by the newly formed single market of 1 trillion dollars and 1 billion people.

Success means the AfCFTA has a positive impact on jobs and economic transformation as well as poverty reduction.[2] The review simulations by Keita in Chapter 3 of the book indicated that the AfCFTA could significantly contribute to long-term growth. For example, the implementation of the Agreement could make the continent's GDP in 2035, 5.5% higher than the level expected without the AfCFTA (Chauvin et al. 2016; Vanzetti et al. 2018, and Saygili et al. 2018). Specifically, in the 10 years preceding the full implementation of the Agreement, the level of GDP could be increased by 0.5 to 5% each year. Simulations also identify other economic impacts of the AfCFTA including an increase in intra-Africa's exports, an increase in Africa's exports to the rest of the world (both will concern mainly products from the manufacturing and agriculture sectors), job creation, welfare gains, and poverty reduction.[3] However, all the existing studies are also very clear that the realization of the gains is strictly conditional on substantial efforts in favor of trade facilitation and the removal of non-trade barriers (NTBs).

The AfCFTA could lead to the reduction of the number of poor substantially in a 10-year horizon. The simulations in Chapter 4 of the book (Tsimpo, Sanoh, and Coulibaly) show that the AfCFTA could reduce the poor by up to 1/3 in an optimistic scenario and about 10% in a pessimistic scenario. Under the pessimist scenario, the AfCFTA will reduce extreme poverty headcount by a bit less than 2 percentage points, corresponding to about 19 million people lifted out of poverty. These numbers could improve substantially under the most optimistic scenario, with 131 million people lifted out of poverty thanks to the AfCFTA. The latter corresponds to a reduction of 12 percentage points in the extreme poverty headcount. This reduction stems from the capacity of the Agreement to generate long-term growth, boost intra-African trade, foster value addition and expansion in the agriculture and manufacturing sectors, and enhance market access. These cumulative effects will increase productivity and income in the agriculture sector, which is, for now, the biggest employer in most African economies, with more than half the workers (see Beegle and Christiaensen 2019; Christiaensen and Hill 2019). The benefits of the AfCFTA will only be effective if governments strive to enhance the productive capacities in the agriculture sector to ensure that supply meets the increased demand in agriculture and manufactured products that will come with the AfCFTA.

Finally, success means that the AfCFTA creates a continental market for services. Almost all Regional Economic Communities (RECs) in Africa focus on goods, and they all lack relevant provisions for liberalizing services trade between member countries and the flow of investment. Hence, regional integration under the AfCFTA should also cover services, investment, and competition policy (see Kassa and Sawadogo in Chapter 6 of the book). The multiplicity of rules across RECs and the distinction with the AfCFTA rules is a big challenge. Countries need to develop strategies to maximize the gains from existing RECs while restricting the costs of divisions in regulations and rules governing each REC in the transition to the AfCFTA. The AfCFTA must avoid becoming one of the overlapping RECs rather than the all-encompassing Free Trade Agreement (FTA).

1.3 Three foundations to achieve success: Demography, digital, and diversification

Demographic dividend

Africa's demographic dividend may start to pay off soon. Today, African economies are at a unique juncture: demography is in their favor. The median age in the whole of Africa is 18 years, compared with 31 in Asia, 35 in North America, and 42 in Europe. Some 628 million Africans are aged under 24 and, by the year 2050, that figure is expected to jump by half to 945 million. It will make up almost twice the young population of South Asia and South-East Asia, East Asia, and Oceania combined. They can take advantage of a relatively young population and global demand for natural resources to spur high economic growth. This will improve lifestyles across the continent. It will also lead to more jobs, better education and healthcare, and prosperity.

It is essential to provide critical skills to the African population to leverage the benefit of demographic dividend. Critical skills are needed for the AfCFTA to be a game changer for the continent's economic integration and transformation (IMF 2019; Belinga and Nayihouba in Chapter 11 of this book). Chapter 11 of the book shows that the free movement of goods and services across the continent following the suppression of tariffs and non-tariff barriers will create opportunities for further participation in backward global value chains (GVCs) or new continental and regional value chains development. Indeed, most African economies produce primarily commodities for further processing in other countries. A limited number of countries are engaged in the production of limited manufacturing products. Participating in and positioning through these value chains depends critically on countries' workforce skills levels. The book documents substantial skills gaps and cross-countries disparities in several critical technical advanced skills necessary for the positioning into the higher segments of the value chains, specifically in STEM and ICT. In the future, Africa should take a series of interrelated policy interventions to upgrade and close the existing skills gap. Policies should aim to improve access and outcomes of education and training systems, harmonize education systems, ensure recognition of academic credentials, and ease skilled workforce mobility across the continent by implementing the African passport and putting in place incentives to attract the skilled African diaspora.

Digital economy

Digital trade is the next biggest opportunity for Africa. Digital trade means conducting trade digitally with mobile phones and tablets. It offers opportunities for youth and women at the bottom of the pyramid who can sell their products locally or across borders. This cross-border trade in Africa has huge potential, given the AfCFTA prospects for harmonized low tariffs. The time is right for digital trade as mobile phone penetration in Africa is high, 95% in 2020.

The main leverage in the digital economy is people and their skills. Therefore, an AfCFTA strategy focused on developing human and institutional capacity will be valuable to Africa. The youth, representing about 60 percent of the population, are Africa's most precious asset in a competitive world of digital trade. They can be leveraged into a skilled and innovative workforce to achieve inclusive growth and development with new sources of job creation (see Belinga and Nayihouba, Chapter 11 of this book). With 375 million young Africans entering the labor market by 2030, it is critical to ensure the widespread availability of digital skills that can benefit both individuals and businesses.

Mobile money technology is becoming more common in Africa.[4] There are almost 400 million registered mobile money accounts in Africa, and 145 million are active accounts. In addition, Africa uses more mobile banking than all other developing regions put together (African Union Commission (AUC) and OECD 2018), making Africa's Digital Financial Services (DFS) market look very promising. Mobile financial services have become a major part of the African banking system. They go beyond just payments and bank accounts to include savings, loans, investments, and insurance, focusing on cashless economies. Digital regional payment systems are changing how businesses conduct cross-border trade by reducing costs and time (i.e. COMESA Regional Payment and Settlement System, East African Payments System, SADC Integrated Regional Electronic Settlement System). At the continental level, a couple of payments and settlement platforms are also under development, such as the ones by UPU and Afreximbank (African Union 2020).[5]

Digital trade and transactions in Africa are rapidly growing and will contribute to the intra-African trade agreement. Increasing infrastructure and deploying the right policies for e-commerce enables companies to market their products and receive payments. International buyers will be able to participate in the market by paying and making purchases, and the scale of the market will increase as a result. Governments are turning to digital channels to deliver public services. Examples are visa processing and issuance, civil registration, tax payments, and tendering. Trade portals allow businesses to easily find trade information, while single windows streamline completing formalities, reducing the time and cost of clearing goods at ports (African Union 2020).

Africans are often without legal identification. African-centered ID systems are fragmented, and many people have no way of proving their identity to the law or service providers. Given Africa's growing population, many people struggle to get the identification they need to vote, receive government benefits, or simply benefit from services or trade. Currently, about 542 million Africans do not have any form of identification. Around 95 million children under five have never had their births recorded, and 120 million children do not have a birth certificate. An AfCFTA digital identity system can spur innovation and entrepreneurship by reducing transaction costs and improving products' traceability (African Union 2020).

Diversified trade and economy

Africa imports more from outside than it exports. This imbalanced trade relationship needs to be addressed, and the AfCFTA is a step in the right direction (Luke and Macleod 2019). Rebalancing trade towards large emerging markets over time, increasing intra-Africa trade, and improving export sophistication is needed. African nations mostly traded along with colonial ties immediately after independence. But today, large emerging markets play a more prominent role in Africa's exchanges, reflecting a steady diversification of Africa's import and export markets. For instance, the share of Africa's exports directed to the European Union more than halved between the mid-'80s and 2020, dropping from about 60% to below 30%. The diversification in Africa's trade partners occurred to the benefit of large emerging market economies, especially China, and to some extent Brazil, Russia, and India. Similar trends are observed in imports, with African countries increasingly seeking alternative markets to source their consumption and investment needs. The shift away from European countries also supported increased trade among African nations.

One byproduct of the diversification in Africa's trade partners has been a steady increase in intra-Africa trade over time, especially, intra-Sub-Sahara Africa (SSA)—which rose from less than 5% of total trade in the early '60s to about

20% in 2020. The surge in intra-SSA trade has generally been stronger than that observed in other regional blocs worldwide. Exports among SSA countries as a share of total regional exports have surpassed a similar ratio in ASEAN5. They are now at par with the AfCFTA, from a significantly lower level just half a century ago.

Success in economic and further trade diversification will lie in the ability of African countries to integrate GVCs. Because those production networks are typically geared towards relatively complex goods, Africa's readiness to position itself in complex production chains will depend on its ability to manufacture products with high value-added content (see Songwe 2019). Two pieces of evidence suggest that this is achievable. First, Kassa and Sawadogo, in Chapter 6 of the book show that export sophistication is positively correlated with the level of development. Second, and relatedly, many African countries are quite close to the predicted sophistication frontier based on their initial level of development (proxied by GDP per capita) for the years for which data is available (1997–2007). Data indeed suggest that export sophistication improved in all sub-regional blocs in Africa over the 10 years for which data is available. The speed of sophistication surpassed many large economies, partly reflecting the low initial base.

The AfCFTA should learn from RECs' experience to succeed in economic diversification. Most of the RECs in Africa have not achieved their goals of expanding regional trade and creating a network of trade and production structures that enhances the spillovers from economies of scale and larger connected markets. The AfCFTA faces the same challenges that served as barriers to RECs' success. Significant challenges stand in the way of transforming the economies of its members through increased trade and integration in services, infrastructure, communications, and other spheres of economic activity. These range from building the necessary institutions to carve out conducive agreements and implementing them, to realizing them through national and regional strategies that require significant investment in resources and political commitment. To realize the objectives of the AfCFTA and transform the continent, three lessons are worth noting.

- First, it would take more than tariff liberalization to make the AfCFTA successful. Effective economic integration is mainly about removing the key trade barriers and reducing the direct and indirect costs of trading across borders. These include regulatory frameworks, the state of regional infrastructure and logistics, the efficiency of borders and customs operations, and the quality of complementary services to trading both within and across borders.
- Second, high fragmentation and thick borders make regional integration both necessary and challenging. With a population size slightly smaller than either China or India, Africa is home to 54 countries, more than any other continent. The high level of fragmentation presents a significant geopolitical challenge for the AfCFTA and poses additional costs to African economies. The stark fragmentation that characterizes Africa, geographically and in economic size and disparity, and the associated costs is one of the key reasons why continental integration is even more important to troubleshoot the continent's economy.

- Third, it is crucial to avoid shallow trade agreements and sticky transitions from RECs to the AfCFTA. Almost all RECs in Africa focus on goods and lack relevant provisions for liberalizing services trade between member countries as well as the flow of investment. RTAs in other parts of the world have a relatively higher number of RTAs with services and investment provisions, while SSA has the lowest number. Continental integration under the AfCFTA should cover services, investment, and competition policy in addition to goods. Because the free flow of investment and services is essential in facilitating the emergence of regional value chains, increasing economic diversification, and spurring growth.

The AfCFTA should also build on AGOA and EBA (two landmark non-reciprocal preferential trade agreements (NRPTA) extended by the US and EU to some African countries) and on trading with Asia to boost greater economic diversification. Kassa and Coulibaly (2019) found that most countries registered gains in exports due to AGOA. It found that much of the gains are attributed to commodity exports such as petroleum, mineral, and agricultural products, whose prices are volatile in the global market. Some countries managed to expand into manufacturing and other industrial goods. Despite the non-existence of trade agreements between Asia and Africa, the trade relationship between the two continents has increased substantially over the last two decades. Exploiting the AfCFTA to increase south-south cooperation would increase trade values and potentially the complexity of the products.

1.4 Call for action to achieve success

How best to leverage these foundations to achieve success? In addition to political economy, changing geopolitical context, and trade policy, African policymakers should strengthen fiscal and monetary policy coordination, adopt and implement the appropriate regulatory environment, and build suitable connectivity infrastructure.

Fiscal policy coordination and harmonization will be critical

To strengthen integration and expand African firms' participation in the continental value chain, a reduction in income and profit tax rates would be needed. This should be compensated by the enlargement of the tax base, strengthening fiscal administration, and increasing indirect taxes and property taxes. In Chapter 7 of the book Tchana argues that efforts should be made to harmonize external tariffs for all African countries to avoid downward tax competition and foster greater cooperation. There is a need to mobilize enough revenue to provide public investment in connectivity infrastructure, and social spending in education, health, and social protection. Revenue mobilization efforts should focus more on the increase of indirect taxes and the tax base. These efforts should be adapted to the country's participation level in the continental and global value chain.

Attention should be paid starting from now on exchange rate policy within the continent to avoid competitive devaluation and depreciation, leading to a downward spiral. Efforts should be made to ensure that the exchange rate keeps countries and the entire region competitive globally. Reforms are needed to ensure that the banking sector finances the sufficiency of the private sector. Additional reforms to ease the movement of capital between countries will support continental and global foreign direct investments (FDI). Lonkeng and Tchana, in Chapter 8 of the book, consider the practicality of a common currency in Africa, contrasting the potential trade benefits of a currency union against the monetary policy constraints imposed by currently unsynchronized business cycles across the continent and find that a common currency could significantly boost intra-Africa trade. They conclude that at this stage, a monetary union is not a necessity, and they advocate for monetary policy coordination and harmonization.

Which regulatory framework to the AfCFTA?

The AfCFTA will be dependent on African policy makers developing and implementing industrial, competition and trade policies that support manufacturing value addition in the continent and intra-Africa trade; and developing appropriately empowered institutions (e.g., providing political muscle to key continental institutions such as the African Union Commission) to develop and implement supranational policies. Attention should be given to i) incentivizing private investment and investing in infrastructure; ii) constituting a supranational competition authority, something akin to the European Competition Commission; and iii) developing a framework for inter-country transfers to address possible concerns about distributional injustice. According to Simbanegavi and Gwatidzo, in Chapter 12 of the book, the AfCFTA must not allow narrow national interests to trump the continental interests regarding the regulatory environment. They propose that: i) the AU Heads of State and Government empower the AU Commission with political muscle to drive the AfCFTA agenda, including the power to enforce implementation of agreed-upon protocols; ii) the AU harmonize competition laws and policies; starting with harmonizing policies in RECs and then harmonizing across the RECs; iii) the AU ensures competition commissions (or equivalents) are independent; iv) the AfCFTA Secretariat leads the development of a common trade policy framework, in partnership with the AU Commission; and v) the AfCFTA Secretariat develop and implement the framework for trade facilitation across African countries.

The Covid-19 pandemic showed Africa's pressing need for a modern and effective pharmaceutical industry. Currently, trade in pharmaceutical products between African countries is relatively small, due to low drugs production capacity but also to differences in the regulations of these countries relating to manufacturing, import, export, and distribution of pharmaceutical products. Attention should be given to i) adopting compulsory licensing of drugs; ii) pooling their resources and strengthening their capacity to manufacture the needed generic pharmaceutical products; and iii) adopting "parallel importation" as a way of increasing access to medications. There is a need for regional trading blocks to collaborate in harmonizing such regulations. Elbeshbishi, in Chapter 13 of the book, argues that the AfCFTA must be Trade-Related Intellectual Property Rights (TRIPS) compatible. The AfCFTA should be harnessed as a vehicle to strengthen Africa's ability to ensure TRIPS flexibilities are fully utilized to enable local production and access to essential medicines. African institutions such as the AU and the AfCFTA Secretariat can play an important role in coordinating efforts and guiding appropriate specialization strategies based on comparative advantage. The AU should also network with its members to negotiate bulk procurement of raw materials for generic production since the costs will be lower than what countries can negotiate individually.

Besides, special attention should be given to the regulation of natural resources. Unprocessed commodities still dominate the bulk of Africa's exports. Yet, continental markets provide opportunities for value addition in resource-rich countries and the establishment of regional value chains (RVCs) in various sectors ranging from agricultural food to value-added mining products. The African Continental Free Trade Area is expected to address the fragmentation of African economies and improve their competitiveness. Tsowou, in Chapter 10 of the book, argues that regulatory efforts are required to establish wide-reaching RVCs; effective implementation of the AfCFTA should be complemented by concerted efforts to address non-tariffs barriers to production and trade, especially infrastructure bottlenecks. Interconnecting regional trade and production hubs and AfCFTA markets efficiently start with the domestication of the Agreement and effective implementation of its provisions.

Connectivity infrastructure

A successful AfCFTA will lead to the construction of relevant continental connectivity infrastructure. Transport infrastructure (roads, ports, airways, waterways, and other intermodal connectors) serves as a crucial link for this trade and plays an important role in boosting countries' economic growth. Despite both the substantial infrastructure gaps and the overall deficit in financing for infrastructure, especially in transport, continental integration remains a critical ingredient that must be reconciled to ensure increased intra-Africa trade through the successful implementation of the AfCFTA.[6] Bougna, in Chapter 9 of the book, argues that attention should be given to i) solving inefficiencies in building infrastructure and effectively implementing private financing and Private-Public Partnerships throughout the process of Africa's regional transport infrastructure network development; ii) designing a broader inter-modal and competitive transport system which will contribute to the regional integration and socio-economic development of the continent; iii) prioritizing the construction of trans-African highways; and iv) increasing the collaboration with Latin America and Southeast Asia regions in building infrastructure.

In addition to goods' transport infrastructure, IT infrastructure will be needed to reap the full potential of the continental market for services. Efforts to improve mobile phones and, most importantly, access to the internet by extending optic fiber infrastructure are essential. Continental policy to optimize the installation of optic fiber across the country and coordination to acquire other infrastructure such as satellites will be critical. Finally, the harmonization of the tax policy of digital infrastructure will be needed. Moreover, Africa needs Data Center Infrastructure designed to host mission-critical servers and computer systems with fully redundant subsystems.[7] The main benefit of this infrastructure localization on the continent will be cost savings on international connectivity and the latency decrease that will deliver a better application performance. The second interest is respect for data sovereignty, even though Africa is at the moment less restrictive, soon it will be necessary to ensure the localization of all personal data of Africa's citizens.

The lack of digital security impedes interaction and better trade. Digital security creates barriers for individuals, businesses and governments to communicate freely about intellectual property, intellectual property rights, financial information and other sensitive information. The use of strong encryption is increasing in Africa, but the lack of high-quality end-to-end encryption will remain a significant challenge to Africa's digital transformation efforts. As mobile access increases across Africa, there is a growing demand for secure and reliable ways for citizens to exercise their rights on a range of issues related to health, good governance and identity management (including income tax), communication with government organizations and the ability to interact with other citizens.

Notes

1 The views and opinions expressed in this paper are those of the authors and do not necessarily reflect the views or positions of their employers or institutions.

2 According to Echandi et al. (2022), the AfCFTA is likely to attract cross-border investment by eliminating tariff and non-tariff barriers and replacing the existing patchwork of bilateral and regional trade deals with a single, unified market. Investors in any one of 55 member countries will have access to a continent of 1.3 billion people with a combined GDP of US\$3.4 trillion. Integration in global and regional value chains offers a further magnet for FDI and the jobs, investment, and know-how that FDI brings.

3 Public revenue losses are also expected but will be minimal.

4 For example, Kenya is ranked 26th worldwide in the Digital Financial Inclusion Rankings.

5 The UPU–Ecom@africa initiative aims at establishing an integrated, inclusive and innovative e-commerce ecosystem provided by designated Operators through e-commerce (online) platforms using the postal network and products for cross-border logistics, deliveries, returns and payments, while the one for Afreximbank is expected to allow cross-border payments wherein both the sender and receiver transact in local currencies.

6 The book argues that AGOA and EBA implementation showed the need to establish adequate infrastructure, a meaningful reduction in trade barriers, ICT development, maintenance of effective institutional and regulatory frameworks (Coulibaly et al., Chapter 5 of the book).

7 Currently, a very large part of the IT content consumed in Africa comes from outside and Data Centers are the digital infrastructure that will allow the development of local digital industry.

References

African Union Commission (AUC)/OECD. 2018. Africa's Development Dynamics 2018: Growth, Jobs and Inequalities. AUC, Addis Ababa/OECD Publishing: Paris. https://doi.org/10.1787/9789264302501-en

African Union. 2020. The Digital Transformation Strategy for Africa (2020–2030). Addis Ababa, Ethiopia. Available at https://au.int/sites/default/files/documents/38507-doc-dts-english.pdf

Beegle, K. and Christiaensen, L. eds. 2019. *Accelerating Poverty Reduction in Africa.* Washington, DC: World Bank. https://doi.org/10.1596/978-1-4648-1232-3.

Bouet, A., Pace, K. and J. Glauber. 2018. "Informal Cross-Border Trade in Africa: How Much? Why? And What Impact?" IFPRI Discussion Paper 01783, International Food Policy Research Institute.

Chauvin, D., Ramos, N., and Porto, G. 2016. "Trade, Growth, and Welfare Impacts of the CFTA in Africa." https://arodes.hes-so.ch/record/2006/files/Depetris-Chauvin_2017_t rade_growth_welfare.pdf

Christiaensen, L. and Hill, R. 2019. Poverty in Africa. https://doi.org/10.1596/978-1-4648-1232-3_ch1

Echandi, R., Maliszewska, M., and Steenbergen, V. 2022. *Making the Most of the African Continental Free Trade Area: Leveraging Trade and Foreign Direct Investment to Boost Growth and Reduce Poverty.* Washington, DC: World Bank. © World Bank. https://openknowledge.worldbank.org/handle/10986/37623 License: CC BY 3.0 IGO.

International Monetary Fund (IMF). 2019. "Is the African Continental Free Trade Area a Game Changer for the Continent?" Regional Economic Outlook: Sub-Saharan Africa Chapter 3 (October), International Monetary Fund, Washington DC.

Kassa, W. and Coulibaly, S. August 20, 2019. Revisiting the Trade Impact of the African Growth and Opportunity Act: A Synthetic Control Approach. World Bank Policy Research Working Paper No. 8993, Available at SSRN: https://ssrn.com/abstract=3440369

Luke, D. and Macleod, J. (Eds.). (2019). *Inclusive Trade in Africa: The African Continental Free Trade Area in Comparative Perspective* (1st ed.). Routledge. https://doi.org/10.4324/9780429401121

Saygili, M., Peters, R., and Knebel, C. 2018. "African Continental Free Trade Area: Challenges and Opportunities of Tariff Reductions." United Nations Conference on Trade and Development Research Paper 15, Geneva.

Songwe, V. 2019. "Intra-African Trade: A Path to Economic Diversification and Inclusion." Brookings Institution. Intra-African Trade: A Path to Economic Diversification and Inclusion (brookings.edu).

Vanzetti, D., Peters, R., and Knebel, C. 2018. "Non-tariff Measures: Lifting CFTA and ACP Trade to the Next Level." United Nations Conference on Trade and Development Research Paper.

2 Africa's trade patterns

Trends and benchmarking[1]

Constant Lonkeng Ngouana

2.1 Introduction

Africa's trade patterns have undergone significant shifts since political independence in the 1960s. This chapter puts those trends into perspective, benchmarking them against other regional blocs around the globe, including the ASEAN[2] Free Trade Area (AFTA), the European Union (EU), and the Southern Common Market (MERCOSUR).

The chapter highlights growing intra-Africa trade as one of the brightest spots of the African Continental Free Trade Area (AfCFTA). It also examines the composition of Africa's trade in comparison to other regional blocs, and in that context, the implications of Africa's growing population.

Many papers have analyzed Africa's trade landscape (see, e.g., International Monetary Fund (IMF) 2019, Lonkeng Ngouana 2012, and Songwe 2019, among others). Songwe (2019) argues that the AfCFTA offers a path to economic diversification and inclusion. IMF (2019) provides a comprehensive analysis of policies to foster regional trade integration. In delving into Africa's trade patterns, this chapter of the book departs from existing studies on Africa's trade along two important dimensions. First, it uses longer historical data, aggregating trade flows from the bottom up based on all bilateral flows since 1960 comparing the experience of Africa with that of other major regional blocs and contrasting the experiences of sub-regional arrangements within Africa. Second, by examining the composition of intra and extra-trade among different regional blocs, based on granular data on what countries trade among each other, the chapter identifies areas where there is potential for larger intra-Africa trade, including food and light manufacturing, considering Africa's growing population. The focus on food trade is particularly relevant in light of ongoing disruptions in supply chains and the ensuing threat to food security on the continent (see, e.g., World Bank 2021 and FAO, IFAD, UNICEF, WFP and WHO 2021).

The chapter documents that intra-Africa trade has grown faster *post-independence* than trade among member countries of other trade blocs around the globe. Moreover, intra-Africa trade has also surpassed intra-trade in its regional economic communities (RECs), which suggests that the AfCFTA could accelerate

DOI: 10.4324/9781003456568-2

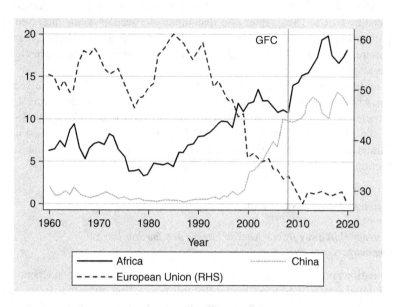

Figure 2.1 Diversification of Africa's trade partners (share in total Africa's exports).

Sources: IMF's Direction of Trade Statistics (DOTS) and author's calculations.

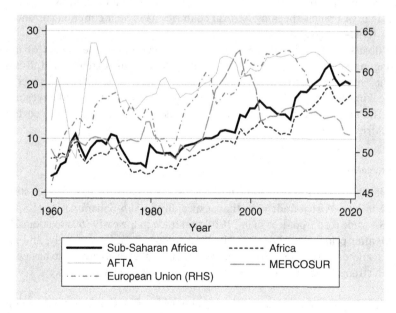

Figure 2.2 Intra-exports in selected regional blocs (% of total exports for each regional bloc).

Sources: IMF's Direction of Trade Statistics (DOTS) and author's calculations.

even further intra-Africa trade by reducing some of the potential inefficiencies introduced by RECs. The chapter also documents the secular continental trend of trade partner diversification, with a growing role for emerging market economies. Furthermore, the chapter documents a steady move toward more sophisticated products in Africa.

The remainder of the chapter is as follows: Section 2 documents the secular shifts in Africa's trade partners since independence, including the rising intra-Africa trade. Section 3 examines the current composition of Africa's trade—in comparison to other regional blocs—and, relatedly, the scope for increased intra-Africa trade in food and light manufacturing. Section 4 looks at export sophistication. Section 5 concludes and draws policy implications.

2.2 Who has Africa traded with historically?

2.2.1 A steady shift away from advanced Europe and towards large emerging markets over time

African nations mostly traded along colonial ties immediately after independence (see estimated gravity model in Chapter 6 of this book). Fast forward to today, large emerging markets play a more prominent role in Africa's exchanges, reflecting a steady diversification of Africa's import and export markets. For instance, the share of Africa's exports directed to the European Union more than halved between the mid-'80s and 2020, dropping from about 60% to below 30% (Figure 2.1). The decline in the share of Euro Area trade was even more dramatic, notwithstanding the fact that 14 French-speaking African countries have their common currency—the CFA franc—pegged to the euro.

The diversification in Africa's trade partners occurred to the benefit of large emerging market economies, especially China, and to some extent Brazil, Russia, and India. Similar trends were observed in imports, with African countries increasingly seeking alternative markets to source their consumption and investment needs. The shift away from European countries also supported increased trade among African nations.

2.2.2 Increasing intra-Africa trade

One spinoff of the diversification in Africa's trade partners has been a steady increase in intra-Africa trade over time, especially in Sub-Sahara Africa (SSA)—intra-SSA trade rose from less than 5% of total trade in the early '60s to about 20% in 2020, after peaking at about 24% in 2016 (Figure 2.2). Interestingly, and contrary to common perception, the surge in intra-sub-Saharan Africa trade has generally been stronger than that observed in other regional blocs worldwide:

- Exports among Sub-Saharan African countries as a share of total regional exports have surpassed the similar ratio in ASEAN5 and are now at par with AFTA, from a significantly lower level just half a century ago. Notwithstanding the overall positive developments for Africa, the decline that preceded the pandemic deserves some consideration—it should be averted to avoid the experience of the early 2000s which saw a prolonged decline in intra-Africa trade.

- Moreover, the size of intra-Africa trade is likely under-estimated, considering informal trade in some corridors, a mirror image of the large informality on the continent—official trade statistics are therefore likely to be a lower bound of the intensity of trade between African nations (see Bouet et al. (2018) on a review of efforts to measure informal cross-border trade in Africa).
- While intra-trade is still the highest in the European Union, reflecting an advanced level of economic integration, it lost some momentum in the 2000s, and partially recovered with the subsequent entry of new member countries. This integration is supported by a common currency in the case of the subset of Euro Area countries and convergence efforts by new member countries (see Chapter 7 of this book).

The observed disparity in intra-regional trade may reflect the extent to which member countries have similar levels of development (and taste) and/or operate similar production technologies. Interestingly, the share of intra-Africa exports surged in the wake of the global financial crisis (GFC), as demand collapsed in advanced economies. This suggests that intra-trade could be a prime tool for African nations to insulate themselves against economic shocks emanating from

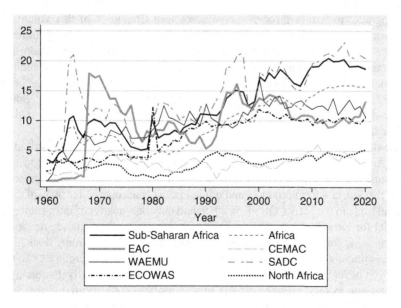

Figure 2.3 Intra-trade in regional blocs in Sub-Saharan Africa (% of total trade of each bloc).

Sources: IMF's Direction of Trade Statistics (DOTS) and author's calculations.

outside the region. Our computations based on data from the IMF's Direction of Trade Statistics (2021) and the IMF's World Economic Outlook (2021) suggest a negative correlation between the US output gap (proxy for the World's output gap) and intra-Africa trade, especially in bad times.

The rise in intra-Africa trade has not always been mirrored by trends everywhere on the continent, with some divergence among sub-regional blocs seemingly coinciding with the GFC (Figure 2.3). More generally, intra-trade has been particularly buoyant in the SADC, partly driven by regional trade with South Africa. While WAEMU-intra-trade has generally surpassed the broader ECOWAS', the CEMAC region has lagged in regional integration, notwithstanding the common currency, a structural issue that likely reflects a similar production structure (see Section 4). Notwithstanding those diverging trends, Figure 2.3 clearly suggests that Sub-Saharan Africa is greater than the sum of its parts—intra-SSA wide trade has generally stood above intra-trade in its sub-regional blocs.

2.3 What does Africa trade?

Consistent with its stage of development, food-related products, crude materials, and mineral fuels currently account for about 60% of Africa's exports (Figure 2.5). Manufacturing, machinery, and transport equipment combined account for only a third of Africa's exports. Interestingly, manufacturing is currently more prominent in intra-Africa trade than in Africa's trade with the rest of the World. This is a positive development to be leveraged going forward, considering the expanding middle class on the continent. Such exchanges will be facilitated by infrastructure upgrade, including through e-commerce (see Chapter 8 of this volume on infrastructure needs). Relatedly, Hagan (2021, *forthcoming*) provides quantitative evidence that intra-Africa trade fosters industrialization, significantly more than extra-trade, as the latter is heavily tilted towards goods with limited value addition. For instance, crude material and fuels and chemicals still accounted for just below half of Africa's total exports to the rest of the World in 2019. Moreover, limited intra-trade in the CEMAC region reflects the fact that crude oil is a major tradable for Chad, Cameroon, Equatorial Guinea, and Gabon.

The difference in the composition of intra and extra-trade is more striking in South American countries. MERCOSUR member countries indeed tend to trade more sophisticated products among themselves relative to what they export to the rest of the World—food products and crude materials accounted for 60% of extra-regional trade in the MERCOSUR in 2019, and only one-quarter of intra-trade. The potential for intra-Africa trade in essential manufacturing products seems large—manufacturing imports from outside Africa currently account for more than 22.5% of the continent's overall import bill. This suggests that African countries can reap the benefit of regional integration in the manufacturing space relatively quickly, as they continue to seek greater strategic integration into sophisticated global value chains (GVC). This is however not a one-size-fits-all—the strategy underpinning the balance of the export mix ultimately depends on the specific endowment of individual countries.

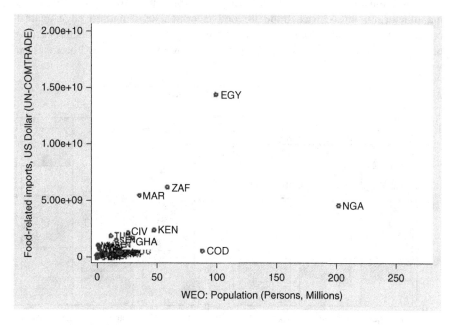

Figure 2.4 Population size and food imports in Africa.

Sources: UN-COMTRADE, IMF-WEO, and author's calculations.

There seems to be a strong case for fostering intra-Africa trade in food-related products:

- First, the potential is large, considering the demand side. For instance, Sub-Saharan Africa imported food—including products from the agroindustry—in excess of 5% of GDP in 2019, about three-quarters of which were purchased from outside the continent. Africa is quite unique in this "food trade imbalance." For example, the value of food imported from within South America was twice as large as the amount imported from outside the region; the overall import bill was much lower at less than 1.5 % of GDP, closer to food self-sufficiency. The split was near half-half for South East Asian nations in the same year.
- Second, the demand for food-related products on the continent is bounded to increase dramatically over time as African countries seek to feed their growing populations. Figure 2.4 indeed depicts a strong positive association between population size and the food import bill across Africa. For instance, the food import bill was as high as US$15 billion (4.2% of GDP) in Egypt in 2019 and about US$5 billion (1.2% of GDP) in Nigeria.[3] To put things in perspective, the import food bills of Egypt and Nigeria were close to the GDP of Benin and Togo respectively in 2019.

In addition to these obvious macroeconomic benefits from trade in food and manufacturing, intra-Africa trade in food is critical as a natural edge against country-specific food supply shocks. These shocks—mostly weather-related—often pose a threat to food security; they could, by exerting upward pressure on

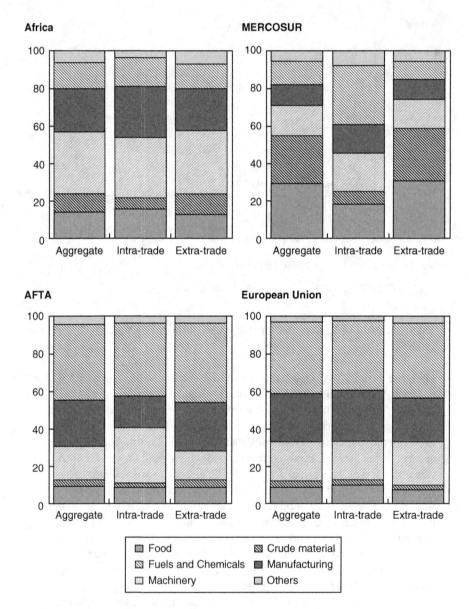

Figure 2.5 Composition of exports (% of total exports if each regional bloc, 2019).

Sources: UN-COMTRADE and author's calculations.

food prices, push far too many into undernourishment and poverty. In addition to intra-Africa trade, countries could consider strategic food reserves to cushion international food shocks. In any case, local production ought to play a key role towards self-sufficiency in food.

2.4 Potential in the horizon—convergence in export sophistication

As shown in Figure 2.6, one important dimension of the success of the AfCFTA will lie in the ability of member countries to integrate GVCs. Because those production networks are typically geared towards relatively complex goods, Africa's readiness to position itself in complex production chains will depend on its ability to manufacture products with high value-added content. Two pieces of evidence suggest that this is achievable. First, we find that export sophistication is positively correlated with the level of development. Second, and relatedly, many African countries are quite close to the predicted sophistication frontier based on their initial level of development (proxied by GDP per capita) for the years for which data is available (1997–2007) (Figure 2.7).

Data indeed suggest that export sophistication improved in all sub-regional blocs in Africa over the 10 years for which data is available. The speed of sophistication surpassed many large economies', partly reflecting the low initial base (see Figure 2.8).

2.5 Conclusion and policy implications

An historical look at Africa's trade patterns suggests important shifts in import and export markets *post*-independence. While African nations mostly traded along colonial ties immediately after independence in the '60s, significant shifts occurred over the past half-century, with large emerging economies such as China gaining more prominence at the expense of advanced Europe. Intra-Africa trade also increased dramatically during that time, surpassing South America and now at par with AFTA. These significant shifts suggest large opportunities ahead, as the level of income in low and middle-income countries converge towards advanced economies. In particular, the fast-growing Africa's population means a sustained demand for food going forward, and for manufacturing products for the expanding middle class—already, the bill of Africa's food imports from outside the region exceeded 5% of GDP in 2019. Alleviating constraints to trade on the continent (see IMF 2019) would position African countries to reap the continent's demographic premium. This not only provides a unique opportunity for Africa to achieve self-sufficiency in basic needs but is also a tool for countries on the continent to insulate themselves against idiosyncratic food supply shocks, including weather-related, as well as economic downturns in advanced economies. Our analysis also suggests that Africa's economy is larger than the sum of its parts and the AfCFTA, by reducing potential inefficiencies in existing RECs could foster intra-Africa trade.

The facts presented in this chapter suggest that, as policymakers on the continent continue to pursue integration in sophisticated global value chains with high

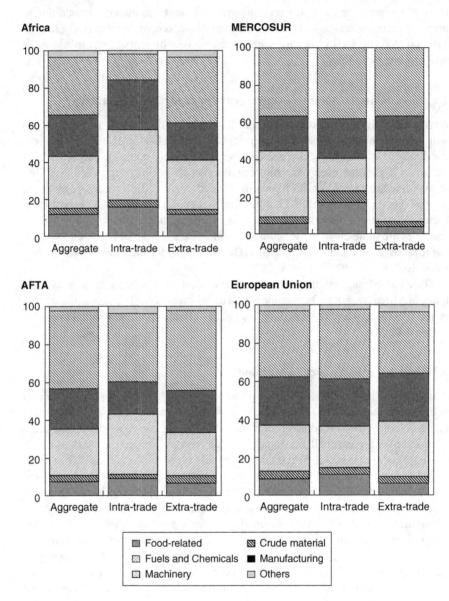

Figure 2.6 Composition of imports (import contribution for each regional bloc, 2019).

Sources: UN-COMTRADE and author's calculations.

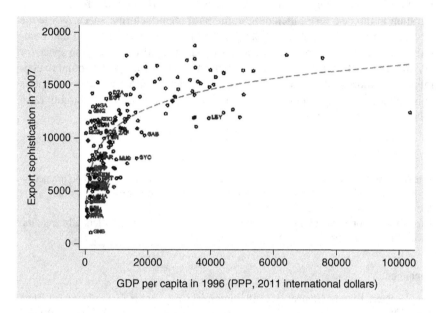

Figure 2.7 Convergence to the export sophistication frontier (ISO code of African countries marked).

Sources: CEPH, WHO, and author's calculations.

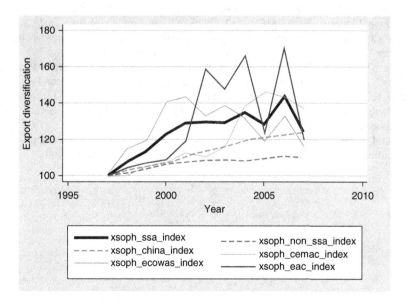

Figure 2.8 Comparing Africa export sophistication.

Note: *Xsoph* stands for export sophistication.

Source: CEPII and author's calculations.

value-added content, they should equally seek to reap the benefits from regional integration in the near term, including in the light manufacturing space. While the trade policy mix will ultimately depend on each country's endowment and comparative advantage, the opportunities ahead are large and diverse, leaving space for every country in a fast-growing continental market. Interestingly, data point to convergence in export sophistication, with notable progress in Africa. Many chapters of this volume elaborate on how Africa can leverage the AfCFTA to durably raise the living standards of its people.

Notes

1 The views and opinions expressed in this paper are those of the authors and do not necessarily reflect the views or positions of their employers or institutions.
2 Association of Southeast Asian Nations.
3 The cross-sectional representation insulates the relationship from potentially trending prices. Prices are expressed in US dollar for cross-country comparison.

References

Bouet, A., Pace, K., and Glauber, J. 2018. "Informal Cross-Border Trade in Africa: How Much? Why? And What Impact?" *IFPRI Discussion Paper 01783*, International Food Policy Research Institute.

FAO, IFAD, UNICEF, WFP and WHO. 2021. "The State of Food Security and Nutrition in the World 2021. Transforming Food Systems for Food Security, Improved Nutrition and Affordable Healthy Diets for All." Rome, FAO. https://doi.org/10.4060/cb4474en

Hagan, M.A. 2021. "Revisiting the Promises of South-South Trade." *Forthcoming*.

International Monetary Fund (IMF). 2019. "Is the African Continental Free Trade Area a Game Changer for the Continent?" *Regional Economic Outlook: Sub-Saharan Africa* Chapter 3 (October), International Monetary Fund, Washington DC.

Lonkeng Ngouana, C. 2012. "Exchange Rate Volatility Under Peg: Do Trade Patterns Matter?" *IMF Working Paper* 12/73, International Monetary Fund, Washington DC.

Songwe, V. 2019. "Intra-African Trade: A Path to Economic Diversification and Inclusion." Brookings Institution. Intra-African Trade: A Path to Economic Diversification and Inclusion (brookings.edu).

The World Bank. 2021. "Agriculture and Food." The World Bank, Washington DC. Agriculture and Food: Development News, Research, Data | World Bank.

3 Long-term growth impact of a well-functioning AfCFTA for the continent and by sub-region

A comparative analysis based on historical experience[1]

Mama Keita

3.1 Introduction

African countries aspire to long-term growth and prosperity. This is well expressed in "Agenda 2063", the long-term strategic framework adopted by African Heads of States in 2015 under the African Union's aegis to achieve sustainable development. Agenda 2063 has seven (7) aspirations, and the first of these reads as follows: "A Prosperous Africa, based on Inclusive Growth and Sustainable Development".

The signing of the AfCFTA, which is one of the 13 flagship projects identified by Agenda 2063 to materialize these aspirations, has raised tremendous hope both from public and private sector stakeholders, Africans and non-Africans. The two citations below attest to the faith of the private sector in the AfCFTA potential and its determination to make it work and take advantage of it (AfroChampion Initiative and the Africa Union, 2020).

> Afreximbank strongly believes that the AfCFTA will unleash a trove of investment opportunities for the private sector, both from outside and within Africa. There was however a need for an investment framework which covered the various layers of the integration process and that's what AfroChampions' "One Trillion Dollar Framework" does. It is just as important as the products like (i) the Pan-African Payment and Settlement System (PAPSS), and (ii)A Fund for Africa's Export Development (FEDA), which we are also rolling out to catalyse investments that will drive the AfCFTA.
>
> (Prof. Benedict Okey Oramah, President, Afreximbank)

> Only a few investors have noted the opportunities in Africa and they are exploiting that to make quite high returns. The AfCFTA Private Sector Investment & Financing Framework can break this cycle. We look forward to leveraging it to help bring Japanese investors to partner with African industrialists to realise tangible projects.
>
> (Masa Sugano, Representative in Africa, JETRO
> (Japan External Trade Organization))

DOI: 10.4324/9781003456568-3

The vivid interest in the AfCFTA's potential is also seen in the number of research papers that focus on its socio-economic potential. In the same vein, this chapter seeks to document the magnitude of the impact that the AfCFTA could have on long-term growth in Africa and to understand the necessary conditions for that to happen.

With a view to provide an analytical framework for understanding the potential of the AfCFTA to promote economic growth in Africa, the paragraphs below review the variables and mechanisms by which economic growth is generated and assess how the AfCFTA is likely to impact this outcome. According to the theoretical and empirical economic literature, prominently among the drivers of growth is productivity supported by technological and private sector development. Other drivers include human capital, infrastructure development, conducive business environments, capital market development, economic governance and related regulatory and legal systems, and trade openness. Economic diversification with the production of tradable and high-value-added goods is necessary. Kaldor (1967), Kuznets (1979), and Lin and Monga (2010) have established the determining role of expanding the manufacturing sector and related structural change to fasten economic growth and increase productivity. The role of the government is vital to promote adequate institutions, reforms, policies and strategies.

It must be emphasized that both trade openness and the development of manufacturing have empirically proven significant drivers of long-term growth. Trade openness increases imports and exports of goods and services and thereby permits the development of technology and the improvement of production processes. These in turn lead to increased productivity and faster economic growth. Trade openness also allows consumers, including the poor, to have access to cheaper goods and services, which result in enhanced purchasing power and living standards, with the potential to reduce poverty and sustain economic growth (World Bank, 2018a). The expansion of the manufacturing sector permits higher economies of scale, economic returns, and efficiency gains acquired through learning by doing, which contribute to productivity rise in both manufacturing and non-manufacturing sectors (Kaldor, 1967). Then higher productivity results in long-term growth.

The AfCFTA's objectives are related to most of the drivers and enablers of growth mentioned above (see Articles 3 and 4 in African Union, 2018). Indeed, among others, the AfCFTA seeks to promote market liberalization and trade openness; attract investments; enhance competitiveness; foster industrialization, diversification and structural transformation, with agricultural development, value chains development; and improve food security.

The rest of the chapter is organized as follows. Section 2 explores the economic impacts that the AfCFTA could generate. It finds that significant potential benefits exist; however, these could only be unleashed if beyond tariff liberalization, trade facilitation is promoted and non-tariff barriers are considerably reduced. Section 3 tries and cross-checks from empirical facts whether the positive results generated by the simulations are plausible. It reviews some successful experiences where long-term growth was promoted through free trade areas and / or other trade-related development strategies, then it identifies the success factors of these experiences that could also be stimulated by the AfCFTA and lead to similar results in Africa. Section 4 takes stock of Africa's growth performance over the past three decades, with a view to further assessing whether it is realistic to believe that Africa can experience long-term growth in the years to come, particularly through the AfCFTA. Section 5 recaps the ability of the AfCFTA to unleash Africa's enormous growth potential and suggests some recommendations to turn the potential into reality.

3.2 Growth and socio-economic impacts of the AfCFTA

Several empirical studies estimated the potential magnitude of the expected impact of the AfCFTA. These studies include international organizations (African Development Bank (AfDB), the International Monetary Fund (IMF), the United Nations Conference on Trade and Development (UNCTAD), the United Nations Economic Commission for Africa (UNECA), the World Bank) and academics such as Chauvin et al. (2016); Vanzetti et al. (2018), and Saygili et al. (2018). Their findings indicate that the implementation of the AfCFTA is expected to increase Africa's GDP, income and welfare, intra-African exports of both goods and services, and export of goods from Africa to the rest of the world. It will also create new jobs. The agreement is also expected to induce public revenue losses; however, these would be rather small due to the low level of intra-African trade currently, and they could be compensated by specific measures in the short term and should be offset in the long term by the gain induced by the agreement. All the studies come to the same conclusion that the AfCFTA is beneficial to Africa in several ways, but the benefits can only be maximized if the tariff elimination implied by the Agreement is accompanied by dedicated efforts for trade facilitation and the removal of non-tariff barriers (NTBs). Indeed, there are several factors that make both the cost of trading and the time required to trade higher than should be.

They include burdensome customs and administrative entry procedures, technical barriers to trade, sanitary and phytosanitary measures, legal restrictions to cross-border financial flows and transactions; unharmonized payment systems, complex or unclear rules of origins; limited quality of trade logistics, infrastructure gaps, particularly in the areas of ports and road networks. There are other factors that are also critical to promoting intra-regional trade, notably an enabling business environment, access to credit, and adequate human capital (Abrego et al., 2020 and AfDB, 2019). The adoption of targeted reforms and Trade facilitations measures are necessary to remove these barriers and improve intra-regional trade. Tables 3.1a and 3.1b provide an overview of estimates of the AfCFTA's macroeconomic impacts. These studies measure the change that each variable will experience by 2035 or so, when the AfCFTA is implemented.

Apart from Chauvin et al. (2016), most studies are static and examine the effects of the agreement in a long-term perspective only, informing about what could be expected around the year 2035, after full implementation. The compilation of the simulations existing to date gives an idea of the highest level of impact that the AfCFTA could have on Africa's economic growth. It indicates that with dedicated

Table 3.1a AfCFTA's macroeconomic changes (in percentage of 2020 values)

	Income gains (%), AfDB (2019)	Poverty reduction gains (millions of people), World Bank (2020a)
Central Africa	6.8	9.0
Eastern Africa	4.3	4.8
North Africa	4.1	—
Southern Africa	2.7	3.8
West Africa:	5.3	12.0

Source: Author regrouping.

Table 3.1b Estimates of AfCFTA socioeconomic gains by sub-regions, from different studies

	AfDB (2019)	IMF (2020)	UNCTAD (2018)	UNECA (2017)/1	WB (2020)	Ind. Research/2
GDP growth			1–3	0.01	0.13–4.2	0.1–5.5
Income / Welfare gains	0.1–3.5	0.05–2.1			7	0.2–2.6
Intra-regional Export	14.6–132	80	33	52.3	22–81	
Exports outside Africa	-0.8–40				19	
Total exports	1–51.1	8			29	
Intra-African imports					22–102	
Imports from outside Africa					27	
Total imports					41	
Public revenue (ratio of GDP)		0.03–0.22				
Jobs creation			1.2			

Source: Author regrouping.

Note: In the table, when an interval of numbers is provided rather than a single number, it represents the range of the impact (minimum and maximum change), based on the different assumptions or scenarios adopted by the authors.
(1) Based on Mevel and Karingi, 2012
(2) Chauvin et al. (2016); Vanzetti et al. (2018), and Saygili et al. (2018)

efforts to facilitate trade and eliminate NTBs, the continent's GDP in 2030 (or beyond) will be at least 5.5% higher than if the agreement is not implemented. More specifically, the agreement will add around 0.5 percentage points to Africa's GDP growth rate every year in the years leading up to full implementation. This maximum impact is found by Chauvin et al. (2016). According to World Bank (2020a), the maximum GDP increase is 4.2% while UNCTAD (2019) estimates it at 3.0%.

The AfCFTA could also increase Africa's income by more than 7% by 2035 (this is the highest estimate found in the literature so far), corresponding to US$ 450 billion (World Bank, 2020a). It is computed under the optimistic scenario whereby the gradual removal of 97% of tariffs on intra-African trade planned under the AfCFTA agreement is accompanied by a 50% reduction in NTBs and by Trade facilitation measures,[2] without which the estimate falls to a mere 0.2%. Other studies find that the income gains from the AfCFTA could be much smaller. For AfDB (2019), the income gain will vary between 0.1% and 3.5%, while IMF's estimates range from 0.05% to 2.6%. Among the individual researchers, the income gains go from 0.2% (Mevel and Karingi, 2012) to 2.6% (Chauvin et al., 2016).

The other macroeconomic benefits estimated by the existing quantitative analyses indicate that with the implementation of the AfCFTA, intra-Africa exports could increase by up to 132% and that Africa's exports outside the continent could also be increased by up to 40% (AfDB, 2019; Table 3.1a). Furthermore, job creation could be increased by 1.2% according to UNCTAD, 2018. Some revenue losses are also expected from the removal of tariffs; however, this negative impact is expected to be relatively small because intra-Africa trade remains low at about 18% of total Africa exports, corresponding to $62 billion in 2016.[3] Among the benefits of the AfCFTA are also the possibility of improving trade deficits of African countries with the increase of their exports and the trade diversion that it could entail, from international markets to the regional single market. According to the studies mentioned above, the gains from the AfCFTA will be generated from increased employment, enhanced consumption with access to cheaper products; better use of resources to increase agriculture and manufacturing production.

Among the existing studies, all those who push the details beyond the continental aggregates, find that the benefits of the AfCFTA will be uneven: the economic gains will not be distributed equally across African regions and countries; tariff revenue losses will vary across countries; job and welfare losses also could take place as part of the cost to pay to adjust to competition. The IMF's study finds that countries with the highest levels of openness, which also tend to be those with the smallest economies, will register the highest level of welfare gains (see, Abrego et al., 2020). In terms of magnitude, Central Africa is poised to reap the greatest economic benefits, with a real income increase projected at about 6.8% of the GDP; next is West Africa (5.3%). They are followed by Eastern Africa and North Africa (4.3% and 4.1%). Southern Africa would derive a 2.7% increase in its income. Along the same lines, Central Africa is also poised to be among the top beneficiaries of the AfCFTA as far as poverty reduction is concerned (Table 3.1b). These orders of magnitude are likely to be commensurate to the amount of NTBs and TF efforts that would have to be addressed in every sub-region (see AfDB, 2019). Central Africa is indeed Africa's region with one of the lowest levels of intra-African trade (they import significantly from the rest of the world and export to the same, essentially oil and other natural resources). Central Africa also posts the lowest levels of business environment and governance indicators, as can be seen in Figure 3.1. Therefore, it is likely that if those shortcomings are fixed, the relative gains from the AfCFTA could be higher than in the other sub-regions.

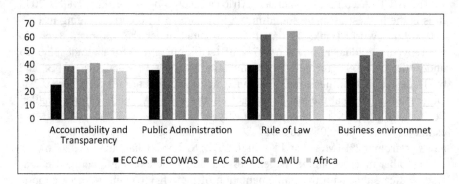

Figure 3.1 Comparing performance of African RECs in some indicators of business environment and economic governance (2019).

Source: Mo Ibrahim database and author's calculation.

Economic gains will also not be distributed equally across sectors, with
Manufacturing and Agriculture poised to be the biggest winners in terms of
the possibility to expand and increase exports. Within Africa, exports from the
manufacturing sector and the agriculture sectors could rise by up to 110% and
46% respectively while the exports of these sectors outside the continent could
rise by 46% and 10% respectively. These two sectors are also the key drivers of
welfare gains that will arise (Abrego et al., 2020; World Bank, 2020a; UNECA,
2019a; AfDB, 2019; UNCTAD, 2018) (Figure 3.2). According to the IMF (2020),
Manufacturing and Agriculture will account for over 60% and 16% of welfare
gains respectively. The World Bank (2020a) included the service sector in its analysis. It finds that the gains in the service sector will be relatively low at a 14%
increase in services' exports within Africa and a 3% increase in services exported
to the rest of the world.

The discussion above predicts that the AfCFTA will have a significant impact on
Africa's long-term growth. There are good reasons to believe that the Agreement
has the potential to deliver that much or even more. For instance, most models are
static and ignore the dynamic arising through learning by doing, which could lead
to efficiency gains and productivity rise over time; also, most of the analyses don't
capture the effect of liberalizing trade in services and its potential effect on the
other sectors, notably agriculture and manufacturing. Yet, a number of economies
on the continent, especially in Eastern Africa, are predominantly service-driven,
and for them, an increase in services' trade tends to have a higher impact on GDP
compared to merchandise trade (UNECA, 2021). The Abrego et al. (2020) notes
that its findings could be substantially underestimated given the static nature of the
model, which does not include the potential effects of the agreement on increased
investments, innovation, and knowledge diffusion. Similarly, the World Bank
(2020a) identifies five reasons why its results could be underestimated, notably a
lack of adequate consideration given to informal trade in the analysis.

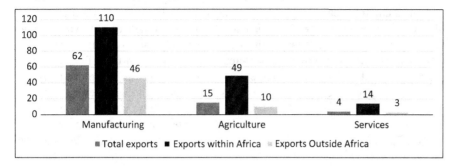

Figure 3.2 AfCFTA's potential impact on Africa's export by main sector (2035 change in %).

Source: World Bank 2020a data, author's compilation.

UNCTAD (2018) argues that Africa's gains from the Free Trade Area can go beyond their current estimates in the longer terms. This optimism rests on the potential of the Agreement to generate dynamic economic gains from improved trade facilitation and customs operations, services trade reform and collaboration on investment, intellectual property and competition. It could also attract investment and stimulate the development of regional value chains, as well as diversification and industrialization in the continent.

3.3 Examples of successful promotion of long-term growth and how the AfCFTA can help achieve similar results: A historical perspective

This section provides additional reasons to believe in the potential of the AfCFTA to promote Africa's long-term growth. In particular, it explores the drivers and catalysts of long-term growth from successful experiences, and, by analogy, infers likely AfCFTA effects on growth drivers and outcomes in Africa.

3.3.1 Insights from existing Free Trade Areas (FTAs): EU and ASEAN

3.3.1.1 The case of the EU in promoting growth

The European Union offers a good success story that illustrates the benefits of trade integration for economic growth. First, Portugal, Ireland, Greece and Spain joined the union and subsequently registered an accelerated and strong economic growth over the following decades which elevated them to the status of high-income economies in the late 1980s (Licandro, 2004).

Second, on a more general note, recent studies indicate that the European single market, after three decades of operation, has increased the EU's GDP by up to 9%.[4] Increases in trade in goods are estimated between 55% and 109% while the figure ranges between 33% and 58% for trade in services (European Commission,

2019; Mayer et al., 2018). For these studies, some models were static, which would prevent them from capturing dynamic gains; the calibration of parameters was different, such as exchange rates; the elasticity between trade and growth; and the weight put on pairs of countries with large levels of trade. Hypotheses on NTBs were also not same.[5] Gains in economic growth arose from the FTA's ability to increase trade flows, increase competition, and reduce prices and profit margins. The enhancement of competition which is promoted with the lowering of tariffs is alone contributing to 2% of the GDP gains. Interestingly, studies conducted ex-post found higher macroeconomic gains than those done ex-ante.[6] This suggests that the current estimates of the macroeconomic effects of the AfCFTA might be underestimated.

The lesson that emerges from this case is twofold. First, FTAs have the potential to generate economic benefits for countries, notably by increasing trade flows, competition, and by reducing prices and profit margins. The AfCFTA is expected to contribute to realizing such conditions. It is then likely to foster growth. Second, the magnitude of the gains really depends on the assumptions and specifications of the models. As such, the models may not be able to capture all the gains. This suggests that in the case of the AfCFTA as well, some dynamic gains might not be captured well in the studies being conducted now and its eventual impact might be greater than the results generated by existing simulations.

3.3.1.2 The case of ASEAN in promoting growth

Trade liberalization among ASEAN countries,[7] has contributed to enhanced cooperation and led to positive economic outcomes for many member countries, notably an increase in net FDIs, trade and financial flows (Capannelli et al., 2009). Oncel and Lubis (2017) look at the effect of the zero-tariff policy adopted in 1992 on the GDP per capita in 5 of the 6 member countries that constituted the ASEAN at that time. It finds an acceleration of the GDP per capita growth for all of these countries over the years that followed 1992. It also finds, using econometric regressions, that variables such as FDIs and trade, had a significant effect on GDP per capita after the introduction of the policy. Several papers suggested that ASEAN would benefit from a larger level of regional integration and recommended extending cooperation to more Asian and Pacific countries (Sharma and Chua, 2000; Frankel, 1993; Petri, 1993). The ASEAN acted in that direction as the Association extended cooperation to China, Japan and South Korea and established ASEAN+3 in 1997. This was followed by ASEAN+6 with cooperation strengthened with Australia, India and New Zealand.

The insights drawn from this experience are twofold: i) FTAs can improve long-term growth and development prospects for member countries and ii) large FTAs increase the profitability of member countries. This hints at the fact that the AfCFTA, with its large size, has the potential to boost growth and foster development in Africa.

Among the ASEAN countries, Singapore and Malaysia present the highest development performance. Therefore, in addition to examining the effects of their

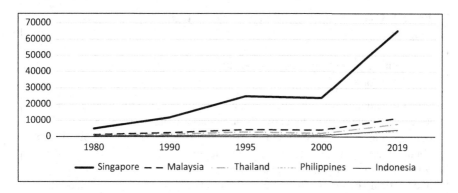

Figure 3.3 GDP per capita of ASEAN countries (in USD).

Source: Drawn by author, based on Öncel and Lubis (2017); World Bank database (WDI), 2021.

membership in an FTA, it is worth exploring how these countries have used other trade-related strategies to promote long-term growth and to see how the AfCFTA could serve to create similar favorable conditions for African countries. This is done in Box 3.1. It appears that while joining an FTA has helped the rapid development of Malaysia and Singapore, being strategic in choosing policies and fully engaging in their implementation, including taking advantage of the ASEAN cooperation framework, was obviously decisive. Likewise, the AfCFTA offers a great opportunity to all African countries, but it will have to be exploited with dedication and strategic policy choices.

3.3.2 Insights from Africa

3.3.2.1 The current economic structure of Africa suggests that a demand exists for African products

Currently, intra-African trade is made up of more transformed and sophisticated products than trade from Africa to the rest of the world, the latter being essentially characterized by the export of raw materials. This observation is supported by both the structure of exports and the technological content of exported goods. Indeed, intra-African exports comprise 46.3% of manufactured products; 21% of agricultural and food products, and 32% of raw material (unprocessed). On the contrary, Africa's exports that go outside the continent include only 22.3% of manufactured products; 16% of agricultural and food products; and 62% of natural resources. In the same vein, 27.1% of technology used to produce the merchandise exported in the intra-African market are high and medium technology while the figure drops by half for the goods exported outside the continent (UNCTAD, 2018).

These observations provide a few insights in connexion to the potential of the AfCFTA. First, it is a sign that African countries are inclined to buy manufactured

Box 3.1 Overview of long-term growth strategies in Malaysia and Singapore

Malaysia: Leveraging abundant natural resources to promote long-term growth

Since its independence in 1957, Malaysia has been able to achieve remarkable improvement in its level of development, moving from a US$ 235 GDP per capita in 1960 to US$11,414 in 2019 (World Bank, 2021). Endowed with abundant natural resources, including agricultural, mineral, hydrocarbon and forestry resources, Malaysia has worked diligently to promote horizontal and vertical economic diversification through local transformation and processing. The overall strategy was to expand the export base and gradually improve its quality with a view to improving growth prospects. Rubber and palm oil, then tin ore were the first commodities produced; they contributed significantly to the nation's wealth, with the expansion of sources of growth. This was followed by a push to add value to natural resources through local processing. Such efforts led to the development of new economic activities, and the production and export of consumer and industrial products in replacement of mere commodities.

As a result, the economy has witnessed a remarkable structural transformation marked by a drop in the share of the primary sector in GDP, in favor of the manufacturing and services sectors. The share of raw materials in total exports was divided by three, from about 75% to 25% between 1980 and 2012. In contrast, exports of manufactured products based on natural resources and electrical and electronic products became dominant in the country's total exports. The diversification goal was pursued with dedicated efforts to ensure the competitiveness of the products exported; a lid on inflation and wage growth is an example of measures adopted in this regard. Malaysia's sustained growth is attributed to its ability to leverage visionary leadership, political stability, development planning mechanisms, and abundant natural resources. The same strategic ingredients also contributed to attracting both foreign and domestic investment and supported the tourism industry, which has been continuously contributing to economic growth (Cherif et al., 2016; Ahmad, 2016).

Singapore: attracting massive FDIs and developing trade in services as a strategy for growth

In the absence of natural resources and assets, Singapore promoted long-term growth through an adaptative and ever-adjusting utilization of productive factors, from labor, to capital, skills, and currently knowledge. It was all based on attracting external resources to fill the domestic gaps with FDIs, skills and knowledge from foreigners. From the 1980s to the 1990s, the State strove to position the country as a global business center. The strategy was to attract FDIs, develop some key industries, create linkages or commercial relationships between these and technical services, and promote trade in services (Cherif et al., 2016; Yeo, 2016). The government aimed to attract international service companies operating in a wide range of sectors including education, finance, lifestyle, medicine, IT and software. Lately, the government has been also stimulating knowledge-based and innovation-driven development through R&D. In this vein, industries and services fostered included pharmaceuticals and medical technology.

Placing the development of the service sector at the core of its development and trade strategy was crucial for Singapore. The share of the service sector in employment is above 80% in 2021 (World Bank, 2021). The GDP per capita of the country rose from US$ 428 in 1960 to about US$ 65,233 in 2019 (World Bank, 2021). Obviously, strategic leadership was fundamental.

By analogy, lessons for Africa, natural resources endowment, and given that the AfCFTA is a strategic vision of African leaders to foster structural transformation and open additional export markets, improving competitiveness will be at reach with the protocol on competition and property rights.

Source: Author's compilation from different documents indicated in the box and in endnotes

goods from other African countries.[8] It means that the demand is there for the new products that the AfCFTA could generate. Second, in connection with the above, the AfCFTA appears as a concrete opportunity for African countries to accelerate their economic diversification and industrialization process, through the production of even more manufactured products, given the expansion of market access for every single economy. Promoting local processing of natural resources like in Malaysia, together with strengthening the productive capacities and fostering regional value chains are necessary conditions.

3.3.2.2 Ethiopia's experience in creating jobs and promoting manufacturing and industrialization

Over the past decades, Ethiopia has made significant strategic efforts, including trade-related policies to promote long-term growth. As a result, its GDP per capita has more than quadrupled since 2000 and stood at US$ 856 in 2019, thanks to high growth rates. An illustration of this is the development of the floriculture sector and the creation of linkages with the air transport sector through Ethiopian airlines transporting flowers to destination markets, mainly in Europe. With the opening of the AfCFTA, the same model could be reproduced on the African markets.

Another major strategic objective that Ethiopia has set for itself is to become a manufacturing hub. To this end, the country has developed a number of industrial parks, and adopted some dedicated measures to attack FDIs. In particular, Ethiopia provided financial incentives and committed to offering an abundant and very cheap labor force, with the view to competing with Asia. Women are working in the newly established industrial parks, in the garment industry, to produce clothes for well-known brands such as Guess, H&M, and Calvin Klein. They earn just US$26 per month, and this corresponds to half the earnings of workers doing the same activities in Bangladesh. The Hawassa industrial park currently employs about 25,000 workers. This cheap labor strategy is, however, proving somehow challenging as the workers cannot cope with such small salaries and have often threatened to quit.

A lesson from this experience is that the AfCFTA can take advantage of the existence of abundant and cheap labor in Africa to attract investment, promote manufacturing, create jobs and spur economic growth. However, there is a need to strengthen labor laws and guarantee minimum salary policies that enable decent living standards for the population; that will have to be complemented by continuous training activities, in order to raise productivity, which is the condition to fasten growth and also continue to attract FDIs (Barret and Baumann-Pauly, 2019).

3.3.2.3 The mobilization of the private sector to crowd in investments needed to make the AfCFTA a success

The diaspora, the foreign and African private sector, are as mobilized as African leaders to make the AfCFTA work well. The AfroChampion is an initiative emanating from them, trying to mobilize investors to fund some strategic projects that will remove the bottlenecks susceptible to undermining the potential of the AfCFTA. Their target is 1 trillion dollars, and they have designed a framework that will determine the projects that would be funded. Among other criteria, the projects to receive funding under this initiative will have to be in a position to enhance productive capacities, promote structural transformation, and create jobs. Given that investment is a major driver of productivity and growth, this initiative illustrates a concrete channel through which the AfCFTA could be fruitful beyond current estimates. Indeed, 1 trillion dollars represents more than one-third of the GDP of the continent; it could have substantial multiplier effects.

Besides the AfroChampion initiative, investment has actually already started on the African market. Ford recently invested in South Africa with the stated objective of serving the regional market.

3.3.2.4 Some opportunities worth mentioning to leverage the potential of the AfCFTA

Some opportunities deserve to be mentioned because of their aptitude to justify optimism concerning the potential of the AfCFTA. First, endogenously driven innovation and technological development is underway in Africa (e.g., mobile banking such as MPESA in Kenya). The digital commerce is also booming. The protocol on property rights could only enhance this trend as it will boost productivity. In the pre-COVID era, digital commerce was growing at a rate of 18% every year in Africa, which was more than double the global average. COVID has accelerated this pace. A number of e-commerce platforms exist already; however, one targeting the regional market as a whole is yet to be created. The revolutionary success of Amazon and Alibaba in expanding economic activity and creating jobs in the US and China suggests the possibility of emulating also a success story beyond imagination in the African context.

Second, there are many sectors that offer opportunities to foster economic diversification and manufacturing. They include activities needed to feed, clothe, provide energy to, transport, educate, and preserve the health and wellness of 1.3 billion Africans. So far, many of the goods addressing the needs in these areas are imported from the rest of the world. The size of the market is significant and will continue to grow in the years to come as 1 in 4 people in the world will be sub-Saharan African in 2050. In 2030, the ratio will be around 18% (see AUC, UNECA, and AfDB, 2017 and UNECA, 2021).

3.3.2.5 On the challenges to leverage the AfCFTA's potential

It goes without saying that the successful implementation of the AfCFTA will face considerable challenges. However, this chapter will not go into them further, its main idea being rather to identify plausible reasons to believe in the potential of the African market. In addition, many of today's emerging countries have also faced significant challenges; their development potential was unlikely and threw serious doubts at first, but they succeeded against all odds.

3.4 Africa's growth performance in the past three decades

To what extent is it plausible that Africa can grow in the future, notably through the AfCFTA? From 1990 to 2019 (i.e., pre-COVID), Africa has consistently exhibited positive growth rates, which almost always remained above 3%, hence above the world average. The period 2000–2013 was particularly positive with an average growth rate that remained above 5%. The year 2020 was marked by the advent of the global COVID-19 pandemic which plunged the continent into a recession; however, the medium-term outlook is positive again with the continental GDP growth rate predicted around 4% (Figure 3.1; Figure 3.3, UNECA, 2021).

Africa's growth has been driven by different factors over time. Some of them may be qualified as external, however many stemmed from internal strategies and efforts. On the one hand, strong global demand for Africa's exports, increases in commodity prices, and weather conditions being favorable to agriculture have contributed to growth. On the other hand, improved economic management with dedicated reforms towards the improvement of the business environment, strong private consumption, continued investment in infrastructure, agriculture, agro-industry, mining and oil; dynamism of the construction sector, development of modern services sectors including the financial, ICT, transport, and tourism sectors; have underpinned the economic growth of the continent.

Trade openness has always been a significant driver of Africa's growth; first directly through the export of raw materials and commodities, but also indirectly via the import of machinery and intermediary goods needed to realize the investments in all the sectors mentioned above. Trade integration through free trade agreements as well as efforts to diversify and expand the export base have also influenced growth positively in some cases.

Overall, the dynamics and drivers of growth in Africa did not remain identical over time, they rather evolved; they have also been different across sub-regions.

In terms of growth performance by sub-region, East Africa has positioned itself since around 2008 as the fastest-growing sub-region. Trade integration may have played a key role in this regard. The East African Community (EAC) is a customs union; it is also among the best-performing regional economic communities in Africa with the highest level of intra-African trade. Agriculture has been the main activity and the main driver of growth in that sub-region, with tea, coffee and floriculture as flagship sub-sectors. Industry and services are also developing in Ethiopia, Kenya, Rwanda, and Tanzania and the mining sector is very dynamic in Madagascar, Uganda, and the Democratic Republic of Congo. Vibrant activities also included tourism, aviation, ITCs, finance, real estate and distribution.

Thanks to oil export, Central Africa experienced very high growth levels during the years 1995–2010, as some of its countries, notably Chad and Equatorial Guinea, became new oil-exporting countries and all countries benefited from the high international prices of the same product. Over time, growth fell, but recently it recorded positive results, due to the dynamism of agro-industry and services in Cameroon, Congo and Gabon; and tourism and construction in Sao Tome and Principe (before COVID). Growth in Southern Africa has been driven by increased distributive trade, manufacturing and mining. As far as West Africa is concerned, the main drivers of growth have been high private consumption, public investment, and good agriculture production. North Africa's growth has been driven by tourism, agriculture and industry, among others, with negative dynamics registered at different points in time, due notably to the Arab Spring, the war in Libya, the global financial crisis and the inflation in some countries, which has led to a reduction in private consumption (UNECA, 2019).

With the growth rates described above, Africa doubled its GDP per capita over the past three decades, bringing it to around US$2,000 in 2020 (Figure 3.4 and Figure 3.5). Considering the fact that the continent's demographic trends have been on the rise during the period, this result is rather remarkable and suggests that it is not unrealistic to think that growth can also be achieved in the future, especially under the framework of the AfCFTA.

However, compared to Asian countries, particularly to groups like West Asia and East Asia, where the average growth rate has long fluctuated between 6% and 8%, the performance of Africa looks modest and warrants additional efforts. In Asian countries, the combination of declining demographic dynamics and high and sustained growth rates made it possible to increase their GDP per capita by more than six times for certain regions (Figures 3.6 and 3.7).

Scholars are divided over the drivers of Africa's economic growth. The most pessimistic argue that external factors such as demand and price of commodities in international markets are the main drivers. To these pessimistic, one can say that in recent years, countries deprived of natural resources such as Ethiopia, Kenya,

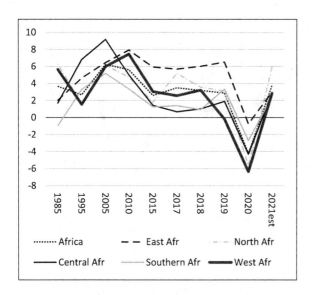

Figure 3.4 GDP growth rates in %–Africa.

Source: IMF (World Economic Outlook) and UNDESA (World Economic Situation and Prospects) databases.

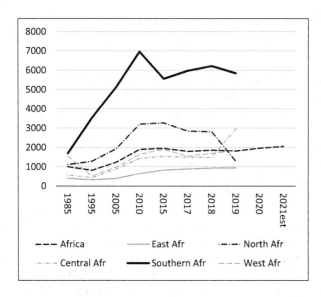

Figure 3.5 GDP per capita in USD–Africa.

Source: IMF and UNDESA databases.

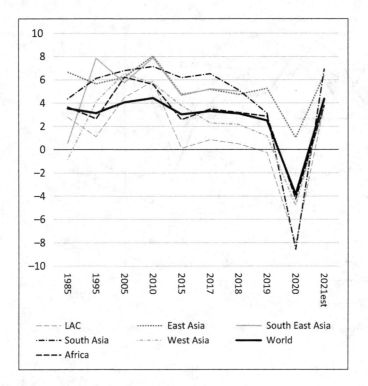

Figure 3.6 Growth rates in %–World.

Source: IMF and UNDESA databases.

and Senegal, have been able to maintain high levels of growth and rank among the most dynamic economies in the world. This has been possible thanks to strategic investments, policy reforms and the promotion of certain promising economic sectors.

In addition, fiscal policy is a key driver of long-term growth and development because it determines the amount of government revenue available to foster development and the wise use of that revenue. In this regard, many African economies have introduced several reforms which have yielded positive results. As of 2020, one-third (18) of African countries have adopted electronic tax declaration and payment systems in place. As a result, Kenya was able to identify data inconsistencies and raised VAT collections by more than US$1 billion between 2016 and 2017; Rwanda was able to boost tax revenues by 6%; South Africa lowered the time and cost of complying with the value-added tax by 21% and 22% respectively. These advances highlight the vast potential for revenue gains for countries that have yet to digitize their tax systems and other administrative services. Moreover, African

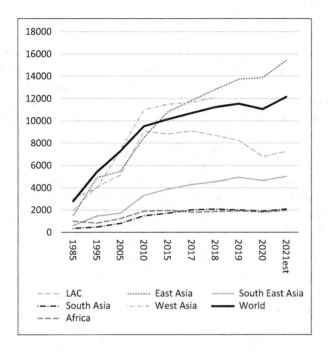

Figure 3.7 GDP per capita in USD–World.

Source: IMF and UNDESA databases.

governments have made notable progress in the social sector over the past decades; spending on education and health started to increase in 2010; the poverty rate fell to 36% in 2016 against 54.3% in 1990, although inequality remains high with a Gini of 0.44 (UNECA, 2019b).

Nonetheless, it is clear that Africa has some structural challenges keeping its growth and development performance subdued. The revenue to GDP ratio remains low at 21.4% in 2019 and cannot provide sufficient resources to support national development strategies. The investment rate is 25% of GDP, significantly lower than the 32% posted in East Asia and the Pacific. Productivity has also plummeted dramatically from an average of 2.4% over the period 2000–2008 to 0.3% over the period 2009–2018, far behind the global average of 9% recorded over the period 2011–2017 (World Bank, 2018b; UNECA, 2019b). The low levels of diversification and sophistication entertained by their high dependence on untransformed products maintain most African economies in a situation of low productivity and limited growth performance. They must improve their growth models, with notably more innovation and competitiveness, and the AfCFTA seems to be an opportunity to seize.

3.5 Conclusion and recommendations

This chapter has explored the potential of the AfCFTA to promote long-term growth in Africa. A review of existing simulations indicated that the AfCFTA could significantly contribute to long-term growth. For example, the implementation of the Agreement could make the continent's GDP in 2035, 5.5% higher than the level expected without the AfCFTA. Specifically, in the 10 years preceding the full implementation of the agreement as well, the level of GDP could be increased by 0.5 to 5% each year.

Simulations also identify other economic impacts of the AfCFTA including an increase in intra-Africa's exports, an increase in Africa's exports to the rest of the world (both will concern mainly products from manufacturing and agriculture sectors), job creation, welfare gains and poverty reduction. Public revenue losses are also expected but will be minimal. However, all the existing studies are also very clear that the realization of the gains is strictly conditional on substantial efforts in favor of trade facilitation and the removal of NTBs.

Several interesting past experiences make it plausible to aim high with the AfCFTA. For example, the FTA has made a significant contribution to the long-term growth of the European Union. In addition, due to conservative assumptions and model specifications adopted, the simulations performed ex-ante were found to be underestimated compared to the long-term real growth that the agreement ultimately yielded. The same situation could be observed with the AfCFTA.

As a second example, overall, ASEAN member countries derived tangible economic benefits from the FTA. Furthermore, a specific focus on Malaysia and Singapore, both founder members of the ASEAN, highlighted also the potential of FTAs and other trade-related strategies to foster growth and development, notably export-led growth, the creation of sectoral linkages, the promotion of trade in services, etc. However, the results stemmed from the determination of these countries to make strategic policy choices and to implement them, which again stresses that the AfCFTA will only deliver if its success factors are identified strategically and implemented diligently.

Success factors of past experiences included the continued pursuit of improved competitiveness with a view to facilitating access to external markets, including markets offered by the FTA to which countries belong. Competitiveness has been sought through the achievement of massive economies of scale, the reduction of production costs, the search for cheap inputs and factors of production, especially labor. Past experiences also highlight the importance of continuously improving productivity, innovating and developing new industries and services with higher technological and knowledge content; and that the development of linkages between industries and services can significantly boost trade in services, attract investment and stimulate growth.

Arguably the AfCFTA relates to most of the dynamics mentioned above. In effect, with the removal of tariffs and NTBs, the AfCFTA is expected to foster access to markets, reduce transaction costs and production costs, and improve access to cheaper inputs due to the abundance of natural resources. The protocol on the free movement of people together with the liberalization of the financial sector can improve access to cheap production factors (labor and capital). It can also give access to a wider range of skills and thereby enhance productivity. Productivity growth, investments, economic diversification and sophistication, technological development, competition, conducive business environments, etc. are critical drivers of growth. The AfCFTA's protocols and disposals on investments; competition; property rights; e-commerce, conflict settlements; Rules of origins; transactions and payments, and monitoring of NTBs removal, will allow fostering them to the benefit of growth.

There are several other additional reasons to believe that the continent can achieve high growth rates in the years to come, notably under the AfCFTA. Among them is that Africa's growth performance over the past three decades has been non-negligible. Plus, the existence of a regional demand from the consumers and firms is a critical success factor of the AfCFTA and a major driver of growth. The current structure of intra-African exports suggests that this demand exists. Moreover, a rapid technological development coupled with an expansion of digital trade; and a large market size constitute additional tangible opportunities that the AfCFTA could leverage.

Against this backdrop, the chapter contends that the AfCFTA has immense potential to influence most of the growth drivers and accelerate Africa's development process considerably. However, unleashing the potential of the AfCFTA warrants a few recommendations.

Strategic and continued leadership is essential for any development opportunity or potential such as the AfCFTA to translate into long-term growth and prosperity. Therefore, the ratification and subsequent official launch of the AfCFTA which took place in January 2021 should not be the end but rather the beginning of every African leader's efforts to make the most of the single market. In particular, they must ensure that all protocols of the agreement are correctly and promptly made operational.

Dedicated efforts must be devoted towards trade facilitation and the removal of NTBs for a smooth circulation of goods and provision of services across the continent at reduced costs. In particular, attention should be paid to improving the services provided by customs administrations; developing infrastructure for better connectivity within the continent; and improving logistics systems, including building the capacity of trade corridors.

The private sector must be encouraged and accompanied to fully engage in trading as well as investing and producing under the AfCFTA. Building the African workforce's capacity and developing the private sector must remain at the heart of every country's efforts. Indeed, besides trading, the private sector will first have to produce more. Innovation, technological development and knowledge must be used as drivers of productivity enhancement, local processing, diversification and industrialization.

Strategic policies and reforms must be implemented to improve the business environment with reduced production and trade costs; deliberate efforts must be devoted to attracting FDIs as well as domestic investments and creating jobs. For example, countries could promote local content policies to foster job creation and help domestic SMEs grow; establish industrial zones to allow economies of scale, reduce production costs, develop niches of competence, improve skills and know-how; promote backward and forward linkages between sectors to foster diversification and expand trade in services; develop or deepen regional value chains for efficiency gains, etc. To sustain long-term growth, countries must also promote peace and security and social inclusion; the management of demographic dynamics is also necessary.

Notes

1 The views and opinions expressed in this paper are those of the authors and do not necessarily reflect the views or positions of their employers or institutions.
2 The assumptions made by these different studies vary. Chauvin et al., 2016, which finds the highest GDP impact of the AfCFTA, considers an assumption of a 50% reduction in Non-Tariffs Measures and a 30% reduction in Transaction Costs in all goods by 2027. UNCTAD, 2018 considers a scenario with 100 removal of NTBs, while IMF, 2020 considers a scenario with a 35% reduction in NTBs. Most of these studies are based on ex ante simulations using multisector, multi-country computable general equilibrium (CGE) trade models.
3 The revenue loss is also already taken into consideration in the calculation of the net income/welfare gains of the different studies.
4 From one study to another, the estimated effects of the EU's FTA on trade vary quite significantly, due to differences in hypothesis adopted and specifications of models.
5 Mayer et al., 2018 and Felbermayr et al., 2018 focus on the effects of NTBs only while European Commission, 2019 takes into account the effects of reducing profit margins and increasing competition, in addition to the removal of tariffs and reduction of NTBs.
6 Computed in 1988 in European Commission, 2019 and Cecchini et al., 1988.
7 ASEAN stands for Association of SouthEast Nations. It was created in 1967 by five countries (Indonesia, Malaysia, Philippines, Singapore, Thailand). Five additional countries joined later on, namely Brunei, Vietnam, LAO PDR and Myanmar, and Cambodia. Brunei joined in 1984 but the four others joined in 1995 and beyond. This group of 10 countries further created cooperation links with other Asian and pacific countries throughout the years, Moving from ASEAN+3.
8 Some of these manufactured products appearing in Africa's export may be produced outside the continent and only proceed from re-export activities. However, in a way, this remains proof that there is internal demand and a sign of Africa's willingness to buy from Africa.

References

Abrego, L.E., de Zamaróczy, M., Gursoy, T., Issoufou, S., Nicholls, G.P., Perez-Saiz, H., and Rosas, J.-N. 2020. *The African Continental Free Trade Area: Potential Economic Impact and Challenges*. International Monetary Fund (IMF), IMF Staff Discussion Note, SDN/20/04. Washington DC: IMF.

AfDB, 2019. Africa Economic Outlook. African Development Bank. Abidjan, Cote d'Ivoire.

African Union, 2018. The Agreement Establishing the Africa Continental Free Trade Area. Accessed in March 2021 at: www.tralac.org/documents/resources/african-union/2162-afc fta-agreement-legally-scrubbed-version-signed-16-may-2018/file.html.

AfroChampion Initiative and the Africa Union. 2020. One Trillion Dollars Investment Framework for Africa in Support of AfCFTA Implementation. Accessed at: https:// afrochampions.org/assets/doc/Contenus%20Trillion%20Dollar%20Framework/THE TRI~1.PDF.

Ahmad, T.A. 2016. Malaysia Move to High Income Economy: Five Decades of Nation Building. A View from Within. In Fouad Assanov and Min Zhu (eds.), *Breaking the Oil Spell by Reda Cherif*. Chapter 4. IMF: Washington DC.

Barrett, P,M. and Baumann-Pauly, D. May 2019. "Report: Made in Ethiopia: Challenges in the Garnment industry's new frontier". Published by NYU/ STERN/Center for Business and Human Rights. New York City. Accessed at: https://bhr.stern.nyu.edu/blogs/https/ issuucom/nyusterncenterforbusinessandhumanri/docs/nyuethiopiafinalonlinee31640827/ 69644612

Cecchini, P., Catina, M., and Jacquemin, A. 1988. *1992-the European Challenge: The Benefits of a Single Market*. Wildwood House.

Chauvin, D., Ramos, N., and Porto, G. 2016. Trade, Growth, and Welfare Impacts of the CFTA in Africa. Accessed at: https://arodes.hes-so.ch/record/2006/files/Depetris-Chauvi n_2017_trade_growth_welfare.pdf.

Cherif, R. et al. 2016. *Breaking the Oil Spell. The Gulf Falcon's Path to Diversification*. Washington DC: IMF.

European Commission, 2019. Quantifying the Economic Effects of the Single Market in a Structural Macromodel. Discussion Paper 094, February 2019. Accessed at: https://ec.eur opa.eu/info/sites/info/files/economy-finance/dp094_en.pdf.

Felbermayr, G., Groschl, J., and Heiland, I. 2018. Undoing Europe in a New Quantitative Trade Model, IFO Working Papers 250-2018, January 2018.

Frankel, J.A. 1993. Is Japan Creating a Yen Bloc in East Asia and the Pacific? In J. Frankel and M. Kohler, ed. *Regionalism and Rivalry: Japan and the United States in Pacific Asia*. Chicago: University of Chicago Press, pp. 53–87.

Ibrahim, M. 2019. Mo Ibrahim Indexo of African Governance dataportal. Accessed at: https://iiag.online/.

IMF. 2020. Lisandro Abrego, Mario de Zamaróczy, Tunc Gursoy, Salifou Issoufou, Garth P. Nicholls, Hector Perez-Saiz, and Jose-Nicolas Rosas The African Continental Free Trade Area: Potential Economic Impact and Challenges. IMF STAFF DISCUSSION NOTE, SDN/20/04.

Kaldor, N. 1967. *Strategic Factors in Economic Development*. New York State School of Industrial and Labor Relations, Cornell University, Ithaca, New York.

Kuznets, S. 1979. Growth and Structural Shifts. In W. Galenson (ed.), *Economic Growth and Structural Change in Taiwan: The Postwar Experience of the Republic of China*. London: Cornel University Press.

Licandro, O. 2004. The Impact of Regional Integration on Economic Convergence and Growth. European University Institute Working Paper ECO. No. 2004/26.

Lin, J.Y. and Monga, C. 2010. The Growth Report and New Structural Economics. Policy Research Working Paper 5336. The World Bank.

Mayer, T., Vicard, V., and Zignago, S. 2018. The Cost on Non-Europe, Revisited. Mimeo, September 2018.

Mevel, S. and Karingi, S. 2012. Deepening Regional Integration in Africa: A Computer General Equilibrium Assessment of the Establishment of a Continental Free Trade Area

Followed by a Continental Customs Union. United Nations Economic Commission for Africa, Addis Ababa, Ethiopia.

Öncel, A. and Lubis, R.F. 2017. What Impact has Free Trade Area on Economies of ASEAN-5 Countries? *Theoretical and Applied Economics*, XXIV (2017), No. 3(612), 51–62.

Petri, P.A. 1993. The East Asian Trading Bloc: An Analytical History, In J. Frankel and M. Kohler (ed.), *Regionalism and Rivalry: Japan and the United States in Pacific Asia*. Chicago: University of Chicago Press, pp. 21–52.

Saygili, M., Peters, R. and Knebel, C. 2018. African Continental Free Trade Area: Challenges and Opportunities of Tariff Reductions. United Nations Conference on Trade and Development Research Paper 15, Geneva.

Sharma, S.C. and Chua, S.Y. 2000. ASEAN: Economic Integration and Intra-Regional Trade. Applied Economics Letters, No. 7, pp. 165–169.

UNCTAD. 2018. Policy Brief N 67: The African Continental Free Trade Area: The Day After the Kigali. May 2018. Summit. Expected effects Ef the African Continental Free Trade Area.

UNECA, AUC and AfDB. 2017. Assessing Regional Integration in Africa VIII: Bringing the Continental Free Trade Area About (Sales No. E.17.II.K.4, Addis Ababa).

UNECA. 2019a. African Continental Free Trade Area Questions & Answers. ATPC, Addis Ababa, Ethiopia. Accessed on February 2021 at: https://au.int/sites/default/files/docume nts/36085-doc-qa_cfta_en_rev15march.pdf.

UNECA. 2019b. Economic Report on Africa: Fiscal Policy for Financing Sustainable Development in Africa. UNECA, Addis Ababa.

Vanzetti, D., Peters, R., and Knebel, C. 2018. Non-tariff Measures: Lifting CFTA and ACP Trade to the Next Level. United Nations Conference on Trade and Development Research Paper 14, Geneva.

World Bank. 2018a. Stronger Open Trade policies Enable Economic Growth for All. Results Briefs, April 2018. Accessed in May 2021 at: www.worldbank.org/en/results/2018/04/03/ stronger-open-trade-policies-enables-economic-growth-for-all.

World Bank. 2018b. Africa's Pulse: Boosting Productivity in SubSaharan Africa: The Role of Human Capital. Washington.

World Bank and Emi Suzuki. 2019. Published in Data Blog. Accessed in 2021 at: https:// blogs.worldbank.org/opendata/worlds-population-will-continue-grow-and-will-reach-nearly-10-billion-2050.

World Bank. 2020a. The African Continental Free Trade Area: Economic and Distributional Effects. Washington, DC: World Bank. © World Bank. https://openknowledge.worldb ank.org/handle/10986/34139 License: CC BY 3.0 IGO.

World Bank. 2020b. Doing Business 2020. Washington, DC: World Bank.

World Bank. 2021. *World development indicators.* Washington, D.C.

Yeo, P. 2016. Going Beyond Comparative Advantages: How Singapore Did It. In R. Cherif, F. Assanov and M. Zhu (eds.), *Breaking the Oil Spell*, Chapter 3. Washington DC: IMF.

4 The Africa Continental Free Trade Area and poverty reduction in Africa[1]

Clarence Tsimpo, Aly Sanoh, and Mohamed Coulibaly

4.1 Introduction

Since the independences in the 1960s (*for most*), the development process has been a bumpy road for most African countries. Economic growth has been affected by several positive and negative shocks, including the oil boom in the 1970s and around 2004, the global financial crisis of 2008, the oil price shocks in 2014–16, and the COVID crisis now. The latter has caused the continent to go into recession for the first time in 25 years. Africa has also been painted as the continent of natural and man-made shocks/disasters. This is illustrated by the proliferation of conflicts across the continent. Natural disasters have struck often, and the population often suffers from the effects of climate change, such as floods, droughts, and most recently, a major locust invasion that occurred in the Horn of Africa.

Efforts to accumulate human and physical capital have not been very conclusive so far, leading to poor performance in terms of fostering the much-needed structural transformation. Most Africans[2] are still relying on subsistence agriculture, with limited levels of mechanization, technology utilization, and use of improved inputs. Most countries are characterized by the export of raw materials and the import of transformed goods. Alarmingly, the continent has experienced deindustrialization over time and the dependency on natural resources has increased (Beegle and Christiaensen, 2019). African farmers are failing to feed the continent and more and more, a big share of trade deficit is being driven by imports of food items.

Consequently, economic growth has not been sustained in Africa. Besides, due to widespread rent-seeking behavior, the benefit of economic growth has not always been shared properly, resulting in high levels of inequality.

For several decades, there has been a polarizing debate on how the continent will overcome its many development challenges. Many supported that the establishment of the "United States of Africa" will be the way to go to increase Africa's chance of development, and also of becoming a major player in the concert of nations. A consensus was reached to first promote and establish regional union, with the aim of having these integrated at some point. The ratification of the Africa Continental Free Trade Area (AfCFTA) in 2019 marks a key step for Africa's

DOI: 10.4324/9781003456568-4

integration. The agreement provides an incredible opportunity to boost intra-Africa trade, which will result in higher growth and job creation.

The AfCFTA has the power to accelerate economic growth, job creation, and poverty reduction while expanding economic inclusion. The World Bank has estimated that the successful implementation of the AfCFTA could increase Africa's aggregate national income by US$ 450 billion through 2035—a gain of 7 percent—while adding US$ 76 billion to the aggregate national income of the rest of the world (World Bank, 2020). Moreover, the AfCFTA is projected to spur wage growth for women and unskilled laborers by 10 percent while reducing the incidence of extreme poverty across the continent, with gains concentrated in countries with high poverty rates. Under the AfCFTA, the African population living in extreme poverty is anticipated to decline by as much as 30 million, including 12 million in West Africa alone. The AfCFTA is also expected to enable another 68 million people to escape moderate poverty (World Bank, 2020).

Intra-African trade is projected to expand at an unprecedented rate. Africa's total exports are forecast to increase by US$ 560 billion over 2020–2035, driven by manufacturing. Moreover, the AfCFTA is projected to deliver US$ 450 billion in aggregate national income gains, of which US$ 292 billion would be generated by lowering the cost of cross-border trade. Trade-facilitation measures designed to streamline customs procedures and lower the administrative costs of trade are expected to have a major impact on regional and global trade flows, whereas reducing tariffs—though essential—is projected to boost the continent's income by just 0.2 percent.

Yet, these potential gains are not guaranteed. As with all trade agreements, some countries will inevitably experience temporary adjustment costs, and all countries will face direct implementation costs associated with introducing the reforms required by the trade agreement. Policymakers in Africa's smallest, most fragile, and least diversified countries will need to implement complementary reforms to enable their economies to take full advantage of the AfCFTA while shielding vulnerable groups from the adverse effects of changes in trade policy. Across Africa, the private sector will likely incur costs arising from the structural realignment of the economy, as firms will need to adapt to a new context marked by emerging opportunities and intensifying competitive pressures.

The main purpose of this chapter is to investigate how the AfCFTA could contribute to poverty[3] reduction in Africa. It documents that Africa's performance in poverty reduction over the past three decades has been unsatisfactory and much lower than the rest of the developing regions, making it currently the continent home to more than half the total poor in the world. It estimates that the AfCFTA could reduce by up to 1/3 of the poor in an optimistic scenario and about 10 percent in a pessimistic scenario.

In addition to the introduction, this chapter is organized into six sections. Section 4.2 provides recent trends of poverty in Africa, with some cross-continent comparisons, and focuses on both monetary and non-monetary dimensions of poverty. Section 4.3 describes the profile of the poor in Africa. Building on the existing literature, Section 4.4 elaborates on key constraints to poverty reduction in Africa and Section 4.5 discusses how the AfCFTA will affect these constraints. Using PovcalNet data and a micro-macro simulations approach, Section 4.6 estimates the impact of the AfCFTA on the poverty rate in Africa. The chapter then concludes that AfCFTA's impact on poverty reduction could be substantial; however, this will require significant dedicated and specific support from governments.

4.2 How has Africa fared so far?

Over the past decade, the poverty headcount, measured by the proportion of the population living below the $1.90 international poverty line, has declined significantly (Figure 4.1). In 1990, 55.1 percent of the African population were poor. Despite a slight increase in the early 1990s, the poverty headcount has since gone down by 15 percentage points to reach 40.4 percent in 2018. In the meantime, due to a high population growth (2.7% annually), the number of poor has increased from 280 million in 1990 to 435 million in 2018. This hints at the significant role that demographic transition could play in reducing poverty in Africa; however, the literature suggests that most African countries are yet to harness demographic dividends.

The pace of poverty reduction in Africa has been much slower than that observed in other regions of the world (Figure 4.2). In the early 1990s, poverty was higher and concentrated in three regions in the world: (i) East Asia and Pacific; (ii) South Asia; and (iii) Sub-Saharan Africa. In fact, in 1990, the poverty headcount was higher in East Asia and Pacific, at 60.9%. By 2015, poverty was almost eradicated in East Asia and the Pacific, with an incidence of 2.1% only. In the same period, South Asia also managed to reduce poverty substantially, from 49.1% to 15%. Regrettably, poverty reduction in Africa was much lower, and as a consequence,

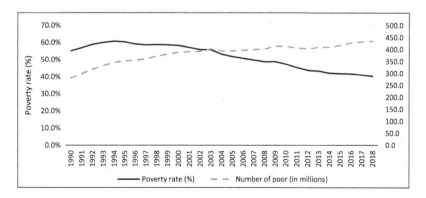

Figure 4.1 Over the past decades, the poverty headcount has gone down, but in the meantime, the number of poor has increased.

Source: Authors using povcal.net.

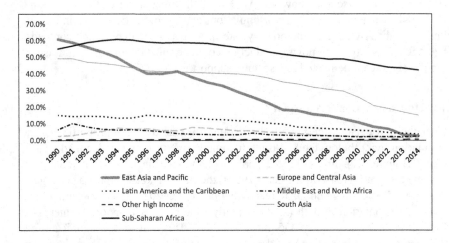

Figure 4.2 The pace of poverty reduction has been much slower in Africa.

Source: Authors using PovcalNet. Note: For South Asia, estimates for the period 1997 to 2002 are derived from linear interpolation because in PovcalNet, survey data coverage was too low for that period, and results for South Asia suppressed.

Africa is now by far the poorest continent both in terms of headcount and number of poor.

Currently, more than half of the world's extreme poor live in Africa. This represents a big shift from the early 1990s (Figure 4.3). Indeed, in 1990, half of the poor were living in East Asia and the Pacific, and this situation prevailed until 2002, when a shift took place, thanks to sustained and sharp poverty reduction in East Asia and the Pacific. Ever since, Africa has become home to most of the poor in the world. The latest robust available data are from the year 2014 and show that 53% of the poor live in Africa, against only 7% in East Asia and the Pacific. After Africa, the other region with the highest concentration of poor is South Asia, which is home to 34% of the global poor. However, similarly to East Asia and the Pacific, South Asia has experienced a much faster reduction in poverty over the last decade. World extreme poverty is more and more concentrated in Africa. Consequently, boosting poverty reduction in Africa will be critical in achieving the world's ambition of eradicating extreme poverty by 2030—as expressed in United Nations (UN) Sustainable Development Goal 1 (SDG 1).

Africa can learn a lot from the success story in reducing poverty in East Asia and the Pacific. East Asia and the Pacific managed to set up a business-friendly environment. In doing so, it was able to attract substantial foreign investments, which boosted the development of a strong industrial sector and connection to the global value chain. Quibria (2002) shows that success in reducing poverty in East Asia and the Pacific was driven by robust economic growth, with several countries growing at double digits. This robust growth was made possible thanks to conducive policy

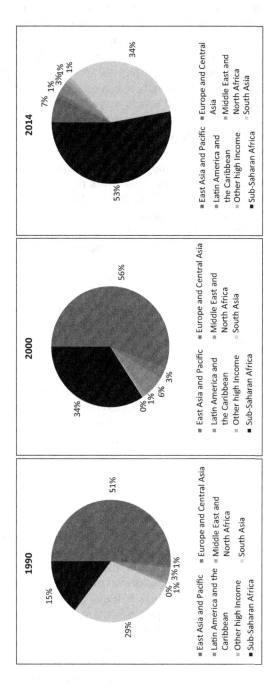

Figure 4.3 Now, more than half of the world's extreme poor lives in Africa.

Source: Authors using poveal.net.

and institutional reforms. The openness of the economy and market-oriented policies and institutions played a key role in capital accumulation. The rapid capital accumulation fueled robust economic growth. The openness of the economy was key to attracting foreign investment, and more importantly in tapping into the virtually unlimited international trading opportunities as well as easy access to new technologies. The robust economic growth resulted in increased employment in the formal sector, which led to rapid poverty reduction. Quibria (2002) notes that the initial conditions such as high initial educational attainment and dynamic agriculture sectors were not that important. Rather, what really mattered was the emergence of an economic framework that allowed critical economic freedoms and a structure of market-supporting institutions. While Africa can learn from East Asia and Pacific success, it will likely not follow the same path in reducing poverty. What works in East Asia and the Pacific may not work in Africa because we are in a different time in the world, and the constraints faced by Africa are different and probably more complex. However, Africa is in a good position to tap into opportunities provided by information and communications technology, and the current economic shift towards a climate-smart or climate-friendly economy.

4.3 A profile of poverty in Africa

There are several socio-demographic characteristics that are associated with poverty in Africa. Existing literature[4] has established that the following factors are strongly correlated with poverty in Africa: dependency ratio, gender, location, and education. A poor family tends to have more children, resulting in a high household size and high dependency ratio. Social norms and order constraints make it more difficult for women to enjoy a quality life. Women are often the backbone of the family, responsible for most household chores and farming activities in order to feed the family. Location matters as well, with rural residents having limited options in terms of jobs and income-generating activities. They rely on subsistence farming, often solely for household consumption, with a limited surplus that could be commercialized. Rurality is also marked by limited access to the market and limited access to amenities that make life enjoyable (electricity, piped water, health facilities, transport, roads, clubs, etc.). Education is often strongly correlated with welfare. A person with a high school attainment is more likely to access quality jobs, which will translate into better income and a higher level of welfare.

Poverty in Africa is both a chronic and a transitory condition (Christiaensen and Hill, 2019). For three in five poor, poverty is chronic. Meaning that these poor have been in this status of poverty for several years in a row (Dang and Dabalen, 2017). This suggests that poverty in Africa remains deeply structural, stemming from a lack of assets, weak access to public goods (infrastructure), and poor income-earning opportunities. Most people are poor because they cannot afford the cost of investing in human capital, or in acquiring minimum technology, which could help them in improving their productivity, and as a result, there is an intergenerational transmission of poverty,[5] thus a vicious cycle. The remaining two in five of Africa's poor are in transitory poverty. This reflects the fact that in Africa, households and firms are exposed to a high incidence of shocks, often with limited formal coping mechanisms available to them. Therefore, eradicating extreme poverty in a sustainable way will be more challenging in Africa.

In Africa, poverty is concentrated in a limited number of countries. Three in four poor live in 14 out of 52 countries. Most of them are large countries in terms

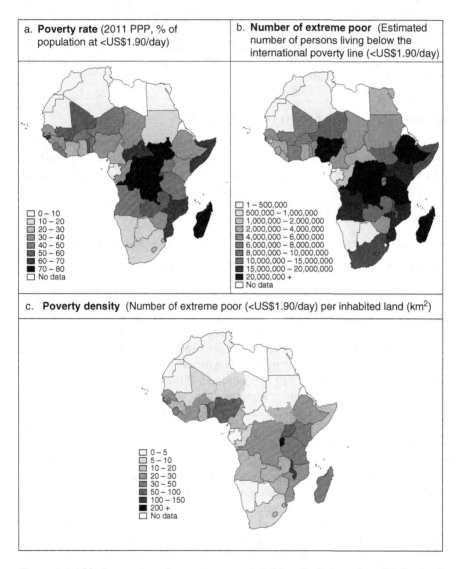

Figure 4.4 Africa's poverty and poor are concentrated in a limited number of (often landlocked) countries and regions within these countries.

Source: Authors using PovcalNet data. Note: data not available for Djibouti, Equatorial Guinea, Eritrea and Libya.

of overall population, but they are not always the poorest countries in terms of poverty rates. Poverty rates are highest in the Sahel countries and the northern regions of the coastal West African countries, extending east into Ethiopia and southeast into the Congo Basin and its eastern surrounding regions in Burundi, Rwanda, Tanzania, and Uganda (Figure 4.4). These are mostly also landlocked regions. Ranking countries from those with the largest number of poor, Nigeria accounts for about one-fifth of Africa's poor (79 million); the next two countries (the Democratic Republic of Congo and Ethiopia) account for another one-fifth; and the next ten (Tanzania, Kenya, Madagascar, Mozambique, Uganda, Angola, Malawi, South Africa, Somalia, Zambia, and Niger) account for the following 38 percent.

4.4 Key constraints to poverty reduction in Africa

From the existing literature, several factors (including: (i) widespread exposure to multiple shocks, such as the ongoing COVID-19 pandemic; (ii) the low productivity of the rural economy; (iii) low overall levels of human capital; (iv) a deep and persistent gender gap; (v) difficulties in accessing markets; and (vi) limited availability of quality jobs are constraining poverty reduction in Africa.[6]

4.4.1 Exposure to Multiple Shocks including COVID-19 and Climate Change

The COVID-19 crisis has reversed much of the progress in poverty reduction achieved in Africa in recent years. Andrew Dabalen and Pierella Paci (2020) estimated that for the first time in 25 years, the Africa region is in recession. The region's gross domestic product (GDP) per capita growth is forecast to be three to five percentage points lower. Based on these macroeconomic indicators, Dabalen and Paci estimated that a decline in GDP per capita of 3%—the optimistic forecast for 2020—will increase the number of Africans living below the international poverty line of $1.90 (2011 PPP) by 13 million. If the containment measures drag on for much longer, the downturn is prolonged or becomes even more severe. For instance, a 5% decline in GDP per capita could lead to poverty rates last seen in 2011 or send 50 million Africans into poverty. It would erase several years of hardwon progress in poverty reduction.

Beyond monetary poverty, COVID-19 is expected to have long-lasting effects on non-monetary dimensions of wellbeing. School closures are expected to further weaken educational outcomes among the current generation of school-age children. The ongoing crisis is also increasing the intensity of poverty for many of the continent's poorest households, and these losses, combined with the pandemic's direct impact on public health, are likely to be felt for decades to come. The COVID-19 crisis has had an especially devastating impact on food security. Most households have experienced a reduction in their income. As a consequence, a standard coping mechanism was to reduce food consumption. Rapid phone surveys done by the World Bank show a significant number of people running out of food. These phone surveys confirmed that issues of food security are increasing in Africa.

Estimates using the Food Insecurity Experience Scale (FIES), the methodology for measuring SDG Indicator 2.1.2. suggest that between 40% to 75% of adults in the sample countries are impacted by moderate or severe food insecurity (Gourlay et al.,, 2021).

Exposure to other types of shock is also high. African households are highly vulnerable to a wide range of shocks. The dependence of the rural population on rain-fed agriculture and pastoralism exposes a majority of the labor force to weather-related shocks and the long-term impact of climate change. Much of the manufacturing and services sectors also depend on agricultural output, intensifying macroeconomic vulnerability to droughts, floods, pests, crop and livestock disease, and conflict-induced disruptions in the rural economy. The impact of health shock is significant. Illness, accident, and death of family members are the most commonly reported idiosyncratic shocks. Given limited coverage of social protection, and limited penetration of insurance/financial services, to cope with shocks, the most commonly used strategy for households is to rely on savings, friends and family, or reduce their food consumption.

4.4.1.1 The low productivity of the rural economy

There is a lot of potential to increase rural income. Most of the African population (59%) resides in rural areas. Consequently, the agriculture sector, including farming and livestock, continues to be the largest employer.[7] Because of the reliance on rainfed agriculture, most farmers only have one main harvest season, resulting in strong seasonality in rural labor demand, income, and prices. Agricultural income is constrained by low productivity due to limited access to inputs, including financial services. Commercialization is also very low. Most households fail to create a surplus and only produce for their own consumption. Opportunities to increase rural income are many: increasing productivity of existing crops, greater commercialization, diversification into animal products and new high-value crops. Agriculture, innovation and technology hold the key to poverty reduction in Africa. Africa must find a way to move from subsistence farming to modern farms. Modern farms operate differently, because of advancements in technology, including sensors, devices, machines, and information technology. Modern farms will provide answers to the structural transformation that is needed and address the increasing demand for food.

4.4.1.2 Low overall levels of human capital

According to the Human Capital Index (HCI), a child born in Africa today can expect to achieve just 40 percent of their lifetime productive potential (Table 4.1), due to a combination of inadequate education access, poor health outcomes, and high mortality rates. The average child can expect to receive only eight years of schooling. The fraction of Children Under 5 Not Stunted remains high (69%). Most African countries are at the bottom distribution of the Human Capital Index (HCI) ranking. The HCI has five sub-indicators, and for all five, Africa has the lowest

Table 4.1 Human Capital Index 2020, averages by World Bank region

	East Asia & Pacific	Europe & Central Asia	Latin America & Caribbean	Middle East & North Africa	North America	South Asia	Sub-Saharan Africa
HCI Component 1: Survival							
Probability of Survival to Age 5	0.98	0.99	0.98	0.98	0.99	0.96	0.93
HCI Component 2: School							
Expected Years of School	11.90	13.10	12.10	11.60	13.30	10.80	8.30
Harmonized Test Scores	432	479	405	407	523	374	374
HCI Component 3: Health							
Survival Rate from Age 15 to 60	0.86	0.90	0.86	0.91	0.91	0.84	0.74
Fraction of Children Under 5 Not Stunted	0.76	0.90	0.85	0.82	–	0.69	0.69
Human Capital Index (HCI) 2020	0.59	0.69	0.56	0.57	0.75	0.48	0.40

Source: World Bank calculations based on the 2020 update of the Human Capital Index.

Notes: The table reports averages of the index components and the overall HCI by World Bank Group regions. "—" indicates data are unavailable.

score. A successful fight against poverty will include supporting efforts for Africa to close the human capital gap.

Gender inequality is a major cross-cutting challenge, despite Government efforts to address the issue. The incidence of child marriage continued to be among the highest in Sub-Saharan Africa (Wodon et al., 2020). Estimations from available data reveal that a staggering 37 percent of women got married at the age of 18 or below. African countries account for 15 of the 20 countries with the highest rates of child marriage. Child marriage contributes to maintaining high fertility rates. In addition, early marriage has a negative consequence on girls' ability to achieve a high level of education and also limits girls' ability to participate in the labor market. Decision making within households is dominated by men.

4.4.1.3 *Weak access to markets*

As discussed above, the East Asia and Pacific success story was made possible by economic openness and connection to the global value chain. Africa is currently far from that position. Currently, Africa accounts for just 2 percent of global trade, and only 17 percent of African exports are intra-continental, compared with 59 percent for Asia and 68 percent for Europe (Kende-Robb, 2021). There are several issues that must be dealt with in order to increase Africa's share in global trade. One of them has to do with the colonial heritage which designed Africa's economy to be a provider of raw materials for the Western world. A deep structural transformation is warranted. Successful integration of Africa into the global value chain will require a shift and a change of paradigm. Africa must boost its industrialization and move from a mere provider of raw materials to become a key player in the industrialized world by taking advantage of new communication and information technology, as well as opportunities provided by the green economy. To be successful, investments are required on several fronts to boost productivity and increase competitiveness, including in human capital, transport, and logistics (Chapter 9 of this book, by Bougna). Achievement of the structural changes that are required to increase Africa's share in the global market will be possible only if the right leadership is put in place—a leadership that will follow East Asia's example and put in place strong institutions, in favor of economic transformation.

4.4.1.4 *Limited availability of quality jobs*

Improvement in labor market conditions has been the main explanation behind many of the poverty success stories observed in the last decade (Inchauste et al., 2012). A decent job will guarantee long-term income security for a household and will ensure better living conditions. Currently, the vast majority of the labor force in Africa is employed either in subsistence agriculture (with limited access to market) for those in rural areas, or in the informal sector for those living in urban areas. These are low-paying jobs, which often are not enough to live above the poverty line; and when such jobs provide enough income to live above the poverty line, the worker remains highly vulnerable to shocks such as climate shocks, robbery, accidents, etc. The types of jobs that can push people out of poverty in a sustainable manner are found in the formal sectors, mostly in the secondary and tertiary sectors. The right equilibrium for Africa will require, on the one hand, a supply of quality jobs, with a population endowed with high skill, and on the other hand, a strong demand by firms. These conditions are needed for Africa to be able to replicate the double-digit growth that is needed to cross the pathways of economic emergence.

4.5 How will the AfCFTA affect constraints to poverty reduction in Africa?

The AfCFTA will have a direct or indirect effect on at least two constraints to poverty reduction highlighted in the previous section: (i) the low productivity of the rural economy, and (ii) difficulties in accessing markets.

Chapter 2 (Lonkeng) of this book indicates that there has been an increase in intra-Africa trade in recent years and estimates about the AfCFTA macroeconomic impacts (Chapter 3 of this book, by Keita) predicts that the AfCFTA will further enhance this trend and boost intra-African trade. So far, the intra-Africa trade is dominated by food, live animals and products from agroindustry to crude materials and mineral fuels. Estimates (Chapter 3) indicate that the agriculture sector and the manufacturing sectors will be those expanding and benefiting most from the AfCFTA. As demonstrated in previous sections, the biggest proportion of the African population relies on subsistence agriculture, therefore all the value addition and expansion that the AfCFTA will generate in that sector will have a significant impact on poverty reduction.

An increased demand for agricultural products will likely boost agricultural production, and yield additional income, especially for poor farmers. However, in most cases, to ensure that there is a supply response by farmers, government interventions will be required. Such intervention will include, but not be limited to, sensitization of and advisory services to farmers, provision of improved input, land reforms, provision of extension services, etc. All these will result in most cases in an increase in farmers' income, and subsequently a reduction of poverty. However, some farmers could be "losers" of the AfCFTA. Particularly, those living in neighboring areas, where the neighbor has a comparative advantage in producing the same good.

With the AfCFTA, African governments will be inclined to put more emphasis on developing regional transport infrastructures that are needed to fluidify regional trade (Chapter 9 of this book, by Bougna). In doing so, this will improve access to markets by farmers, and other non-farms producers. Improving access to the market will improve the competitivity of African products, and subsequently increase the demand and related incomes. Here again, those living in rural areas, who often are not connected to the market are likely to be the main beneficiaries of the new infrastructures. In case these infrastructure projects are well designed, it will also result in job creation for the local population, contributing again to income growth. The development of the manufacturing sector with linkages to the agriculture sector will also lead to the creation of non-farm jobs in rural areas and lead to increased revenues and living standards.

4.6 Poverty impact of the AfCFTA

This section quantifies the potential impact of the AfCFTA on extreme poverty. There are several channels through which trade reforms such as the AfCFTA can affect welfare (Hertel and Reimer, 2005), including: (i) the price and availability of goods; (ii) factor prices, income, and employment; (iii) government transfers influenced by changes in revenue from trade taxes; (iv) the incentives for investment and innovation, which affect long-run economic growth; (v) external shocks, in particular, changes in the terms of trade; (v) short-run risk and adjustment costs. It is not easy to model all these channels, and most papers focus on one or two of these.

Building on the existing literature on poverty simulation, two complementary approaches will be used here: (i) first, we rely on Ravallion (2004)[8] who expressed the growth of the poverty headcount as a function of the GDP per capita growth and the Gini inequality index; and (ii) we grow elasticity of poverty (GEP). The GEP is the percentage reduction in poverty rates associated with a percentage change in

Table 4.2 Impact of the AfCFTA on poverty in Africa

	Baseline	Pessimist scenario (growth =2%)	Optimistic scenario (growth =5%)
Poverty headcount ($1.90) in %			
Ravallion approach	40.4%	38.7%	28.2%
Growth elasticity of poverty approach	40.4%		
Number of poor ($1.90) in millions			
Ravallion approach	435.6	416.8	304.2
Growth elasticity of poverty approach	435.6		

Source: Authors using PovcalNet data.

mean (per capita) income. Here the change in per capita income is assumed to be the same as the GDP per capita growth. Estimations suggest that in the last decade, GEP for Africa was 1.3, meaning a one percentage point increase in per capita GDP will translate to a reduction of 1.3 percentage points of the extreme poverty headcount. Both approaches provide estimates that are very close.

The macroeconomic numbers used here are derived from Chapter 3 of this book, which estimates that the AfCFTA will increase Africa's growth by 0.5 percentage points annually from 2021 until 2030.

Under the pessimist scenario, the AfCFTA will reduce the extreme poverty headcount by a bit less than 2 percentage points, corresponding to about 19 million people lifted out of poverty (Table 4.2). These numbers could improve substantially under the most optimistic scenario, with 131 million people lifted out of poverty thanks to the AfCFTA. The latter corresponds to a reduction of 12 percentage points in the extreme poverty headcount. Clearly if successful, the AfCFTA will provide Africa with an opportunity to increase its chances of achieving the world's ambition of eradicating extreme poverty by 2030—as expressed in United Nations (UN) Sustainable Development Goal 1 (SDG 1).

4.7 Conclusion

Africa's performance in poverty reduction over the past three decades has been unsatisfactory and much lower than the rest of the developing regions, making currently the continent home to more than half the total poor in the world. The AfCFTA represents a great potential for poverty reduction. It could reduce by up to 1/3 of the poor in an optimistic scenario and about 10% in a pessimistic scenario. This stems from the capacity of the agreement to generate long-term growth, boost intra-African trade, foster value addition and expansion in the agriculture and manufacturing sectors and enhance market access. These cumulative effects will increase productivity and income in the agriculture sector, which is for now the biggest employer in most African economies, with more than half the workers. The benefits of the AfCFTA will only be effective if governments strive to enhance the productive capacities in the agriculture sector to ensure that supply meets the increased demand in agriculture and manufactured products that will come with the AfCFTA.

Notes

1 The views and opinions expressed in this paper are those of the authors and do not necessarily reflect the views or positions of their employers or institutions.
2 Agriculture employs 65–70 percent of the African workforce, supports the livelihoods of 90 percent of Africa's population, and accounts for about a quarter of the continent's GDP (OECD and FAO, 2016; World Bank, 2016).
3 Poverty is measured by the US$1.9 international poverty line. The results and conclusions remain unchanged when using the US$2.15 poverty line.
4 See for instance Buddelmeyer and Verick (2008), Anyanwu and Anyanwu (2017), and Haughton and Khandker (2009).
5 See for instance Bird (2013) and De Lannoy (2015).
6 For more information, check the various Poverty Assessment Reports done by the World Bank.
7 According to the AfDB, agriculture currently employs 65–70 percent of the African workforce. Moreover, 83 percent of the poor in Africa live from subsistence agriculture.
8 Ravallion (2004) demonstrates that the following equation expresses the growth of the poverty headcount capita GDP as a function of the GDP per capita growth and the Gini inequality index:

$$\frac{\Delta FGT0}{FGT0} = -9.3 * (1 - Gini)^3 * \frac{\Delta GDPcap}{GDPcap}$$

Where, *FGT0* stands for poverty headcount ratio and *GDPcap* for per capita GDP.

References

Anyanwu, John C. and Joanna C. Anyanwu, 2017. The key drivers of poverty in sub-Saharan Africa and what can be done about it to achieve the poverty sustainable development goal. *Asian Journal of Economic Modelling*, 1, pp. 33–50.
Beegle, Kathleen, and Luc Christiaensen, eds., 2019. *Accelerating Poverty Reduction in Africa*. Washington, DC: World Bank. doi:10.1596/978-1-4648-1232-3.
Bird, Kate, 2013. The Intergenerational Transmission of Poverty: An Overview. In: Shepherd A., and Brunt J. (eds.), *Chronic Poverty. Rethinking International Development Series*. London: Palgrave Macmillan. https://doi.org/10.1057/9781137316707_4
Buddelmeyer, Hielke and Sher Verick, 2008. *Understanding the Drivers of Poverty Dynamics in Australian Households*. Wiley Online Library. https://doi.org/10.1111/j.1475-4932.2008.00493.x
Christiaensen, Luc and Ruth Hill, 2019. Poverty in Africa. https://doi.org/10.1596/978-1-4648-1232-3_ch1
Dabalen, Andrew and Pierella Paci, 2020. How severe will the poverty impacts of COVID-19 be in Africa? World Bank Blogs. https://blogs.worldbank.org/africacan/how-severe-will-poverty-impacts-covid-19-be-africa

Dang, Hai-Anh H., and Andrew L. Dabalen, 2017. *Is Poverty in Africa Mostly Chronic or Transient?: Evidence from Synthetic Panel Data*. Policy Research Working Paper No. 8033. Washington, DC: The World Bank. https://openknowledge.worldbank.org/handle/10986/26471 License: CC BY 3.0 IGO.

De Lannoy, Ariane, Leibbrandt, Murray, and Frame Emily, 2015. A Focus on Youth: An Opportunity to Disrupt the Intergenerational Transmission of Poverty. In: De Lannoy, A., Swartz, S., Lake, L. & Smith, C. (eds) *South African Child Gauge 2015*. Cape Town: Children's Institute, UCT.

Gourlay, Sydney, Akuffo Amankwah, and Alberto Zezza, 2021. Food security in the face of COVID-19: Evidence from Africa. World Bank Blogs. https://blogs.worldbank.org/opendata/food-security-face-covid-19-evidence-africa

Haughton, Jonathan and Shahidur R. Khandker, 2009. *Handbook on Poverty and Inequality*. Washington, DC: The World Bank.

Hertel, Thomas and Jeffrey Reimer, 2005. Predicting the poverty impacts of trade reform. *The Journal of International Trade & Economic Development, Taylor & Francis Journals*, 14(4), 377–405.

Inchauste, Gabriela, João Pedro Azevedo, Sergio Olivieri, Jaime Saavedra, and Hernan Winkler, 2012. *When Job Earnings Are Behind Poverty Reduction. Economic Premise; No. 97*. Washington, DC: The World Bank. © World Bank. https://openknowledge.worldbank.org/handle/10986/17067 License: CC BY 3.0 IGO.

Kende-Robb, Caroline, 2021. *6 Reasons Why Africa's New Free Trade Area is a Global Game Changer*. World Economic Forum.

OECD and FAO, 2016. OECD-FAO Agricultural Outlook 2016–2025. Paris: OECD Publishing. http://dx.doi.org/10.1787/agr_outlook-2016-en

Quibria, Muhammad G., 2002. Growth and Poverty: Lessons from the East Asia Miracle Revisited. ADB Institute Research Paper No. 33.

Ravallion, Martin, 2004. Pro-Poor Growth: A Primer. Policy Research Working Paper No. 3242. World Bank, Washington DC: The World Bank. https://openknowledge.worldbank.org/handle/10986/14116 License: CC BY 3.0 IGO.

Wodon, Quentin, Adenike Onagoruwa, Chata Malé, Claudio Montenegro, Hoa Nguyen, and Bénédicte de la Brière, 2020. *How Large Is the Gender Dividend? Measuring Selected Impacts and Costs of Gender Inequality*. The Cost of Gender Inequality Notes Series. Washington D.C.: World Bank. © World Bank. https://openknowledge.worldbank.org/handle/10986/33396 License: CC BY 3.0 IGO.

World Bank, 2016. *CPIA Africa–Assessing Africa's Policies and Institutions: 2015 CPIA Results for Africa*. Washington, D.C.: World Bank Group.

World Bank, 2020. The African Continental Free Trade Area: Economic and Distributional Effects. © Washington, DC: World Bank. http://hdl.handle.net/10986/34139 License: CC BY 3.0 IGO.

5 The AfCFTA

What it means for the AGOA, EBA, and trading with Asia?[1]

Souleymane Coulibaly, Natnael Simachew Nigatu, and Angella Faith Montfaucon

5.1 Introduction

Africa's international trade participation is rising, though it still accounts for a relatively smaller share of the global trade, see Lonkeng's Chapter 2 of this book. Non-reciprocal preferential trade agreements (NRPTAs) such as Everything But Arms (EBA) and the Africa Growth and Opportunity Act (AGOA) played their part since they were launched in the early 2000s. Africa's export to Europe has increased from US$ 72 billion in 2001 to US$ 212 billion in 2018. Similarly, following AGOA, Africa's export to the USA has increased from US$ 25 billion in 2000 to US$ 35 billion in 2018, after reaching its maximum of US$ 108 billion in 2008.[2] Moreover, Europe's and the US's export to Africa has more than doubled since the entry into force of EBA and AGOA, respectively.[3]

Despite the non-existence of such agreements between Asia and Africa, trade between the two continents has increased substantially over the last two decades. Asia took over Europe's place as the leading trade partner of Africa both as an export destination and import origin since the mid-2010s. Achieving such performance without formal trade agreements *emphasizes the huge trade potential between Africa and Asia that demands to be realized.* The African Continental Free Trade Agreement (AfCFTA) is an opportunity to strengthen the relationship between the two continents to the next level to maximize their mutual benefits. Among other things, the AfCFTA's success will depend on its achievement in engaging with East Asia due to the following four reasons.

First, East Asia is home to the largest cohort of middle-class consumers demanding sophisticated goods and services, which gives Africa a vast market to diversify and transform its economic structure. As of 2020, around 2 billion middle-income consumers reside in the Asia Pacific region. It is projected to grow to 3.4 billion in 2030, which would accommodate two-thirds of the global middle-income population (Malik, 2013).

Second, East Asian economies are strategically trying to move away from their trade and investment dependence (on the US and the EU) for survival and risk mitigation. On the other hand, Africa needs investments in different sectors to utilize its cheap labor force and natural resources fully. The World Investment Report

DOI: 10.4324/9781003456568-5

(UNCTAD, 2020) shows that East Asian countries contribute on average 25% of the global FDI outflow, which is a substantial amount. Once the AfCFTA Investment Protocol is complete, it could facilitate FDI flow between the two continents. In addition, the uniformity of the regulatory environment following the AfCFTA will help to reduce entry costs.

Third, the goods and services that East Asia specializes in can be fragmented to maximize efficiency and access to resources. As the 2020 World Development Report shows, to keep the high growth while engaging in global value chains (GVCs), countries need to move progressively to sophisticated participation forms (World Bank, 2020). As East Asian countries proceed to the more complex production process and specialize in them, Africa could follow by taking over the relatively less complex task and engage in GVCs with East Asian countries to maximize their mutual gains. Such opportunities would increase intra-Africa trade as well, which is the central goal of the AfCFTA.

Fourth, involvement in GVCs and diversifying into these goods and services will make the AfCFTA more trade-creating than diverting. For example, de Soyres et al. (2019) show that countries that are not integrated into the GVC experience a decrease in import and export activities with the rest of the world after signing a regional trade agreement. Hence, more vigorous trade participation in GVCs in general and engagement with East Asia, in particular, will contribute to the success of the AfCFTA.

While AGOA and EBA are still to deliver on their promises, the Covid-19 pandemic shattered the world economy and triggered some reconfiguration of GVCs of interest to both Africa and Asia. Recent trends in trade and investment between Africa and Asia suggest a huge potential still to be tapped. Now is the time to engineer a scaling up of trade and investment between the two regions. Learning from AGOA and EBA mixed performance, the private sector is to drive this reengineering.

This chapter aims to explore the impact of the AfCFTA on accelerating trade between Africa and East Asia. It finds that by utilizing the current opportunities created by the AfCFTA and the RCEP, Africa should apply lessons from Asia to participate in global value chains to advance the trade relationship between the two regions and the rest of the world. The AfCFTA and the RCEP are very timely and can potentially transform the trade and investment relations between Africa and East Asia. For example, the current developments in the automotive industry where major car manufacturers are choosing hubs to delocalize assembly plans could be accelerated by the success of the AfCFTA.

The remainder of the chapter is as follows. Section 2 explores the legacy of non-reciprocal preferential trade agreements; Section 3 explores the prospects of the African Continental Free Trade Agreement; Section 4 focuses on the prospect of trade and investment with Asia; Section 5 analyses the process from political NRPTAs to reciprocal private trade and investment; and Section 6 concludes and provides policy recommendations.

5.2 The legacy of non-reciprocal preferential trade agreements

AGOA and EBA are two landmark non-reciprocal preferential trade agreements (NRPTA) extended by the US and the EU to some African (also non-African for EBA) countries that have been in effect for nearly two decades now. They were expected to boost the exports of eligible products from designated countries.

Coulibaly and Kassa (2019) examine the impact of AGOA on the export of African countries using a synthetic control method, which addresses major limitations in the existing empirical approaches. The study finds that most countries registered gains in exports due to AGOA. Nevertheless, the gains were varying across countries and periods. Notably, they find that much of the gains are attributed to commodity exports such as petroleum, mineral, and agricultural products, whose prices are volatile in the global market. Some countries managed to expand into manufacturing and other industrial goods.

Coulibaly (2017) compared the trade elasticities of AGOA and EBA by focusing on Western African countries' export between 2001 and 2015. He employed the Pseudo-Poisson Maximum Likelihood (PPML) estimation approach to properly account for bilateral trade flows' heteroscedasticity and zero trade values. Over the sample period, AGOA's effect on the textile sector exports was stronger than non-textile ones. Moreover, when examined in a short period, the estimated impact of the textile provision of AGOA is even more substantial. However, when focused on West African countries, the textile sector's effect was statistically insignificant. By contrast, the estimated EBA coefficients are large and positive, although not statistically significant. The study used the estimated coefficients on AGOA and EBA for each year to simulate export potentials of ECOWAS countries, if all ECOWAS countries are allowed to earn the full benefits of the NRPTAs. The simulations' overall result indicates that ECOWAS exports of non-textile products to the EU or the US could have been 2.5 times more than the registered levels, on average. Furthermore, the exports of textile products could have been four times more. The results imply that stronger commitment to more economic integration would substantially help to nurture the unexploited export capacity of the region, which calls for a revision of the AGOA and EBA provisions to incentivize cooperative behaviors.

What determines the success of NRPTAs? Among other things, the success of the NRPTAs depends on the strictness of the rules of origins (RoO) involved in them. De Melo and Portugal-Perez (2014) examined the role of RoO in the case of AGOA and EBA, particularly by focusing on the garment and apparel trade. AGOA allows more than half of the beneficiary countries to use a fabric of any origin and still maintain their beneficiary status (single transformation) through its special rule. In contrast, the EU requires the beneficiary of EBA to use fabric produced within the exporting country itself only (double transformation). The study exploits this variation to study the effect of the rules of origin clause included in NRPTA. The result showed that the simplification of the AGOA procedure increased the beneficiaries' export to the US by approximately 168% for the top seven beneficiaries, or approximately four times as much as the 44% growth effect from the initial preferential access under AGOA without single transformation. However, at least in the case of apparel produced by the low-income African countries, the double transformation requirement by the EU has discouraged developing exports at the intensive and extensive margins. Brenton and Hoppe (2006) look at AGOA apparel exports from 2000 to 2004 and find that all of the growth during this time has been from countries utilizing the third-country fabric rule. SSA exports of apparel to the US under the third-country fabric rule increased from 158.9 million to 234.4 million square meter equivalents between 2001 and 2004, signifying the role of RoO.

There are also other factors that determine the success of NRPTAs. As an extension of their impact evaluation work, Coulibaly and Kassa (2019) investigate and identify major determinants that resulted in variation of AGOA across the beneficiaries. The results show that four factors largely explain the variations in the trade impacts of AGOA: the availability of ICT infrastructure, the efficiency of institutional and legal frameworks (including property right protection), the ease of labor market regulations, and sound macroeconomic environment (including the stability of exchange rate and inflation levels). The degree of effective protection NRPTAs provide is another critical factor that determines their success. Sorgho and Tharakan (2019) argue that given the trend of trade liberalization in the EU (with non-NRPTA beneficiaries) and the further erosion of preferences, developed countries need to supplement such trade agreements with other policies to support exports from developing countries.

Overall, NRPTAs played a positive role in increasing African countries' export, though more is expected, and the results are sometimes mixed depending on different factors. These results lend relevant lessons for the success of the AfCFTA regarding the need to establish adequate infrastructure, provision of meaningful reduction in trade barriers (both tariff and non-tariff), ICT development, maintenance of effective institutional and regulatory frameworks, etc. Moreover, the issue of rule of origin needs to be carefully considered, as it is one of the main factors affecting the success of regional integrations. In fact, the UNCTAD dedicated its 2019 report on African development to the issue of RoO and noted that rules of origin could be a game-changer for the success of the AfCFTA as long as they are simple, accessible, transparent, business-friendly, and predictable.

5.3 The prospects of the African Continental Free Trade Agreement

GVCs are characterized by the division of the production process into a series of stages, with each stage adding value and at least two stages in different countries. A country's positioning in GVCs is a determining factor of the available gains from trade and foreign investment, such as the number and quality of jobs, transfers of capital, infrastructure, skills, and technology. Thanks to GVCs and the access to global markets, it is now possible for developing countries to participate in the gains from producing sophisticated products by specializing in tasks, rather than having to master the entire production process of a good from large domestic firms, as was common in the earlier waves of industrialization. Countries can join GVCs by facilitating the entry of domestic firms or by attracting foreign direct investment (FDI). The FDI option includes more direct access to foreign know-how and technology.

Countries hosting lead GVC firms have been hard hit by the COVID-19 outbreak, disrupting production and trade across many other countries. In late March 2020, one month after COVID-19 was declared as a pandemic, China, Japan, South Korea, Germany, and the US, five countries central to manufacturing GVCs across the world, represented 42% of cases worldwide, and robust measures to contain the spread of the virus there thus disrupted production and trade from GVCs across many other countries. Given how critical GVCs are to the integration of developing and emerging countries into the global economy, the outbreak of COVID-19 quickly had severe impacts globally, generating more widespread disruptions as workers in other parts of the world went into quarantine, triggering an increasing shortage of labor across many sectors and leading to a sharp slowdown in production and trade (Baldwin and Di Mauro, 2020).

While AGOA and EBA are still to deliver on their promises, the COVID-19 pandemic shattered the world economy and triggered some reconfiguration of GVCs that is opportune for the AfCFTA. For example, the redundancy in suppliers or diversity location of production is a strategy for resilience against disruption to supply value. This creates an opportunity for previously unpopular GVC destinations for the private sector. Javorick (2020) argues that the benefit of such destinations from the reconfiguration process depends on their investment promotion and business friendliness efforts.

There are already ongoing reconfiguration efforts in several sectors. The Industrial, Manufacturing, and Transport (IMT) GVC cluster is one of them. Companies within this sector were already engaged in GVC reconfirmation after the US-China trade dispute, but COVID-19 created a more urgent need to improve their resilience against reoccurring health, climate, or natural disasters that could disrupt their supply chain. For example, Tata Motors of India has decided to diversify its sourcing from China and look for alternative solutions. Moreover, the German African Business Association argues that Africa could become a new player in the game of globalized production. There are ongoing efforts among European car manufacturers to diversify their sourcing strategies to North African countries due to their geographic advantages.[4] The AfCFTA could help African countries to claim their fair share in the overall reconfiguration process. For example, the reduction of tariff and non-tariff barriers between African countries could attract regional value chain that can produce desired intermediate products to European car manufacturers at a cheap cost and a nearby place, assuming a cordial rule of origin clause would prevail.

Even prior to COVID-19 the IMT cluster was showing interesting trends especially in the automotive industry. Many African countries almost exclusively import used cars, which is a challenge to promote domestic production in the sector. This is progressively changing. For example, Volkswagen expressed its desire to start a small-series assembly in Ghana and also showed interest in Kenya, Rwanda,

Nigeria, and Ethiopia.[5] Although Ghana has around 30 million people, their access to ECOWAS allows Volkswagen to access 350 million people. Toyota is cementing its position in Africa by investing in Cote d'Ivoire and South Africa. Cote d'Ivoire's government signed an agreement in 2019 with Toyota to build a vehicle assembly plant in the West African nation.[6] In January 2020, Toyota South Africa announced it would invest 4 billion Rands in its parts distribution and manufacturing projects in the country. Toyota has a warehouse in Johannesburg and a car assembly plant in prospection, south of Durban.[7] Nissan has a commercial and industrial presence in South Africa, Nigeria, Egypt, and Ghana. The company is still evaluating the Kenyan market.

Morocco is showing a significant progress in Africa's automotive sector. The arrival of the PSA Peugeot Citroën plant in Kenitra, northern Morocco, has led to a wave of investments by automotive equipment manufacturers. Notably, firms from China. Moroccan Association for automotive industry and car manufacturers (AMICA) claims that as of 2019, the industry consists of more than 150 companies, 160,000 jobs, and nearly €10 billion in exports. Morocco plans to produce more than 700,000 vehicles per year by 2022—90% of them for export—and thus become the number-one manufacturer on the continent, ahead of South Africa, which manufactured 610,854 vehicles in 2018.[8]

These developments are not only relevant in advancing the IMT GVC cluster and creating jobs. They also play a critical role in reducing pollution and environmental problems. Between 2015 and 2018, the EU, Japan, and the US exported 14 million used vehicles worldwide—40% of which went to African countries (UNEP, 2020). The UNEP report concludes that the gap in policy measures between exporting and importing markets has led to global trade in used vehicles that are very old, unsafe, and polluting. Thus, a continental level and stricter regulations on the import of used vehicles would help lower emissions and air pollution levels, improve road safety and promote the continent's rising automotive sector.

The development of the automotive industry as well as the efficiency of ports in South Africa and Morocco makes them natural candidates to be continental hubs. As figures 5.1 A to 5.3A in the appendix section show, the port efficiency of the SADC region is better, the transport cost to selected Asian markets is lower and it performs better than other African RECs in terms of logistics performance index. Other African countries could take advantage of these through regional value chains that would be relatively easier under the AfCFTA framework. The technology, media, and telecommunication (TMT) GVC cluster is also undergoing reconfigurations to de-risk and improve its efficacy. After COVID-19 related disruptions, firms embraced digital transformation to improve efficiency and reduce risks. Multinationals are using AI, machine learning, and Big Data to monitor their productions' entire supply network and use ICT advances to plan, develop, and oversee production remotely. Another example could be the shift towards online shopping, which is a vital resilience mechanism when in-person contacts are not possible. New technology platforms are developing across the continent, from Ride in Ethiopia to health care platform Bylos in Rwanda. In Kenya, nearly 50% of all transactions are done through mobile payment.

Telecom, media and tech investment and consolidation activity in Africa is predicted to rise further. A number of significant deals are scheduled, including the opening up of Ethiopia's telecom sector in 2021. Pan-African telecom operators such as MTN, Safaricom and Vodacom are among those vying to enter Ethiopia for the opportunity to serve its 105 million population following progress in the telecom privatization process, as per the TMT Finance.[9] Privatizations of telecom assets are also planned for Togocom and Benin Telecom in West Africa, with consolidation investments expected in Kenya and Tunisia. Meanwhile, Airtel has hired banks for an IPO of its entire Africa portfolio while several telcos are bidding for Millicom's assets. The acceleration of investment into mobile and broadband infrastructure across the region continues as operators and investors try to meet the need for data services.

Global giants such as Facebook have had offices in Johannesburg since 2015. Facebook is now expanding to Lagos. The Nigerian office is set to become operational in the second half of 2022 and will support the entire Sub-Saharan Africa region. It will be the first on the continent to house a team of expert engineers building for the future of Africa and beyond. X (formerly known as Twitter) has recently decided to open its first African office in Ghana.

The expansion of information and technology can also enhance business processing outsourcing (BPO) activities in Africa. Moreover, the service sector expansion can be useful to promote the export of goods. Coulibaly and Mirza (2017) show that the share of employment in foreign affiliates in Egypt, Morocco, and Nigeria is correlated with the export of goods. However, they find no effect for South Africa. (see figure 5.4 in the appendix section). Innovations in these promising tech sectors will however require effective Intellectual Property (IP) protection. The AfCFTA's discussions over harmonizing key IP issues could help facilitate the growth of the TMT GVC cluster in particular, and the other GVC clusters in general (Songwe, 2020).

The Health and Life Science (HLS) GVC cluster is perhaps one of the clusters undergoing the fastest reconfiguration process following the COVID-19 outbreak. There were more than 120 new export bans on medical goods by April 2020 (Evenett et al., 2021), which exposed the vulnerability of the current system and triggered reshoring activities. For example, the Italian company Coccato & Mezzetti Srl resumed the production of a disposable biodegradable face mask in Italy after stopping production in 2005 due to competition from low-cost alternatives coming from China (Barbieri et al., 2020).

Export bans and rising protectionism in the health sector put stronger pressure on Africa, which fulfills 80% of its pharmaceutical needs via import. The vulnerability was recognized earlier, and the African Union and the head of States agreed on the Pharmaceutical Manufacturing Plan for Africa (PMPA) in 2005. However, COVID-19 has made more apparent and urgent the need to implement this plan. The AfCFTA could facilitate the implementation of the PMPA and the creation of regional value chains as it involves over 1.3 billion people, which creates a significant economy of scale and scope. Moreover, a pooled procurement mechanism will encourage leading global generic pharmaceutical manufacturers to build plants in

Africa or partner with African pharmaceutical companies to manufacture generic products (Byaruhanga, 2020).

The development of a biotechnology supply chain is predicted to create over 16 million jobs across the continent (Songwe, 2020). Hence, the AfCFTA can facilitate Africa's active participation in the global HLS GVC cluster via IP protection laws. Especially, those countries which are already involved in pharmaceutical production would benefit more. However, the industry is challenged by differences in regulations concerning production and trading of pharmaceutical products among African countries. The AfCFTA is an opportunity that can allow African countries to enhance regional and international cooperation, improve countries' enforcement standards and move towards a harmonized, predictable, and reliable regional IPRs enforcement system building from TRIPS and other treaties (Elbeshbishi, 2021, i.e. Chapter 13).

The COVID-19 pandemic has clearly shown the continent's vulnerability in the production of pharmaceutical products. Though Africa depends on others for a significant proportion of its pharmaceutical product demands, 34 out of 55 African countries have some level of pharmaceutical production,[10] with countries offering an array of incentives to encourage pharmaceutical investment. The industry has been undergoing visible shifts over the past few years and is responding to the well-recognized vulnerability of the continent during the COVID-19 period. For example, European drug makers—including GlaxoSmithKline (GSK), Sanofi and Novartis—are investing in Africa to capture a larger market share. Sanofi is spending EUR 70 million (US$ 94.15 million) on a new plant in Algeria, while GSK just spent US$ 98 million to raise its stake in its Nigerian consumer products unit. GSK is also working to boost its market penetration in other countries, with the goal of increasing volumes fivefold within five years, partly by keeping prices very low. The European Investment Banks is launching a EUR 50 million pharmaceutical investment initiative, together with ENUP Foundation. It will contribute to reducing dependency on drug imports and address medical supply chain weaknesses linked to COVID-19.

Following the US decision to temporarily suspend intellectual property rights on COVID-19 vaccines, African Union officials hope that at least three countries—South Africa, Senegal and Rwanda—will develop the capacity to produce vaccines for the continent, including the mRNA-type vaccines that emerged as an innovative technology against COVID-19. Such African hubs could be very helpful to combat future pandemics if the AfCFTA agreement includes the provisions of the Paris Convention, which is also included in the TRIPS agreement, on compulsory licenses. The agreement allows countries to provide compulsory licenses to interested third parties in extreme situations to provide otherwise unaffordable drugs in their domestic markets. Exporting drugs manufactured through compulsory licensing is not normally allowed but sharing among members of the same regional economic grouping could be exempted (Elbeshbishi, 2021). Hence, African countries should strive to use these hubs and produce critical drugs for the benefit of the whole continent under the AfCFTA framework.[11]

5.4 The prospect of trade and investment with Asia

Despite the non-existence of trade agreements between Asia and Africa,[12] the trade relationship between the two continents has increased substantially over the last two decades. As the two panels on the left side of Figure 5.1 show, the import and export relationships between Africa and Asia have increased in multiple folds. Asia took over Europe's place as the leading trade partner of Africa both as an export destination and import origin since the mid-2010s.

We find a similar result when we investigate the percentage shares of Africa's export to the Asian, European, and US markets as depicted in the lower two panels in Figure 5.1. Africa's exports share to the US market declined from 16% in 2000 to 6% in 2018. Similarly, Europe's market share has declined from 50% to 34% during the same period.

However, Asia's market share in African exports has increased from 16% in 2000 to 40% in 2018 (bottom right panel). Africa's market share in the exports of Asia, the EU and the US is substantially smaller than these values. Nevertheless, one has to note that Africa's exports to Asia has doubled between 2000 and 2017. Still, the data indicates there is wide room to enhance the Africa-Asia trade.

The trade relationship between Asia and Africa is unbalanced. As the top right panel in Figure 5.1 shows, the trade balance between Africa and Asia has deteriorated from 2000 to 2015; it has been improving since then. Nevertheless, it is still far away from being balanced.

The deteriorating trade balance between the two regions may not necessarily be a good sign if it cannot ensure long-lasting benefits for both participants. Understanding the type of imported and exported products between the two regions can highlight some relevant facts. The top-left panel in Figure 5.2 shows Africa's export to Asia. Africa mainly exported fuel and lubricants in the mid-2000s, but both exports of primary and processed industrial supplies are increasing and represent the highest share for the latest year.[13] It is an encouraging signal for African countries aiming to play a significant role in the reconfiguration of the IMT sector. Further examination of the data (not reported in the figures) shows that the relationship between SADC and China plays the major role. The top right panel shows the export of Asia to Africa. The industrial supplies, capital goods, and transport equipment and parts represent over 50% of the products. Such products are essential to establish a vibrant manufacturing sector in Africa. Despite the anecdotal evidence on trade with Asia, notably China, the share of consumer goods is relatively smaller compared to capital goods or industrial supplies.

Analysis has shown that exports to third markets of countries with a greater degree of competition with China tend to rise/fall significantly more as the renminbi appreciates/depreciates, with a greater magnitude for homogeneous goods which constitute the bulk of African exports (Mattoo et al., 2020). Other studies have found this negative effect specifically for Africa. For instance, exports of manufactured goods by China and other countries to African countries mainly exert a negative effect on African manufacturing. It is not all bad news however, as China also provides relatively cheaper imports of machinery and other intermediate and

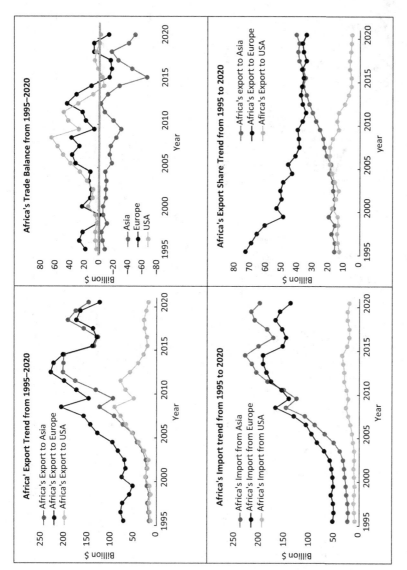

Figure 5.1 Africa's trend of export and imports in value and shares.

Source: Authors' illustration based on BACI data.

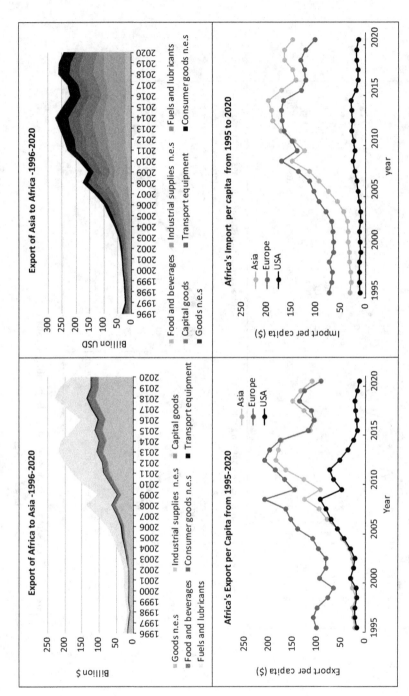

Figure 5.2 Africa's trend of export and imports based on BEC classification.

Source: Authors' illustration based on BACI data.

capital goods, such that a moderate real appreciation of African currencies vis-à-vis the renminbi positively influences manufacturing value added (Guillaumont and Hua, 2015).

With its 1.3 billion people (which represents 20% of the world population), Africa should be able to export more to Asia and simultaneously be a dependable market for Asian products.

More rigorously, the export potential could be predicated by calculating the counterfactual level of trade that would be predicted based on demand, supply, and easiness of export under a frictionless economy. Based on International Trade Center (ITC) data, we have plotted the percentage share of the actual and untapped (unrealized) exports compared to the predicted potentials (for Africa's five geographic regions).[14] Figure 5.3 shows that the five African geographic regions have not utilized more than 40% of their potential to export to the four Asian regions considered (ASEAN, East Asia, South Asia, and Central Asia & East Europe) between 2015 and 2019. In relative terms, Southern Africa's performance is better. Further examination of the data at the country level reveals exporting to China has the highest untapped potential in terms of value, which calls for a stronger linkage between Africa and China.

We further disaggregate our analysis to focus on the trade among the ASEAN and three African Regional Economic Communities (ARECs), namely the EAC-IGAD, the ECOWAS, and the SADC. Disaggregated analysis helps to identify region-specific challenges, which is relevant to suggesting targeted solutions.

As Figure 5.4 shows, export has been increasing in the four economic communities over the last 25 years, but the ASEAN countries' performance is substantially higher. The ASEAN countries steadily increased their export values by more than threefold from less than US$ 500 billion in 1995 to US$ 1,500 billion in 2018. Meanwhile, the EAC-IGAD, ECOWAS, and SADC only managed to increase their export values by a few US$ billion during the same period.

The four regional communities experienced a reduction in exports right after the global financial crisis but managed to bounce back in the subsequent years. Nevertheless, the three African Regional Economic Communities' (ARECs) export has lost its momentum and stagnated since the 2014's commodity price shock.

Exports of the four regional communities has been increasing over the past two decades, with their intra-regional trade growing substantially higher than inter-regional trade. However, the performance of the four regional blocs was uneven. ASEAN countries steadily increased their exports to the three African regional blocs, but the intra-ASEAN trade growth dwarfs it. The ARECs also increased their exports to the ASEAN region since the mid-2000s with varying degrees. The SADC takes the bigger share, and the ECOWAS and EAC-IGAD follow. One notable takeaway from the figure below is the consistently low level of bilateral trade engagements between the EAC-IGAD and ECOWAS countries. It suggests the presence of strong trade barriers resulting in an east–west trade divide, which the AfCFTA could help to narrow.

A comparison of the three ARECs reveals that the SADC is a better performer, and the ECOWAS follows. The EAC-IGAD countries are the lowest performers

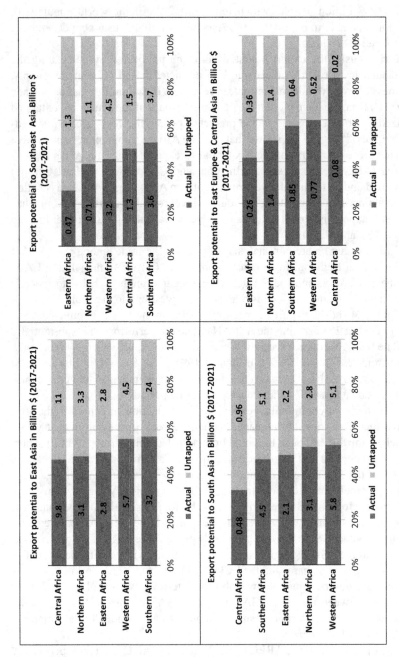

Figure 5.3 Export potential of Asia for African's exports.

Source: Authors' illustration based on ITC data.

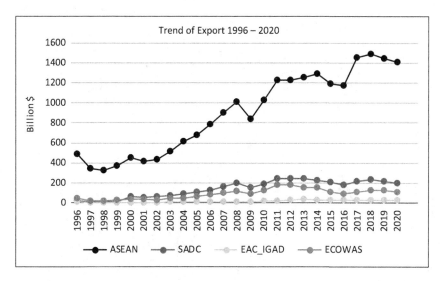

Figure 5.4 Trend of export for ASEAN, EAC-IGAD, ECOWAS, and SADC.

Source: Authors' illustration based on BACI-CEPII data.

and show almost no change from their share in the mid-90s. Another fact worth mentioning is that the global export share of the AREC has also stagnated since 2014. In contrast, the ASEAN demonstrated a visible change in its share of global exports. The ASEAN countries account for 8% of the global exports in 2018, a 2-point increase over their performance in the mid-90s. Also, their share has been steadily increasing since the global financial crisis.

We also conducted the product space analysis based on Hidalgo et al. (2007) to understand the complexity of exports by the RECS. Figure 5.5 shows that the complexity of exports has not increased for all the regional communities over the last two decades, suggesting the countries are not moving up the technology ladder. The ASEAN countries were exporting fairly advanced products even in the mid-1990s; hence, there may not be substantial room to push further. However, the ARECs have ample room to improve their export's complexity; nevertheless, it has not been realized yet. Therefore, they need to address structural and policy bottlenecks to promote production and export complex products and earn a higher and steady foreign exchange flow. The result of the product space analysis also shows that the Manufacturing of Machines and Electrical Equipment, Agriculture and Food Processing, Textile and Mineral sector has the highest potential to accelerate economic integration among the ASEAN and the three ARECS.

The ARECs export more sophisticated products to fellow member countries compared to their export to the ASEAN and China. It suggests the latter are mainly importing less-complex products located at the lower end of the global value chain. The presence of trade on more complex products among the ARECs could have

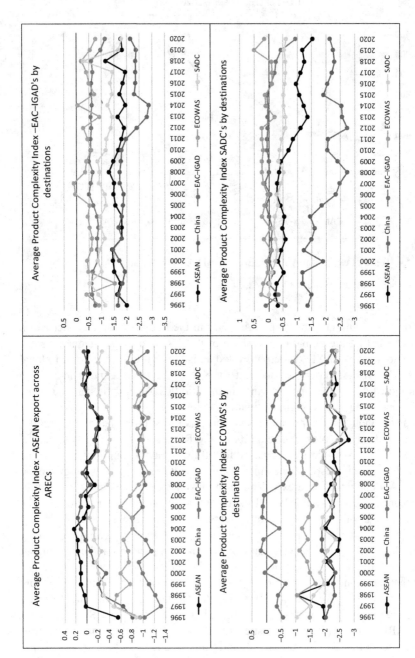

Figure 5.5 Average complexity of export in 2018.

Source: Authors' computation based on COMTRADE data.

a significant implication on the role of south–south trade. It can lend suggestive evidence about how south-south trade could promote economic transformation by providing a market platform to experiment with complex and non-traditional export products.

Exploiting the AfCFTA to increase south–south cooperation would not only increase trade values but potentially the complexity of the products as well. Overall, the ASEAN-Africa trade is asymmetric, low, less complex, and less integrated but with the potential to grow if actions are taken to facilitate trade between the two regions and to develop new investment opportunities between them. The recent regional integration in the two respective regions (AfCFTA and RCEP) opens a new door to enhance their inter-regional relationships.

In 2015, the global middle-class spending was about US$ 35 trillion (in 2011 purchasing power parity terms) and approximately evenly divided between developed and developing countries (Kharas, 2017). Today, it accounts for one-third of the global economy. By 2030, global middle-class consumption could be US$ 29 trillion more than in 2015 (left panel in Figure 5.6a). Only US$ 1 trillion of that will come from more spending in advanced economies. Lower-middle-income

---

Box 5.1 Trade partnerships

The AfCFTA is one of the flagship projects of the First Ten-Year Implementation Plan (2014–2023) under the AU's Agenda 2063—"The Africa We Want". It became operational on January 2, 2021, after a delay due to COVID-19. The AfCFTA can create a continental free-trade zone with a combined GDP of US$ 3.4 trillion and a population of 1.2 billion, which will make it a huge potential importer and exporter in the global market in the years to come. A simultaneous development in East Asia led to the creation of the Pacific Regional Economic Partnership (RCEP) on November 15, 2020. RCEP negotiations started in 2012 with 16 countries, including the 10 ASEAN countries, China, Japan, India, South Korea, Australia, and New Zealand. Although India eventually withdrew in 2019, the agreement is the world's largest, encompassing 30% of global GDP and 27% of global merchandise trade. The RCEP also comprises over 18% of services trade and 19% of FDI outflows.

Driven by China, the RCEP trade bloc has gained prominence in global trade and investment and has outstripped the growth of large high-income trade blocs over the past decades. The remarkable growth of China and South-East Asian economies is reflected in the rising share of the RCEP bloc in global GDP, trade, and FDI over the past two decades. This has also propelled the RCEP to overtake trading blocs that were much larger at the beginning of the century, including the North America Free Trade Agreement (NAFTA) and the European Union.

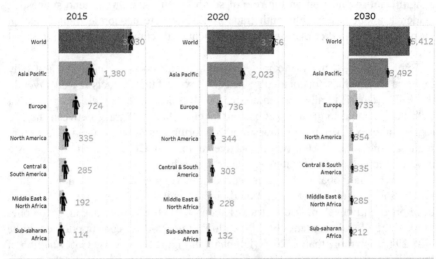

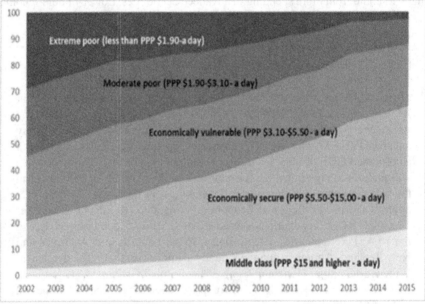

Figure 5.6 Middle-income consumer base of East Asia and Pacific region. (a) Size of the
Middle Class, by Region (millions) (b) Population distribution by economic
class in East Asia and Pacific.

Source: Adapted from Kharas 2017; East Asia and Pacific Team for Statistical Development.

countries, including Indonesia, Malaysia, Philippines, Thailand, and Vietnam,
will have middle-class markets that are US$ 15 trillion bigger. The success of the
AfCFTA partly depends on effectively utilizing the huge market potential being
created in the RCEP region as it contributes over 60% of the global middle-income

consumer, who are the main drivers of demand for a variety of commodities sophisticated products.

Moreover, the linkage between Africa and Asia could be strengthened through investment cooperation. Although there is an investment slump in 2020 due to COVID-19, several major investment partners outside the continent are increasingly engaged in initiatives to strengthen investment ties in infrastructure, resources, and industrial development (UNCTAD, 2020). The implementation of the AfCFTA, especially its investment protocol, is expected to affect bilateral ties positively. Africa has a significant infrastructure development deficit, and inter-regional cooperation could result in mutual gains. Figure 5.7 (adapted from Rentschler et al., 2019) highlights the effect of the utilization rate losses in electricity, water, and transport on GDP for the most affected low- and middle-income countries, including 21 African countries. African countries comprise at least half of the top 15 most-affected countries in each category of infrastructure disruption. The African Development Bank estimates that to close this gap, Africa's infrastructure needs between US$ 130 billion and US$ 170 billion per year; however, financing for African infrastructure currently falls short by between US$ 68 billion and US$ 108 billion per year. Such significant challenges could be transformed into opportunities for cooperation and mutual gain through deeper integration and investment agreements between Africa and Asia.

Taking the trade and investment relationship between Africa and Asia to the next level requires addressing some major bottlenecks, especially among the ARECs. First, they need to improve their port connectivity in several ways. For example, they need to increase their bilateral connectivity to lower their trade costs. Moreover, improvement in the logistic performance index should continue. It should be followed consistently in all of the yardsticks (i.e., competency and quality, ease of arranging shipment, the efficiency of the clearance process, improving the quality of infrastructure, timeliness, and tracking related abilities). Second, countries need to lower tariff and non-tariff trade barriers. The ARECs could draw relevant lessons from the ASEAN and China as to how trade costs could be lowered without too much fiscal strain.[15] Last but not least, the ARECs should focus on enhancing digital connectivity as it is a key instrument in facilitating information and financial flows which are critical to trade and investment in the 21st century.

5.5 From political NRPTAs to reciprocal private trade and investment

Despite the developments since the inception of AGOA and EBA, there is still a significant challenge to fully utilize the preferential treatments. The gains from AGOA are concentrated in a few commodities such as petroleum and minerals (Kassa and Coulibaly, 2019). Few countries manage to diversify manufacturing and textile industries. Moreover, the short-term nature of AGOA and the need for annual approval do not encourage long-term investments that are vital to increasing the export capacity of SSA. Furthermore, the annual renewal process involves some political considerations, which create uncertainty for private sector actors. For example, Table 5.1 shows different AGOA recipients that were excluded for

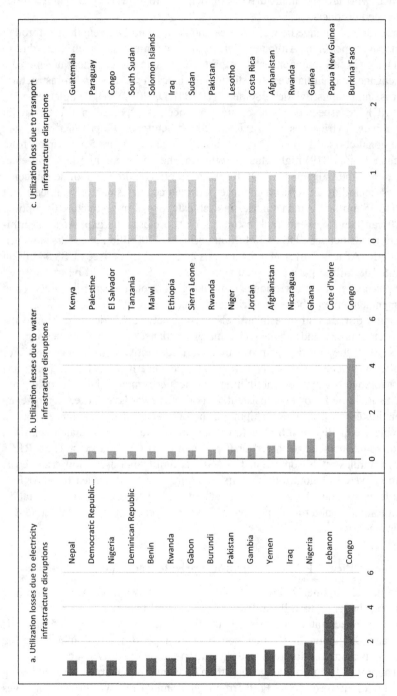

Figure 5.7 Top 15 countries with greatest utilization rate losses, by type of infrastructure disruption.

Source: Adapted from Rentschler et al. (2019).

failing to fulfill AGOA criteria (many of the times due to political instability or human rights considerations).

Such non-reciprocal benefits are not free gifts since strings are attached to the legislation, constraining policy space or sometimes involving some implicit political dimensions. The 2018 suspension of Rwanda's AGOA eligibility by the Trump administration following the former's decision to ban second-hand clothes in its market is an interesting example. Political considerations play in the case of EBA as well. For instance, Sorgho and Tharakan (2019) showed that attaining EBA beneficiary status depends on maintaining a good level of freedom of expression and a high level of human development. The latest suspension of Cambodia could be a recent reminder. Moreover, AGOA and EBA do not address major structural challenges in Africa, such as infrastructural development, investments and financial constraints. The missing investment agreements are among the factors which limited their success. Unfortunately, without comprehensive agreements which address such challenges, it is difficult to make progress.

Focusing on reciprocal private sector-led trade and investment can promote economic relationships between Africa and non-African actors and abate undesired political influences and conflicts. For example, when uncertainties over the extension of AGOA were becoming major concerns in 2013, the US private sector industry groups active in the textile and apparel sectors made a plea for the US government to extend the provision.[16] They made sensible arguments about how the African and the US labor market would suffer if it was not extended. The private sector could form regional networks that strengthen regional integration and interdependence to produce goods and services as well as investments, making political conflict more costly.[17] Moreover, the private sector could be a source of capital to address structural bottlenecks such as infrastructure development based on economic considerations. It could also lobby based on economic considerations, which improves the business environment.

AGOA is expected to expire in 2025 and renewal is not yet guaranteed. The AfCFTA could lend a platform to collectively negotiate and replace AGOA with a reciprocal trade deal with the US to deepen the trade relationship with Africa. Although it could be tempting for some AfCFTA member countries to sign unilateral trade agreements with the US, that should be avoided to ensure a long-lasting and win-win trade deal at a continental level.

The AfCFTA and RCEP provide opportunities for private-sector-led trade and investment in the post-COVID-19 world. The private sector is a key stakeholder and beneficiary of such initiatives as they are the actual traders and investors; responsible for moving goods and services across borders and continents. Both agreements can contribute to the ongoing GVC reconfiguration process following COVID-19. Notably, the clauses included in the two agreements in the following areas are crucial: the investment protocols, competition laws (regulatory uniformity), intellectual property protection, and dispute settlement mechanisms.

Table 5.1 Removal from AGOA eligibility due to political and economic factors

Status	CAR	Eritrea	Cote d'Ivoire	Mauritania	Guinea	Madagascar	Niger	DRC	Mali	Guinea-Bissau	South Sudan	Swaziland	Gambia	Rwanda*
Removed	2004	2004	2005	2006	2009	2009	2009	2011	2012	2012	2015	2015	2015	2018
Restored	2016	-	2011	2009	2011	2014	2014	2021	2014	2014	-	2017	2017	-

Source: AGOA annual reviews of country eligibility.

Note: *Apparel sector.

AfCFTA negotiation involves two phases. The first phase, a negotiation in goods and service trade schedules and dispute settlement mechanism is already finished. Phase 2 negotiations will focus on investment, competition policy, and intellectual property rights. The AfCFTA's draft Protocol on Intellectual Property Rights (IPR) is submitted to the January 2021 Session of the AU Assembly for adoption. The protocol is expected to provide adequate protection for property rights continent-wide, which fosters R&D activities and the private sector's involvement in formerly risky areas such as pharmaceuticals and IT-based startups. The continental investment protocols would also be a relevant tool for the private sector to tackle barriers to investment entry, reduce time and costs of investment approvals, enhance transparency, improve efficiency, and promote investment-related cooperation and coordination across the continent. A vibrant private sector economy also requires effective and fair competition laws, which would be soon negotiated at the continental level. Therefore, the AfCFTA is well aligned with the private sector's interest to utilize the ongoing GVC reconfiguration process, which is partly triggered by COVID-19.

Although these protocols will only apply to intra-Africa investment and trade, they could also benefit Asian investors (and others) and assets indirectly through the most-favored-nation (MFN) principle in the WTO and bilateral treaties. Both market and efficiency-seeking non-African investors would find it attractive. Moreover, the improved governance following the AfCFTA would be shared by them as well. The AfCFTA creates a vast market for Asian goods and services and is shaping a harmonized policy and regulatory regime, meaning that the same rules will be implemented at the continental level, reducing the cost of transactions.

The RCEP is deeper and more comprehensive than the AfCFTA, and it addresses several economic integration issues. Chapter 10, 11, 13, and 19 specifically talk about investment, intellectual property, competition laws, and dispute settlements, respectively. Moreover, Chapter 5 deals with sanitary and phytosanitary standards, and Chapter 6 deals with standards, technical regulations, and conformity assessment procedures. The inclusion of these clauses in the agreement encourages private participation within the member countries and also increases inter-regional cooperation.

Despite the conventional wisdom, recent studies such as Lee et al. (2019) and Baldwin (2014) argue that the theoretical effect of trade agreements on non-member countries could be positive under deep integrations. That is because it makes member countries more similar in terms of the regulatory environment, thus reducing entry costs. Similarly, Mattoo et al. (2020) explain how deep agreements lead to more trade creation and less trade diversion than shallow agreements. Hence, the AfCFTA and RCEP would complement each other to promote active private sector engagement within and between their member countries.

A critical element for the success of the AfCFTA and RCEP is the rule of origin clause (RoO). The AfCFTA's rule of origin has reached its concluding stages. UNCTAD's 2019 report notes that RoO will determine whether the AfCFTA can be a game-changer for Africa's industrialization. RoO should be simple, less costly, business-friendly, easy to use and understand, and accessible to bear the desired fruit. In the case of the RCEP, the rule of origin is already negotiated. By taking their geographic configuration into consideration, the parties ensured that the RoO chapter includes clear, direct consignment rules so that originating goods do not inappropriately lose their originating status. Interestingly the agreement aligns RoO for all 15 countries, allowing RCEP participants to integrate into the same production chain.

Asian countries such as China are currently undergoing a reconfiguration process and pushing out low-end manufacturing. This is an opportunity the African private sector should seize. COVID-19 has created additional incentives to speed up the reconfiguration process. Although the nearby countries are natural candidates, the rising wage in Vietnam, the Philippines, and Indonesia, as well as the proximity considerations for market-seeking FDI make Africa an attractive destination. With secured market access, regional integration momentum, and better governance following the implementation of both the AfCFTA and the RCEP, viable trade and investment cooperation opportunities will emerge between African and Asian countries' private sectors. Stable firm-to-firm linkages would benefit regional blocks from efficiency and risk diversification perspectives. Governments and other stakeholders should therefore commit to strengthening the private sector-oriented Africa-Asia trade and investment relationship to take their economic integration to the next level by exploiting the ongoing reconfiguration processes for their mutual gains.

5.6 Conclusion

The ongoing global economic dynamics augur a time to engineer a scaling of trade and investment between Africa and East Asia for the following four reasons: (1) the reconfiguration of GVCs of interest for both Africa and East Asia in the post-COVID-19 world is an opportunity to be seized; (2) the entry in force of the AfCFTA and the RCEP provides a low hanging fruit entry point to strategize on the reengineering of trade and investment between the two continents; (3) the Asian Aspirations momentum in Africa provides the authorizing environment to consider bold measures and initiatives; and (4) this might be the only chance Africa has left to rebalance its economic relations with Asia.

The COVID-19 pandemic exposed the vulnerability of the current model of global production as multinationals' supply chain disruption hamper the supply of raw materials, intermediate inputs, and final goods, which forced companies to consider risk diversification mechanisms. Moreover, the recent trade tension between the US and China promoted the diversification of American and Chinese production facilities to other East Asian countries. However, the rising wages in East Asia and their advance to more complex production processes make Africa a reasonable choice to take over low-end manufacturing tasks.

The AfCFTA and RCEP clauses make private sector cooperation more attractive for regional and integrational value chain development that ensure mutual benefits and structural transformation. Notably, the ongoing AfCFTA discussions on the rule of origin, IP protection, investment protocol, and other regulations will be essential to facilitate the private sector cooperation between Africa and Asia. That is because it makes member countries more similar in terms of the regulatory environment, thus reducing entry and trade costs. Countries shall focus on industries with low hanging fruits and proceed to the more complex ones as their integration advances. The manufacturing and electrical production sector could be a good starting point.

Asia's economic success over the last few decades created a strong aspiration among African countries and encouraged them to take bold measures. Africa and Asia both had gone through colonization and share some similarities, making it a natural choice to draw lessons from. Moreover, much of Asia's growth is directly linked to active engagement in the global economy and domestic policy measures taken by their governments in the recent past, rather than natural resources or other causes. By utilizing the current opportunities created by the AfCFTA and RCEP, Africa should apply lessons from Asia to participate in global value chains to advance the trade relationship between the two regions and the rest of the world.

Engaging with Asia and the broader RCEP would be beneficial to rebalance the trade between Africa and Asia. So far, Africa is participating as raw material and low-value-added inputs provider, which makes its relative share in the final products very small. Unless it integrates itself with the global economy and starts to participate in light manufacturing, the trade imbalance will continue and finally stifle the progress the two regions can make together.

Therefore, governments and other stakeholders should commit to strengthening the reciprocal, private sector-oriented Africa-Asia trade and take their economic integration to the next level by exploiting the ongoing reconfiguration processes for their mutual gains. The AfCFTA and RCEP are very timely and can potentially transform the trade and investment relations between Africa and Asia. Actively addressing bottlenecks and creating a private sector enabling environment will have a paramount relevance in this regard. The AfCFTA secretariat should initiate trade and investment agreements with Asian countries and blocks by representing all African countries.

Notes

1 The views and opinions expressed in this paper are those of the authors and do not necessarily reflect the views or positions of their employers or institutions.
2 This is mainly due to the United States' decision to move away from importing petroleum from Africa and other countries in favor of consuming domestic production.
3 Europe's export increased from US$ 67 billion to US$ 202 billion between 2000 and 2018. USA's export rose from US$ 11.9 billion to US$ 24 billion during the same period.
4 www.dw.com/en/as-coronavirus-disrupts-supply-chains-could-africa-profit/a-53435112
5 www.volkswagenag.com/en/news/stories/2019/10/the-next-few-years-will-be-exciting-in-africa.html
6 www.reuters.com/article/us-toyota-tsusho-ivorycoast-idUSKCN1VJ1IL
7 www.bloomberg.com/press-releases/2020-01-31/toyota-investing-4-billion-rand-in-south-africa-statement

8 www.theafricareport.com/17953/morocco-sees-big-investment-drive-from-auto-part-manufacturers/
9 www.tmtfinance.com/
10 https://developmentreimagined.com/2021/04/23/qa-how-the-chinese-private-sector-can-help-develop-pharmaceutical-production-capacity-in-africa/
11 See Elbeshbishi (2021) for more details.
12 Except for the China-Mauritius free trade agreement, which comes into effect on Jan 2021.
13 The products are classified based on Broad Economics Categories (BEC) Rev. 4.
14 A detailed methodological explanation can be found on ITC's website. Here the untapped potential refers to the difference between the potential export and the actual export levels.
15 Figures 5.1 A and 5.2A show logistics performance index, transport cost and time for selected African countries and RECS.
16 https://agoa.info/downloads/research/5921.html
17 Please see Massimiliano Calì (2014) "Trading Away from Conflict: using Trade to Increase Resilience in Fragile states".

References

Baldwin, R. E. (2014). *Multilateralising 21st Century Regionalism* (No. Book). OECD.
Baldwin, R., & Di Mauro, B. W. (2020). *Economics in the time of COVID-19*. A VoxEU.org eBook, CEPR Press.
Barbieri, P., Boffelli, A., Elia, S., Fratocchi, L., Kalchschmidt, M., & Samson, D. (2020). What can we learn about reshoring after Covid-19? *Operations Management Research*, *13*(3), 131–136.
Brenton, P., & Hoppe, M. (2006). The African Growth and Opportunity Act, Exports, and Development in Sub-Saharan Africa (August 1). World Bank Policy Research Working Paper No. 3996, Available at: SSRN: https://ssrn.com/abstract=927139
Byaruhanga. J. (2020). How Africa can manufacture to meet its own pharmaceutical needs, blog.   www.un.org/africarenewal/magazine/september-2020/how-africa-can-manufacture-meet-its-own-pharmaceutical-needs
Calì, M. (2014). *Trading Away from Conflict: Using Trade to Increase Resilience in Fragile States*. The World Bank.
Coulibaly, S. (2017). Differentiated Impact of AGOA and EBA on West African Countries. *Manuscript. Africa Chief Economist Office, The World Bank*.
Coulibaly, S. and Mirza D. (2017). Liberalization of Infrastructure Services and Exports of Goods: A Focus on Four African Countries Using FATS Data. Unpublished working paper.
De Melo, J., & Portugal-Perez, A. (2014). Preferential market access design: evidence and lessons from African apparel exports to the United States and the European union. *The World Bank Economic Review*, *28*(1), 74–98.
de Soyres, F., Maire, J., & Sublet, G. (2019). *An Empirical Investigation of Trade Diversion and Global Value Chains*. Policy Research Working Paper; No. 9089. © World Bank, Washington, DC. http://hdl.handle.net/10986/33058 License: CC BY 3.0 IGO.
Elbeshbishi, A. (2021). Intellectual Property and the African Continental Free Trade Area: A Public Health Perspective.
Evenett, S., Fiorini, M., Fritz, J., Hoekman, B., Lukaszuk, P., Rocha, N., Ruta, M., Santi, F., & Shingal, A. (2021). Trade policy responses to the COVID-19 pandemic crisis: Evidence from a new data set. *The World Economy*, *45*(2), 342–364. https://doi.org/10.1111/twec.13119.

Guillaumont Jeanneney, S., & Hua, P. (2015). China's African financial engagement, real exchange rates and trade between China and Africa. *Journal of African Economies*, *24*(1), 1–25.

Hidalgo, C. A., Klinger, B., Barabási, A. L., & Hausmann, R. (2007). The product space conditions the development of nations. *Science*, *317*(5837), 482–487.

Javorick, B. (2020). Global supply chains will not be the same in the post-COVID-19 world, in R. E. Baldwin & S. J. Evenett (eds.), *COVID-19 and Trade Policy: Why Turning Inward Won't Work*. A VoxEU.org eBook, London: CEPR Press.

Kassa, W., & Coulibaly, S. (2019). *Revisiting the Trade Impact of the African Growth and Opportunity Act: A Synthetic Control Approach*. The World Bank.

Kharas, H. (2017). "The Unprecedented Expansion of the Global Middle Class, An Update". Working Paper 100, Brookings Institution, Washington, DC.

Lee, W., Mulabdic, A., & Ruta, M. (2019). Third-Country Effects of Regional Trade Agreements: A Firm-Level Analysis. Policy Research working paper no. WPS 9064 Washington, D.C.: World Bank Group.

Malik, K. (2013). Human Development Report 2013. The Rise of the South: Human Progress in a Diverse World. The Rise of the South: Human Progress in a Diverse World (March 15, 2013). UNDP-HDRO Human Development Reports.

Mattoo, A., Rocha, N., & Ruta, M. (2020). The evolution of deep trade agreements. Policy Research Working Paper Series 9283, The World Bank.

Rentschler, J., Kornejew, M., Hallegatte, S., Braese, J., & Obolensky, M. (2019). *Underutilized Potential: The Business Costs of Unreliable Infrastructure in Developing Countries*. Policy Research Working Paper Series 8899, The World Bank.

Songwe, V. (2020). A Continental Strategy for Economic Diversification Through the AfCFTA and Intellectual Property Rights. *Foresight Africa*.

Sorgho, Z., & Tharakan, J. (2019). Assessing the impact of unilateral trade policies EBA and AGOA on African beneficiaries' exports using matching econometrics. *The World Economy*, *42*(10), 3086–3118.

UNCTAD. (2019). Economic Development in Africa Report 2019: Made in Africa Rules of Origin for Enhanced Intra-African Trade. Geneva: United Nations Publications.

UNCTAD, G. (2020). World Investment Report. New York: United Nations Publications.

UNEP. (2020) Global Trade in Used Vehicles Report.

World Bank. (2020). World Development Report.

Appendix

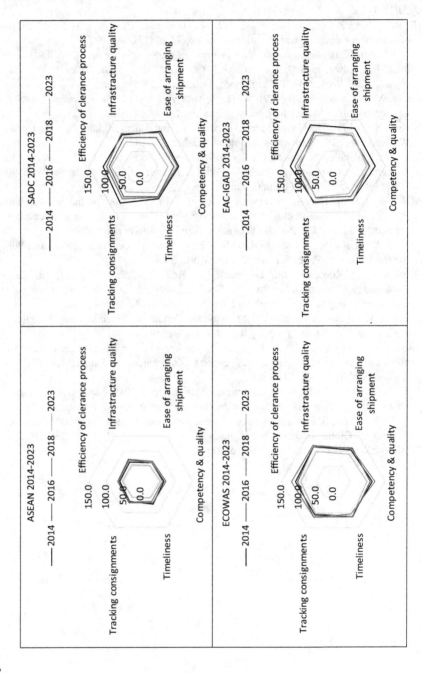

Figure 5.1A Logistics performance index.

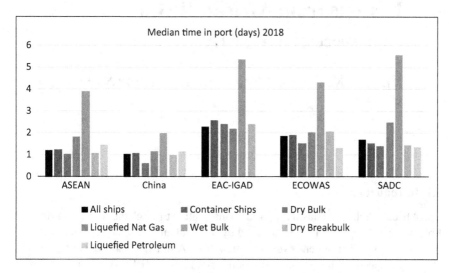

Figure 5.2A Median time in ports (days).

6 Lessons from African RECs

For a successful AfCFTA[1]

Woubet Kassa and Pegdéwendé Nestor Sawadogo

6.1 Introduction

Can Africa's high enthusiasm for regional integration through the Africa Continental Free Trade Area (AfCFTA) be matched by national and regional efforts to achieve its desired goals? It depends on how the AfCFTA draws upon the successes and challenges faced by the regional economic communities (RECs). When it comes to regional integration in the region, the rhetoric often does not match the reality. The rising ambitions of the continent to reduce poverty and promote rapid economic growth could provide additional momentum to achieve the stated goals of regional integration. However, despite some success, the experience of regional integration and RECs in the continent is fraught with failures. This study aims to draw key lessons using evidence from within the continent. Though drawing lessons from the rest of the world is essential, given the unique feature of economies in Africa, the most relevant lessons can be drawn from the experiences of regional economic communities in the continent.

Although intraregional trade still accounts for a very small share of total trade in Africa, it is becoming increasingly important. The establishment of the AfCFTA presents major opportunities and challenges to boost intra-Africa trade. The literature is awash with studies that estimate the potential impact of the AfCFTA on economic growth, exports, investments and welfare. Using a computable general equilibrium model (CGE) model, Saygili et al. (2018) estimate that the full elimination of tariffs among African countries increases GDP by close to 1% and creates an overall welfare gain of about US$ 16.1 billion in the long run. The growth and welfare gains from the AfCFTA could be even larger if the scope of the agreement is extended to non-tariff measures (NTMs) and trade facilitation. Depetris Chauvin et al. (2017) estimate that the elimination of tariff barriers combined with a reduction of NTMs is associated with an increase in GDP of at least 5 percent. A World Bank (2020) report finds that full implementation of the WTO Trade Facilitation Agreement brings the overall welfare gains to 4.7% by 2030 (compared to the baseline). The volume of total exports is expected to increase by over 21 percent. However, intra-continental exports are estimated to rise by over 57 percent. There is some modest trade diversion to the rest of the world, with an export decline of

DOI: 10.4324/9781003456568-6

around 0.5% outside the continent. In monetary terms, intra-continental trade will grow from US$ 196 billion in 2030 in the reference scenario to US$ 310 billion after the implementation of the AfCFTA in 2030.

The assessment of the potential impacts of various agreements under the AfCFTA could only be estimated ex-ante. Hence, despite all the potential, the realization of the expected gains from the AfCFTA depends on the extent of intraregional trade under the new AfCFTA regime and subsequently on the impact of such trade on growth and welfare. To better understand whether the AfCFTA could yield the much-sought gains, it is essential to understand the early successes and failures of regional trade agreements (RTAs) both within the continent and beyond. Of course, many other lessons can be drawn from other regional trade agreements including the European FTA, the North American FTA, and the Association of Southeast Asian Nations (ASEAN). However, the most relevant lessons are from the experiences of past and current regional economic communities in the continent. This study focuses on drawing these key lessons with an emphasis on the experiences of regional economic communities in the African continent.

This chapter draws upon the eight (8) Regional Economic Communities (RECs), which have been recognized by the African Union (AU) as pillars on which the continent will rely to implement the African Continental Free Trade Area (AfCFTA). It evaluates the trade creation and trade diversion impacts of each of the eight RECs and examines their performance with the goal of drawing lessons and identifying challenges for the success of the AfCFTA. It establishes that despite significant heterogeneities, there is more trade creation than trade diversion and a generally positive impact on within-REC trade. Two RECs in particular—EAC and SADC—outperform all the other RECs in terms of boosting intra-REC trade. This is mainly associated with their high level of investment in trade facilitation, the level of synergy between national and regional goals, the density of economic activity and the advancement in the quantity and quality of regional infrastructure. There are also variations among the RECs in terms of whether they promote exports to the rest of the world or displace them.

The key policy implications focus on two key areas—significant investment in trade facilitation and strategic sequencing of integration schemes. Given that the AfCFTA is a much larger FTA compared to the existing RECs, it is important that economies use regional integration to create agglomeration economies to expand supply/production which in turn provides greater impetus to engage in GVCs. Given the costs of distance and the benefits of already existing strong trade corridors, it is imperative that integration efforts start with a focus on selected high-density corridors of trade. Expanding trade on an African level is a daunting task but is achievable and feasible if sub-regional corridors of trade and production integration are strengthened to build regional value chains that serve as key hubs of GVCs. However, there are many challenges that African countries, and regional and global entities need to address to realize the objectives of the AfCFTA and transform the continent. We address some of these key challenges and suggest relevant policy options.

6.2 Regional economic communities (RECs) in Africa: Evaluating their impact on trade

The resurgence of regionalism and regional trading blocs has stirred Africans towards establishing a regional trading bloc to deepen integration. The rise of (mega) regionalism is manifested by the rapidly increasing number of regional trade agreements. The number of RTAs in force has been continuously increasing worldwide, from 142 in 1999 to 176 in 2003 and then to 343 in 2021 (WTO, 2021), while the number of RTA notifications is 548 in 2021 (Figure 6.1). This rise in regional trade liberalization has also contributed to multilateral liberalization, though it could also have fostered increased regionalization at the cost of multilateral trade.

The African continent, like many other regions of the world, has also witnessed a proliferation of RTAs (Figure 6.1). In Africa, the number of RTAs in force (46) is lower than in North and South America, East Asia and Europe, but it exceeds all other regions. The African Union (AU) recognizes eight (8) RTAs as pillars on which the continent will rely to implement the AfCFTA. These include the Arab Maghreb Union (AMU), the Community of Sahel–Saharan States (CEN-SAD), the Common Market for Eastern and Southern Africa (COMESA), the East Africa Community (EAC), the Economic Community of Central African States (ECCAS), the Economic Community of West African States (ECOWAS), the Intergovernmental Authority on Development (IGAD) and the Southern Africa Development Community (SADC). The four major RTAs in terms of the number of member countries are CEN-SAD (29 members), COMESA (21 members), SADC (16 members) and ECOWAS (15 members). Most of these RTAs aim to become a customs union (CU) or a common market (CM) or an economic union in the long run. Many African countries have multiple and overlapping memberships. Figure 6.2 presents the membership and economic size of the major RECs in the region.

The RECs have varying experiences and degrees of integration with uneven progress in their integration drives (Table 6.1). Some RECs have graduated from an FTA and advanced to a higher level of integration including customs unions while most are FTAs. For example, the EAC has advanced beyond the level of FTA in trade integration, being currently a common market. COMESA and SADC have free trade areas in operation, while a subset of SADC called the Southern Africa Customs Union has developed into a CU with higher levels of integration. Almost all the eight RECs have adopted a free movement of persons protocol. However, the degree of implementation varies among them. ECOWAS has been recognized as the best practice in this area since all its member countries have implemented the protocol on the free movement of persons and rights of residence and establishment. They have also adopted a common passport.

6.2.1 Key trends in regional trade across RECs

In line with Chapter 2, the share of intra-African exports to total exports has doubled from less than 10% in 1990 to more than 20% in 2019. However, despite

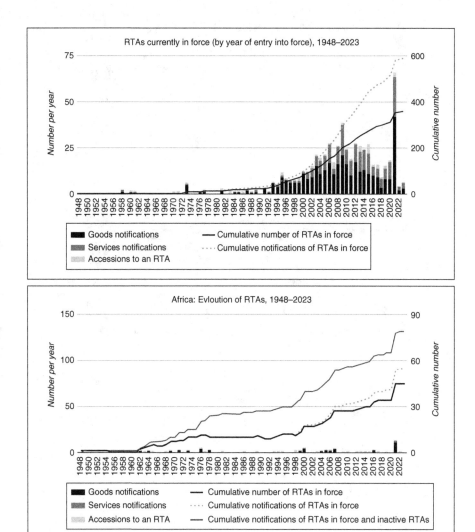

Figure 6.1 Evolution of Regional Trade Agreements, 1948–2021.

Source: WTO, March 2021.

the strong positive trend in intra-African trade since 2008, the African continent remains the least integrated region in terms of trade flows (Figure 6.3).

Africa's low intraregional trade coexists with the region's extremely high dependence on exports to the rest of the world (RoW). The continuously lower level of export diversification explains this lower regional trade and higher dependence on exports to the RoW. Export dependence, defined as the share of regional

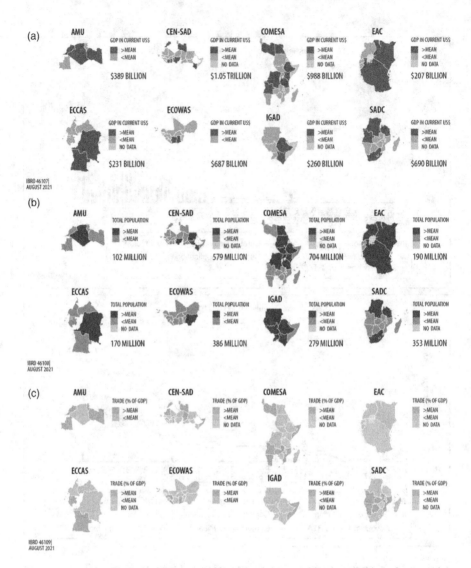

Figure 6.2 Major RECs in Africa—membership and economic size: a) Size of economies
(GDP in Current US$), b) Population size, c) Trade (%GDP). Mean represents
the mean value for all African countries.

Source: Authors' Elaboration based on WDI data.

exports to the RoW to total continental exports, has slowly decreased from around
90% in 1990 to less than 80% in 2019. This high export dependence also reflects
the continent's historical links with the outside world and lack of export diversification. Nonetheless, the lower level of intra-African trade could be underestimated

Table 6.1 Progress in market integration of African RECs

REC	FTA	CU	CM	EMU	SU	FM protocol
ECOWAS	Yes	Yes	No	No	No	All 15
EAC	Yes	Yes	Yes	No	No	3 out of 5
COMESA	Yes	Yes	No	No	No	Only Burundi
ECCAS	Yes	No	No	No	No	4 out of 11
SADC	Yes	No	No	No	No	7 out of 15
AMU	No	No	No	No	No	3 out of 5
IGAD	No	No	No	No	No	No protocol
CENSAD	No	No	No	No	No	Unclear

Source: Author's elaboration based on United Nations. Economic Commission for Africa (UNECA) (2016).

Note: FTA = Free Trade Area, CU = Custom Union, CM = Common Market, FM = Free Movement of persons, EMU = Economic and Monetary Union, SU = Supranational Union.

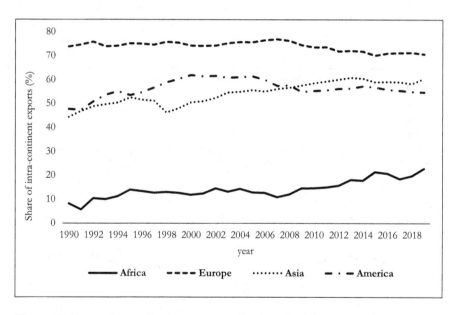

Figure 6.3 Share of intraregional exports to total exports by region.

given the omnipresence of informal trade. It could also be overestimated because of the multiple and overlapping memberships of many countries. There is significant variation in trade and other indicators of regional integration across RECs.

Regional integration, as measured by trade integration as a share of total trade, which is the focus of this study, is deeper in EAC and SADC, followed by CENSAD, ECOWAS, and COMESA (Figure 6.4). The differences in the levels of

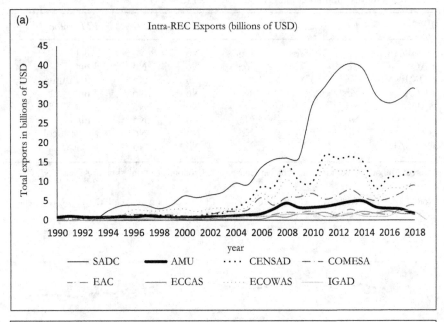

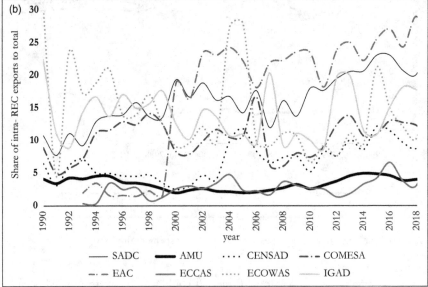

Figure 6.4 Comparison of intra-REC exports trends from 1990 to 2019.

intraregional export performances within the African RECs reflect many factors including the size of economies in each REC, varying levels of integration in infra-structure and policies, institutional quality to implement the agreements and the provisions in each REC, the difference in the level of the industrialization process,

Table 6.2 Top 10 and bottom 10 countries share of intra-African exports over the decade 2009–2019

Top 10 countries			Bottom 10 countries		
Rank	Country	Intra-African export	Rank	Country	Intra-African exports
1	Eswatini	83.03	10	Morocco	8.50
2	Zimbabwe	81.49	9	Guinea	8.4
3	Gambia	78.68	8	Sao Tome & Principe	8.18
4	Togo	68.89	7	Seychelles	6.27
5	Rwanda	63.73	6	Mauritania	6.27
6	Uganda	58.76	5	Gabon	5.40
7	Senegal	57.54	4	Algeria	4.46
8	Djibouti	51.80	3	Angola	3.87
9	Mali	49.09	2	Cabo Verde	2.22
10	Mali	49.09	1	Libya	2.025

Source: Authors' elaboration based on CEPII data.

Note: *Intra-African exports is the % share of intra-African exports to total exports.

and the degrees of complementarity in the production structures. A closer look at the share of intraregional exports by country identifies significant disparities across countries and across RECs. The disparity across countries is more stark compared to the disparity across RECs, and the comparison between the RECs tends to hide this intra-REC disparity in trade integration.

Indeed, some countries are more integrated at the regional level and show a strong share of intraregional exports to total exports. In this respect, the ten countries with the largest share of intraregional trade as a share of total exports, during 2009–2019 include Eswatini, Zimbabwe, Gambia, Togo, Rwanda, Uganda, Senegal, Djibouti, Mali, and Lesotho, respectively (see Table 6.2). Out of the top ten countries leading intra-African exports, three (Eswatini, Zimbabwe, Lesotho) are members of SADC, four (Gambia, Togo, Senegal, Mali) are members of the ECOWAS and three (Rwanda, Uganda, Djibouti) are members of the COMESA, two of which are also EAC members. Similarly, the ten countries with the lowest share of intra-African exports are Libya, Cabo Verde, Angola, Algeria, Gabon, Mauritania, Seychelles, Sao Tome and Principe, Guinea, and Morocco. This indicates that even within each REC there are significant disparities in intraregional trade where some members trade more than others.

The RECs also differ in terms of the extent of tariff liberalization (see Figure 6.5). The EAC stands out as the most advanced REC in terms of tariff liberalization, where all tariff lines are fully liberalized and the average applied tariff is 0%. SADC on the other hand has relatively the highest intraregional tariff, excluding members of SACU. Within COMESA, the proportion of tariff lines fully liberalized is 55% while the average applied tariffs by member countries (using import weighting)

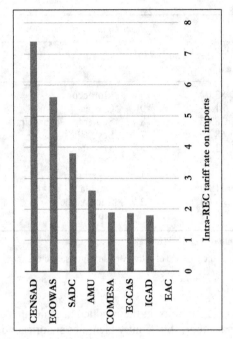

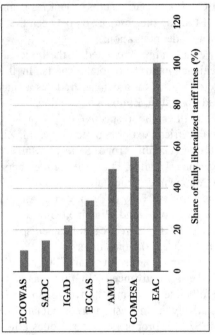

Figure 6.5 Trade costs in terms of tariff within RECs.

Source: Author's elaboration based on United Nations. Economic Commission for Africa (UNECA) (2016).

Table 6.3 Comprehensive trade costs excluding tariff by REC in 2017

Rank	REC	Non-tariff trade costs
1	AMU	131.4
2	EAC	142.7
3	IGAD	169.05
4	ECCAS	174.73
5	ECOWAS	198.39
6	SADC	211.58
7	CENSAD	228.46
8	COMESA	261.97

Source: ESCAP-World Bank Trade Cost Database.

is 1.89%. As for SADC, only 15% of tariff lines are fully liberalized while the average applied tariff amounts to 3.8%.

In addition to tariffs, there is heterogeneity in the levels of trade costs associated with non-tariff barriers. Comprehensive trade cost, here, excluding tariff includes all additional costs other than tariff costs expressed in-advalorum equivalents (%). AMU and EAC have the lowest intraregional non-tariff costs, while COMESA, CENSAD and SADC have the highest trade costs among all the RECs. Table 6.3 shows that, on average, trading goods within African RECs involves, on average for all tradable goods, additional non-tariff costs amounting to approximately 131%–262% of the value of goods—as compared to when each country trades these goods within its borders. AMU stands out as the REC with the lowest non-tariff cost, followed by EAC. While COMESA and CENSAD show the highest levels of non-tariff cost in Africa.

6.2.2 Evaluating the impact of RECs on trade creation and trade diversion

The objective of the empirical investigation is twofold. First, we examine the determinants of bilateral trade flows in Africa following the gravity model framework. Second, we evaluate the effects of African RECs in terms of trade creation (TC) and trade diversion (TD) in accordance with the central theoretical framework of free trade areas.[2] The classic theoretical framework (Viner, 1950) in analyzing the impact of an FTA or customs union suggests that the welfare impact is ambiguous due to the contrasting welfare impacts of trade creation and trade diversion. Viner (1950) notes that trade creation increases welfare while trade diversion reduces it, and pointed out that an FTA could leave countries worse off as a consequence. However, this has largely been focused only on the static gains from trade, without due regard to the dynamic (Balassa, 1961; Cooper and Massell, 1965) and possibly the more important long-term gains.

A free trade area, by allowing competition among FTA members due to reduced trade barriers, may promote a more efficient (re)allocation of resources within the FTA. This is associated with what is often referred to as trade creation—i.e.

there will be a shift in the locus of production from a high-cost producer to a low-cost, relatively more efficient producer, within the FTA. There is a welfare gain associated with reduced prices, increasing consumers' surplus within the FTA and an overall improvement in the efficiency of production within the FTA. There are two distinct effects associated with trade creation—i.e., the production effect and the consumption effect, both of which are expected to increase welfare. On the production side, we will have greater efficiency gains while also contributing to declining prices (consumption effect) and hence increased societal welfare.

On the other hand, there is the possibility of trade diversion—i.e. a shift in the locus of production from more efficient production by non-members of the FTA to inefficient producers within the FTA, depending on the extent of the external tariffs. The impact of trade diversion could be stronger if members raise external tariffs following the FTA. Within the underpinning theoretical framework, this is harmful due to the global efficiency losses. The effect within the FTA, however, could be positive if the 'production' gains of the new exporter outweigh the loss in consumer welfare of the old producer. The net impact of an FTA depends on the totality of trade diversion and trade creation, which is largely an empirical question. According to the 'old theory', an FTA is more likely to have a favorable impact on welfare if trade creation exceeds trade diversion. But, considering the dynamic and long-term impacts could change the outcome and even trade diversion could yield increased FDI, employment and growth. We evaluate the eight RECs by estimating the trade creation and trade diversion impacts.[3]

Table 6.A1 in the appendix presents the results of the basic gravity model estimates without disaggregating the trade creation and trade diversion impacts. Economic size proxied by GDP is a significant determinant of bilateral trade. An increase in a country's GDP leads to a sizable increase in bilateral trade. A strong economic activity is an important driver of bilateral trade. Countries trade more when their bilateral trade costs proxied by distance are low. Trading partners closer to each other or countries that share a border tend to have higher levels of bilateral trade in comparison to more distant partners. These results are in line with the findings of most gravity models estimated in the literature as they reveal that transportation costs are important determinants of bilateral trade between countries (Vicard, 2009; Francois and Manchin, 2013). Consequently, reducing the cost of transportation is crucial to increase bilateral trade.

Results also show that the membership of an RTA is positively and significantly related to bilateral trade flows over the period 1990–2019. The formation of RTAs, by removing trade barriers (tariff and non-tariff barriers depending on the deepness of the RTAs) between member countries, improves bilateral trade between countries, ceteris paribus. The effect of the membership of an RTA on bilateral trade flows is economically significant.

The implication of the findings from the basic gravity model including the significant role of the high density of economic activity and low distance as well as the role of RECs are important for the strategic prioritization of selected corridors of trade and integration. Because, given that the AfCFTA is a continental FTA, it is going to be daunting to think of regional integration on the bigger continental scale.

Table 6.4 Summary of the effects of RECs on TC and TD in Africa

RTAs	Effects	Intraregional	From imports	From exports	Dominant
SADC	TC	yes	no	Yes	TC
	TD	no	no	No	
CEN-SAD	TC	yes	no	No	TC
	TD	no	no	No	
ECOWAS	TC	no	no	No	TD
	TD	no	yes	Yes	
COMESA	TC	yes	no	No	TC
	TD	no	no	Yes	
ECCAS	TC	yes	no	Yes	TC
	TD	no	no	No	
EAC	TC	yes	no	No	TC
	TD	no	no	Yes	
IGAD	TC	yes	yes	Yes	TC
	TD	no	no	No	

Source: Authors' elaboration based on regression estimates.

Note: yes(no) indicates that there is TC or TD either within the region (intraregional), from imports (imports), from exports (exports) or not. The Dominant effect is given by adding up the significant coefficients of our three dummies variables which capture TC and TD for each REC. We discard AMU because of missing data.

There is a need to strategically prioritize key corridors of trade along proximity in selected corridors in addition to key regions and sub-regions where the density of economic activity is relatively higher. Reflected in this prioritization is the need to build on the already high levels of regional integration in East, Southern and West Africa, where based on density and proximity the sub-regional components of the AfCFTA can emerge from and provide the springboard to deepen the continental integration. The existing RECs provide the sub-regional foundation to jump-start and deepen regional integration at the continental level. That is why the RECs are central to the success of the AfCFTA.

Table 6.4 presents a summary of the results for the model that identifies the impact of the eight RTAs in the Africa region on trade creation and trade diversion, both on overall trade as well as separately on imports and exports. Overall, African RECs tend to create more trade than they divert. TC dominates TD (in terms of imports) in 6 RECs out of the eight RECs. However, there are some heterogeneities within African RECs. Our interpretation here focuses on the coefficients associated with three dummies capturing TC and TD effects of RTAs since the coefficients of the traditional gravity variables do not differ significantly from those in Table 6.A1.

If we consider SADC, TC is more important than TD. SADC has generated positive and significant intraregional bilateral trade flows. Similarly, SADC members' exports to the RoW have increased, suggesting a trade creation from exports to the RoW. However, the Africa sample indicates that SADC has diverted trade (both from exports and imports) as its member countries import and export less to the rest of Africa following its formation. The formation of the SADC trade bloc has neither diverted nor created trade from imports since the member countries of this regional community have not significantly changed their imports from the RoW following the bloc's creation. This is an encouraging trend with respect to regional integration in Africa and particularly SADC and that increased trade between members also promotes trade with the rest of the world. This scenario could lead to the rise of regional value chains that would foster agglomeration economies to serve as loci of production and hence promote exports to the RoW.

One key implication of this finding for SADC is that it may not be economically feasible to deepen trade between countries, when the rationale has not been well established. Starting with the RECs and related key trade corridors should precede all other integration efforts under the AfCFTA. Within CEN-SAD, intraregional TC outweighs TD in terms of both exports and imports, though the TC effect is much smaller than what we find for SADC (more than three times smaller). The formation of CEN-SAD has generated a positive and significant intraregional trade. Similar to what we find in SADC, there is also no trade diversion effect with respect to the rest of the world, while there is a TD effect with respect to other African non-members of CEN-SAD. This suggests both exports and imports from other African countries declines as a result of the FTA. This may sometimes come at the cost of loss in efficiency and hence welfare.

ECOWAS seems to exhibit higher TD than TC (mostly TD in terms of imports and exports). More specifically, there is no effect on intra-REC trade within ECOWAS associated with the establishment of the FTA. However, ECOWAS has diverted trade in terms of exports to the RoW given that its member countries have reduced their exports to the RoW following its creation. In addition, ECOWAS has diverted trade in terms of imports from the RoW because its member countries seem to import less from non-member countries following its formation. This requires further investigation. But preliminary evidence suggests that ECOWAS has not succeeded in expanding trade within the FTA as envisioned. If we isolate the West African Monetary and Economic Union (UEMOA) member countries that share a common currency, the results show that there is intra-REC TC. UEMOA member countries trade more among themselves as compared to other ECOWAS member countries. In addition, there is TC from imports while no evidence of TD from exports exists. Trade diversion in ECOWAS reflects a restrictive unilateral trade policy in Nigeria. For instance, in August 2019, Nigeria closed its land borders with neighboring Benin, Cameroon, Chad, and Niger. The authorities argue that it will curb smuggling and dumping of goods and insecurity along Nigeria's land borders. In fact, large quantities of imported goods (especially rice) are re-exported from Benin into Nigeria. This policy leads to high informal trade because people cross the borders illegally. This could also explain TD within ECOWAS.

COMESA results show that intraregional TC is more important than TD from exports on average. As a matter of fact, considering bilateral trade between COMESA member countries with their partners worldwide, intra-COMESA trade has increased following the creation of this trade bloc. However, intra-COMESA trade has decreased when it comes to bilateral trade between its member countries with the rest of Africa. Moreover, the formation of COMESA has diverted trade in terms of exports given that its member countries have reduced their exports to the RoW. Yet, our results show that COMESA has neither diverted nor created trade from imports since imports of its member countries from non-member countries have not significantly changed in the aftermath of its creation.

ECCAS has generated positive and significant intraregional bilateral trade flows. Similarly, ECCAS has created trade from exports because its members' exports to the RoW have increased. However, the formation of the ECCAS trade bloc has neither diverted nor created trade from imports since the member countries of this regional community have not changed their import from the RoW following the bloc's creation. If we consider only Central African Economic and Monetary Community (CEMAC) member countries (a monetary union within ECCAS), the coefficient of intraregional TC is higher than that of TC within ECCAS. This result suggests that the deepness of an RTA is critical to reap the benefits of regional integration. However, contrary to ECCAS, there is no evidence of TC from exports within the CEMAC.

EAC intraregional TC is more important than TD from exports on average. For instance, intra-EAC trade has increased following the creation of this trade bloc. However, the formation of EAC has diverted trade in terms of exports given that its member countries have reduced their exports to the RoW. Finally, we find that EAC has neither diverted nor created trade from imports since imports of its member countries from non-member countries have not significantly changed in the aftermath of its creation.

Finally, TC is more important than TD within IGAD. IGAD has generated positive and significant intraregional bilateral trade flows. In the same vein, IGAD members' exports to the RoW have increased, suggesting a trade creation from exports to the RoW. Similarly, the formation of the IGAD trade bloc has created trade from imports since the member countries of this regional community have increased their imports from the RoW following the bloc's creation. However, the Africa sample indicates that IGAD has diverted trade from imports as its member countries import less to the rest of Africa following its formation.

Most of the RECs in this study have contributed to increasing intraregional trade as a result of the FTA. Many of the results could also be compared to Carrere (2006), Martinez-Zarzoso et al. (2009) and Coulibaly (2009). Carrere (2006) evaluates the total trade effects for seven RTAs over the period from 1962 to 1996, and their evolution over time. Martinez-Zarzoso et al. (2009) evaluate the effects of preferential agreements on trade between bloc members and bloc non-members over the period 1980–1999. Their results provide evidence of positive intra-bloc effects in the EU and NAFTA in the 1980s and 1990s. Coulibaly (2009) examines the trade impact in 22 RTAs around the world over the period 1962–2006. Similar to Carrere (2006), we find that African RTAs have generated trade between member countries. Carrere (2006) shows that UEMOA and SADC succeeded in generating net TC with an increase in the propensity to import from the RoW over the period

1962–1996. Another study, by Longo and Sekkat (2004) finds contrasting evidence that RTA schemes were not able to increase intra-African trade. Carrere (2006), Coulibaly (2009) and this chapter show that African RTAs result in increasing intraregional trade among members.

To summarize, most RECs in Africa have on average created more trade than they divert. Drawing upon these results, the success of the AfCTFA will critically depend on its ability to address the obstacles to trade creation on the continent. SADC has particularly succeeded not only in expanding trade between members but also in expanding exports to the rest of the world as a result of the FTA. This is critical to the success of other RECs and the AfCFTA. Because trade with regional partners and the rest of the world should be considered as complements and not substitutes. Countries need to deepen their integration while at the same time expanding exports and trading with the rest of the world. Regional integration should be a mechanism to increase local supply capacity to engage in global trade to improve access to markets and other suppliers (World Bank, 2009).

6.3 Lessons and challenges in transitioning from RECs to the AfCFTA

Most of the RECs in Africa have not achieved their goals of expanding regional trade and creating a network of trade and production structures that enhance the spillovers from economies of scale and larger connected markets. The AfCFTA faces the same challenges that served as barriers to RECs' success. Significant challenges stand in the way of achieving the goals of transforming the economies of its members through increased trade and increased integration in services, infrastructure, communications, and other spheres of economic activity. These range from building the necessary institutions to carve out conducive agreements and implementing them, to realizing them through national and regional strategies that require significant investment in resources and political commitment. In the following sections, drawing from the experiences of the RECs, we discuss the key challenges that African governments, multilateral and regional organizations, and businesses need to address to realize the objectives of the AfCFTA and transform the continent.

6.3.1 It takes more than tariff liberalization

Effective regional integration is more than simply reducing or eliminating tariffs—it is mainly about removing the key trade barriers and reducing the direct and indirect costs of trading across borders. These include regulatory frameworks, the state of regional infrastructure and logistics, the efficiency of borders and customs operations, and the quality of complementary services to trading both within and across borders. Despite the significant liberalization the region has seen over the last three decades, regional trade remains restricted to a few corridors and at very low levels. Though many factors play a role, much of the low regional trade is associated with the higher cost of trade in the region, much higher than any other region.

A significant part of the drag on trade costs derives from the higher cost and time associated with the inland transit (Freund and Rocha, 2009) of merchandise from production to the point of exit at the border and the cross-border transactions. Out of the bottom ten economies with the worst logistic performance index (LPI), eight were from Africa, the other two being Afghanistan and Haiti.[4] These include Angola, Burundi, Niger, Sierra Leone, Eritrea, Libya, Zimbabwe and Central African Republic. Only South Africa, Botswana, Kenya, Rwanda, Cote d'Ivoire, Tanzania, Uganda and Malawi have a relatively higher logistic performance index, in some cases even higher than non-African middle-income economies. Except for Cote d'Ivoire, all the African economies with a higher LPI are members of either SADC or EAC. Among RECs, EAC is the top performer in terms of customs efficiency and border management while AMU has the lowest score in this area. In addition, the quality of trade and transport-related infrastructure is higher within the EAC compared to the other African RECs. The lowest score for the quality of trade and transport-related infrastructure is recorded by the ECOWAS. Although the LPI indicators are low in Africa on average, the RECs with relatively higher customs efficiency and border management, better quality of infrastructure and timely shipments experience a strong intraregional trade flow.

Figure 6.6 presents a correlation between the share of intraregional export to total exports and trade costs measured by: (i) the time to export (in hours) and (ii) the cost to export (in terms of documentary compliance). On average, trade costs are high in Africa as compared to other regions around the world. These higher trade costs are associated with lower levels of the share of intraregional exports to total exports.

This underscores the significant investments in reducing the cost of trading in these two RECs. As discussed in Box 6.1 and 6.2, below there are multiple initiatives focused on reducing the costs of moving goods across borders. In the EAC, it is mainly through doing away with all tariffs and hence the associated need for documentary requirements, establishing one-stop custom shops across borders, and sharing customs personnel across borders to ease the drag from differences in regulations. The regional strategy is well bolstered by various national efforts to foster trade in the customs union. On the other hand, in SADC, in addition to similar initiatives within EAC, member countries have deliberate priorities to build regional infrastructure.

Hence, despite the high levels of tariff and non-tariff barriers within SADC, the high levels of both availability and quality of cross-border infrastructure provide for a better trading environment. Both SADC and EAC have advanced their investments in one-stop border shops, strategic collaboration between members to address the specific challenges associated with differences in regulations and customs procedures across borders as well as a concerted effort and investment in regional infrastructure including roads, payment systems and electronic transaction facilities. Many African countries still encounter significantly higher costs of trading due to the low quality of infrastructure, particularly roads and trucks, lack of seamless processing of transactions across and within borders as well as poor levels of overall logistic services both in transport and trade facilitation.

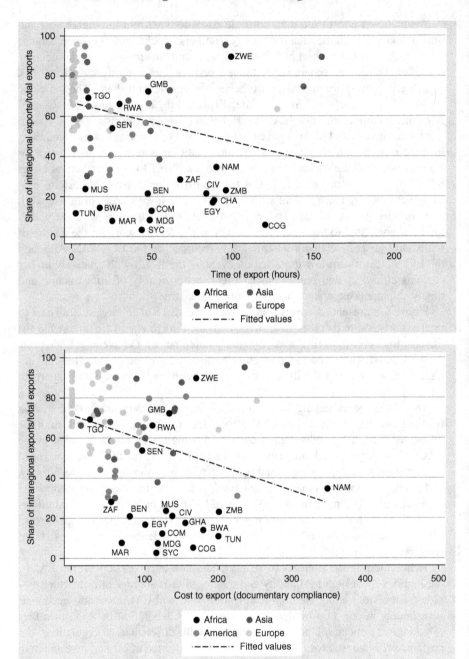

Figure 6.6 Correlation between trade costs and the share of intraregional trade.

Source: Authors elaboration based on CEPII Data and World Bank's Doing Business Indicators: i) time to export: documentary compliance (hours) and ii) Cost to export: documentary compliance (USD).

Box 6.1 Why are some RECs more regionally integrated than others? The case of EAC

Integration in infrastructure, better alignment of national and regional priorities often reflected in the degree of political commitment for regional integration and density of economic activity are key drivers, though other factors also play a role. Geographical proximity explains a good share of bilateral trade flows between partner countries. In addition, socioeconomic factors (common language), historical links and economic factors played a key role in promoting trade and integration within REC. The success of regional integration in EAC lies in an adequate infrastructure (e.g., transport networks, information and communication technologies—ICT). Investing in digital infrastructure is critical to bolstering intraregional trade in a highly technological world with strong linkages in economic, finance, trade, and social development.

EAC regional integration hinges on its higher levels of infrastructure development also associated with the density of economic activity. EAC stands out as the most densely populated region in Africa with roughly 170 people per square kilometer of land area over the period 1990–2019 (the less densely populated region being the AMU with around 31 people per square kilometer of land area). The success of EAC is also driven by the Customs reforms it has undertaken (including the Single Customs Territory, One-Stop Border Posts, and the electronic cargo tracking system.). For instance, customs officers from Rwanda, Uganda, and Burundi are deployed and are operating in Kenya and Tanzania. Similarly, Tanzania has deployed officers in Nairobi and Mombasa. This initiative has simplified the administrative burden and reduced the turnaround time of trucks from Mombasa to Kampala and from Mombasa to Kigali. These reforms, by reducing the time of customs clearance in the region, have helped boost intraregional trade. In short, investments in joint customs processes, in easing the costs of transactions across borders, and concerted effort to address continuously emerging issues due to the national governments' adoption of regional integration as part of national development efforts has been central to the success of EAC. Although EAC is the top performer among the African RECs in terms of trade, there still exists ample room for improvement in terms of infrastructural integration for a successful implementation of the AfCFTA.

6.3.2 High fragmentation and thick borders make regional integration both a necessity and a challenge

With a population size slightly smaller than either China or India, Africa is home to 54 countries, more than any other continent. The high level of fragmentation presents a significant geopolitical challenge for the AfCFTA and poses additional costs to

---

Box 6.2 Why are some RECs more regionally integrated than others?The case of SADC

Cross-border infrastructure combined with a One-Stop-Border Post initiative have contributed to boosting intra-SADC trade by eliminating trade barriers through the reduction of clearance time and cost. Development corridors within this region have driven industrial growth (mainly in landlocked countries) by providing cheaper alternative transport routes to seaports. As an illustration, the highway linking South Africa and Mozambique has contributed to improving the businesses of many entrepreneurs in these two countries. SADC's Integrated Regional Electronic Settlement System (SIRESS)—a SADC electronic payment system developed by member States to settle regional transactions among banks within the countries— has boosted intra-SADC as well as SADC trade with non-SADC members by reducing transactions clearing time between banks and across different currencies. This has also enhanced the production of goods and services in this region. The success of SADC in boosting intraregional trade also lies in the implementation of a regional electricity market in this region. An excel- lent example of a successful regional infrastructure is the Southern African Power Pool (SAPP)—a cooperation of the national electricity companies in Southern Africa under the auspices of SADC—which has given planners and managers additional options to meet growing demand since 1995. In sum, all these investments in the much-needed infrastructure could explain the above subpar intra-SADC performance in regional trade and integration.

Source: Authors' elaboration.

African economies. Most of the economies are small, with half of the region's econ- omies with a GDP of less than US$ 10 billion. Close to 30% of the countries (16 coun- tries) are landlocked. The high cost of trading faced by landlocked countries is well documented. Trading costs for an average landlocked country are 40–50% higher than those for a representative coastal country. Severe economic and geographic fragmentation of economies leading to limited-scale economies has long restricted economic expansion by restricting large-scale investment. Small markets often restrict competition and result in monopoly power creating an incentive for incum- bent firms to actively pursue strategies that deter the entry of new firms (Venables and Collier, 2008). This contributes to low productivity and limited potential to reap the benefits of economies of scale associated with large size. The fragmentation of African economies makes regional integration a challenge. The stark fragmentation that characterizes Africa, geographically and in economic size and disparity and the associated costs is one of the key reasons why continental integration is even more important to troubleshoot the continent's economy.

Historical factors have contributed to the current patterns of trade that are biased toward outside the continent. Infrastructure and trade networks were designed with

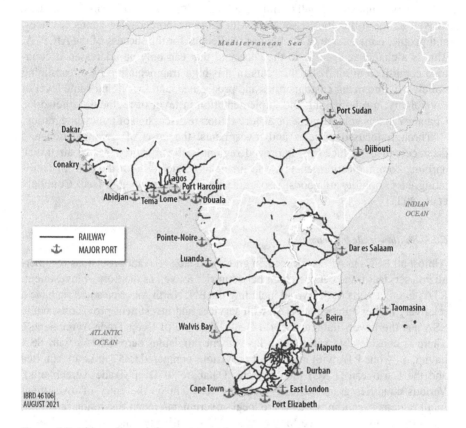

Figure 6.7 Africa railway infrastructure and connected ports.

Source: Africa Infrastructure Country Diagnostic (AICD), database (World Bank, 2009).

the goal of transferring natural resources outside the continent. As a result, the continental transport networks are poorly developed. Most transport networks, including rail lines, run from the location of a mine or agricultural production hotspot to a port, with a focus on exports to the rest of the world (see Figure 6.7). This situation still characterizes most of the countries in the region and is reflected in the higher costs of trading within Africa. Transport costs in Africa are 136% higher compared with other developing regions (see, Limao and Venables, 2001). The persistent cost of the deep fragmentation is reflected beyond the costs of transportation. Even with increased transportation networks, there is a multiplicity of rules and procedures in trading across multiple countries and ports. The redundant procedures associated with each country's customs procedures present a significant barrier to trade. The average customs transaction involves 20 to 30 different parties, 40 documents, and the rekeying of 60 to 70% of all data at least once (UNCTAD, 2019).

The large number of small countries, with a multiplicity of rules and procedures, as well as the difficulties associated with crossing borders, for goods, services, and people, remains one of the biggest challenges for the success of the AfCFTA. This is a challenge specific to the continent that can only be addressed if countries commit to minimizing the costs of this high fragmentation by streamlining policies, harmonizing customs rules and procedures, and sacrificing some level of sovereignty in rule-making and implementation in favor of regional frameworks. Chapter 7 in this volume presents a more elaborate discussion of policy integration.

Through focused policies and investments, the costs of fragmentation and distance can be reduced by improved regional infrastructure—roads, air travel, harbors, communication, energy, and financial services—with the goal of facilitating easy mobility of goods, services, people, and knowledge (see, Coulibaly et al., 2021).

6.3.3 Shallow trade agreements

Almost all RECs in Africa focused on goods and lack relevant provisions for liberalizing services trade between member countries as well as the flow of investment. RTAs in other parts of the world including the EU, North America and Asia have a relatively higher number of RTAs with services and investment provisions, while SSA has the lowest number (World Bank Database of Deep Trade Agreements). There is considerable variation in investment provisions across RTAs with SSA having only one PTA with investment provisions compared to 57 in Latin America and the Caribbean (LAC) (World Bank Database of Deep Trade Agreements). Various countries grant members national treatment on the entry of investment in all regions except in SSA, where local governments retain discretion regarding the entry of investment (see Mattoo et al. 2020). Africa has the lowest number of free trade areas with services provisions. Regional integration under the AfCFTA should cover services and investment as well as competition policy in addition to goods. Because the free flow of investment and services are essential in facilitating the emergence of regional value chains.

6.3.4 Avoiding a sticky transition from RECs to the AfCFTA

One of the core principles of the AfCFTA is that the RECs serve as building blocks for the AfCFTA, and the program aims to 'resolve the challenges of multiple and overlapping memberships' between the eight RECs functioning at various levels of integration. The RECs may remain active during the operation of the AfCFTA, although 'in the event of inconsistency, the AfCFTA agreement shall prevail'.

Still, the multiplicity of rules across RECs and the distinction with the AfCFTA rules remain a big challenge. The transition from RECs to the AfCFTA is expected to be challenging, and members need to develop strategies to maximize the gains from existing RECs while restricting the costs of divisions in regulations and rules governing each REC in the transition to the AfCFTA. For example, recent efforts to establish the Tripartite Free Trade Area (TFTA), at the same time the AfCFTA is becoming operational, by merging SADC, EAC and COMESA, while fostering regional integration on a bigger scale, could also restrict the pace of adoption and deepening of the AfCFTA. Hence, the AfCFTA needs to avoid becoming one of the overlapping RECs rather than the all-encompassing FTA it is destined to become.

Still the RECs present a significant opportunity in prioritizing integration across the region. Even though the AfCFTA is a continental free trade area, much of the deeper trade integration will be across key regional corridors with a relatively higher economic density. These include key trading corridors along SADC in Southern Africa; EAC and IGAD in East Africa; and Nigeria and neighbors in West Africa. Though regional trade overall is low, about 80% of all intra-Africa trade flows through RECs and trade across RECs has been extremely low. This implies the key role the existing RECs could play in serving as key corridors of regional trade upon which the AfCFTA can build.

For Africa, the gains from continental integration either through RECs or the AfCFTA go beyond the static analysis of trade creation and trade diversion. Much of the benefits arise from the dynamic gains associated with the potential to exploit economies of scale advantages both in production and markets, to build regional value chains and promote industrialization giving rise to Factory Africa, and to promote the transfer of technology through increased trade and FDI flows. To achieve these, the AfCFTA members must develop strategies to maximize the gains from prioritizing trade within the existing RECs, while restricting the intricate political challenges of multiple rules and regulations governing each REC in the transition to the AfCFTA (see Coulibaly et al., 2021). Setting a clear path to this transition is essential to the success of the AfCFTA, which also depends on the success of RECs to deepen trade and integration in the region. Both at the national level and at the REC level, countries may need to sacrifice some level of national and sub-regional sovereignty in policymaking, expand the horizons of trade liberalization and ease the cost of trading associated with multiple and overlapping rules, regulations and other domestic policies.

6.4 Conclusion

In this paper, we evaluate the effects of African RECs with respect to trade creation (TC) and trade diversion (TD). Despite significant heterogeneities, there is more trade creation than trade diversion, and a generally positive impact on within-REC trade. Except for ECOWAS, the effect of regional integration is dominated by trade creation. The absence of any intra-REC trade effect associated with ECOWAS could be explained by the existence of significant barriers to trade (tariff and non-tariff barriers) between members. Two RECs—EAC and SADC—outperform all the other RECs in terms of boosting intra-REC trade. This is mainly associated with their high level of investment in trade facilitation, the level of synergy between national and regional goals, the density of economic activity and the advancement in the quantity and quality of regional infrastructure. There are also variations among the RECs in terms of whether they promote exports to the rest of the world or displace them. In this respect, SADC presents an exemplary instance where trade integration leads to increased exports to the rest of the world. This provides the ideal form of regional integration that regional entities should aim for. That is, deepen integration to promote trade and linkage with global value chains and distance partners particularly the key centers of high economic density including North America, the EU and East Asia.

The key policy implications focus on two key areas—significant investment in trade facilitation and strategic sequencing of integration schemes. Given that the AfCFTA is a much larger FTA compared to the existing RECs, it is important that economies use regional integration to create regional value chains to expand supply/production which in turn provides greater impetus to engage in GVCs. Given the costs of distance and the benefits of already existing strong trade corridors, it is imperative that integration efforts start with a focus on selected high-density corridors of trade. Expanding trade on an African level is a daunting task but is achievable and feasible if sub-regional corridors of trade and production integration are strengthened to build regional value chains that serve as key hubs of GVCs.

A large number of small countries, with a multiplicity of rules and procedures, as well as the difficulties associated with crossing borders, for goods, services, and people, remains one of the biggest challenges for the success of the AfCFTA. The transition from RECs to the AfCFTA is expected to be challenging, and members need to develop strategies to maximize the gains from existing RECs while restricting the costs of divisions in regulations and rules governing each REC in the transition to the AfCFTA. In addition, many structural factors impede the process of integration and could explain the limited effects of RECs in driving intra-Africa trade. These factors include tariff and non-tariff barriers, high fragmentation and thick borders, and shallow trade agreements. Our findings suggest that policymakers should focus on eliminating obstacles (tariff and non-tariff barriers) to trade to reap the benefits from the implementation of the AfCFTA. Given that the AfCFTA is a continental scheme, fostering trade is going to present a more daunting task compared to the existing RECs. It is hence essential to ensure a smooth transition from RECs to the AfCFTA and avoid the possibility that the AfCFTA could remain another overlapping REC in the region.

Notes

1 The views and opinions expressed in this paper are those of the authors and do not necessarily reflect the views or positions of their employers or institutions.
2 Tinbergen (1962); Anderson (1979); Anderson and Van Wincoop (2003); Baier and Bergstrand (2009). We employ Ordinary Least Squares (OLS) estimator and Poisson Pseudo-Maximum Likelihood (PPML) estimator. The PPML estimator not only addresses zero trade flows but also performs best to the possibility of specification errors and is consistent in the presence of heteroscedasticity (Silva and Tenreyro, 2011).
3 See the appendix for a complete discussion of the estimation framework and results of estimation for each REC. Here we present a summary of the results.
4 Arvis et al. (2018). Logistic performance index (LPI) is composed of measures of the efficiency of customs and border management, quality of trade and transport infrastructure, quality of other logistic services including trucks, among others.

References

Anderson, J. E. (1979). A theoretical foundation for the gravity equation. *The American Economic Review*, 69(1):106–116.

Anderson, J. E. and Van Wincoop, E. (2003). Gravity with gravitas: A solution to the border puzzle. *American Economic Review*, 93(1):170–192.

Arvis, J.-F., Ojala, L., Wiederer, C., Shepherd, B., Raj, A., Dairabayeva, K., and Kiiski, T. (2018). Connecting to Compete 2018: Trade Logistics in the Global Economy. World Bank.

Baier, S. L. and Bergstrand, J. H. (2009). Bonus vetus ols: A simple method for approximating international trade-cost effects using the gravity equation. *Journal of International Economics*, 77(1):77–85.

Balassa, B. (1961). *The Theory of Economic Integration*. London: Routledge.

Carrere, C. (2006). Revisiting the effects of regional trade agreements on trade flows with proper specification of the gravity model. *European Economic Review*, 50(2):223–247.

Cooper, C. A. and Massell, B. F. (1965). A New Look at Customs Union Theory. *The Economic Journal*, 75(300): 742–747. https://doi.org/10.2307/2229672

Coulibaly, S. (2009). Evaluating the trade effect of developing regional trade agreements: A semi-parametric approach. *Journal of Economic Integration*, 709–743.

Coulibaly, S., Kassa, W., and Zeufack, A. G. (2021). *Africa in the New Trade Environment: Market Access in Troubled Times*. World Bank Group: Washington, DC.

Depetris Chauvin, N., Ramos, M. P., and Porto, G. (2017). Trade, Growth, and Welfare Impacts of the CFTA in Africa. In CSAE Conference 2017: Economic Development in Africa, Number Conference.

Francois, J. and Manchin, M. (2013). Institutions, infrastructure, and trade. *World Development*, 46:165–175.

Freund, C. and Rocha, N. (2009). What is Holding Back African Exports. VOXEU Column, London: CEPR Press.

Limao, N. and Venables, A. J. (2001). Infrastructure, geographical disadvantage, transport costs, and trade. *The World Bank Economic Review*, 15(3):451–479.

Longo, R., and Sekkat, K. (2004). Economic obstacles to expanding intra-African trade. *World Development*, 32(8):1309–1321.

Martinez-Zarzoso, I., Felicitas, N.-L. D., and Horsewood, N. (2009). Are regional trading agreements beneficial?: Static and dynamic panel gravity models. *The North American Journal of Economics and Finance*, 20(1):46–65.

Mattoo, A., Rocha, N., and Ruta, M. (2020). The Evolution of Deep Trade Agreements, Policy Research Working Paper Series 9283, The World Bank.

Saygili, M., Peters, R., Knebel, C., et al. (2018). African Continental Free Trade Area: Challenges and Opportunities of Tariff Reductions. Technical Report. United Nations Conference on Trade and Development.

Silva, J. S. and Tenreyro, S. (2011). Further simulation evidence on the performance of the poisson pseudomaximum likelihood estimator. *Economics Letters*, 112(2):220–222.

Tinbergen, J. (1962). Shaping the World Economy; Suggestions for an International Economic Policy. Twentieth Century Fund, New York. hdl.handle.net/1765/16826

United Nations Conference on Trade and Development (UNCTAD) (2019). Roadmap for Building a National Trade Information Portal. Transport and Trade Facilitation Series No. 16.

United Nations. Economic Commission for Africa (UNECA) (2016). *Assessing Regional Integration in Africa VII: Innovation, Competitiveness and Regional Integration*. Addis Ababa: UNECA.

Venables, T. and Collier, P. (2008). Trade and Economic Performance: Does Africa's Fragmentation Matter. In Annual World Bank Conference on Development Economics.

Vicard, V. (2009). On trade creation and regional trade agreements: Does depth matter? *Review of World Economics*, 145(2):167–187.

Viner, J. (1950). The Customs Union Issue. London: Stevens and Sons.

World Bank (2009). World Development Report 2009: Reshaping Economic Geography. World Bank.

World Bank (2020). *The African Continental Free Trade Area: Economic and Distributional Effects*. Washington, DC: World Bank.

WTO (2021). Regional Trade Agreements Database. RTA Database: http://rtais.wto.org/UI/ Charts.aspx

Appendix

Table 6.A1 Gravity model controlling for MRT

	OLS		PPML		OLS		PPML	
	[1]	[2]	[3]	[4]	[5]	[6]	[7]	[8]
	World	Africa	World	Africa	World	Africa	World	Africa
ln(GDP importer)	0.56***	0.42***	0.60***	0.04	0.56***	0.42***	0.60***	0.05
	(0.01)	(0.04)	(0.02)	(0.06)	(0.01)	(0.04)	(0.02)	(0.06)
ln(GDP exporter)	0.56***	0.72***	0.64***	0.27***	0.56***	0.71***	0.64***	0.26***
	(0.01)	(0.06)	(0.02)	(0.08)	(0.01)	(0.06)	(0.02)	(0.08)
ln(distance)	-1.66***	-2.12***	-0.72***	-0.72***	-1.66***	-2.12***	-0.72***	-0.72***
	(0.00)	(0.03)	(0.01)	(0.05)	(0.00)	(0.03)	(0.01)	(0.05)
Border	0.75***	1.49***	0.66***	1.14***	0.75***	1.49***	0.66***	1.14***
	(0.02)	(0.05)	(0.02)	(0.07)	(0.02)	(0.05)	(0.02)	(0.07)
Common colonizer	0.80***	0.60***	0.10***	-0.14*	0.80***	0.60***	0.10***	-0.14*
	(0.01)	(0.05)	(0.03)	(0.07)	(0.01)	(0.05)	(0.03)	(0.07)
Common language	0.77***	0.59***	0.18***	0.79***	0.77***	0.59***	0.18***	0.79***
	(0.01)	(0.04)	(0.02)	(0.06)	(0.01)	(0.04)	(0.02)	(0.06)
SADC_M	**-0.09****	**-0.57****	**0.01**	**-0.59****	**-0.09****	**-0.58****	**0.01**	**-0.67****
	(0.04)	**(0.13)**	**(0.07)**	**(0.19)**	**(0.04)**	**(0.13)**	**(0.07)**	**(0.19)**
SADC	**1.39****	**0.48****	**2.00****	**1.23****	**1.39****	**0.22**	**2.41****	**0.44**
	(0.07)	**(0.13)**	**(0.09)**	**(0.18)**	**(0.08)**	**(0.16)**	**(0.14)**	**(0.28)**
SADC_X					-0.01	-0.29***	0.42***	-0.76***
					(0.05)	(0.11)	(0.11)	(0.23)
Constant	-3.18***	5.32***	-6.92***	-2.04***	-3.18***	5.52***	-6.92***	-1.42**
	(0.29)	(0.44)	(0.25)	(0.60)	(0.29)	(0.45)	(0.25)	(0.62)
Observations	496975	30252	994815	69448	496975	30252	994815	69448
R^2	0.732	0.593	0.817	0.656	0.732	0.593	0.817	0.656
Importer/FE	YES	YES	YES	YES	YES	YES	YES	YES
Exporter/FE	YES	YES	YES	YES	YES	YES	YES	YES
Time/FE	YES	YES	YES	YES	YES	YES	YES	YES

Source: Authors' elaboration based on CEPII data.

7 Fiscal policies coordination for the success of the AfCFTA[1]

Fulbert Tchana Tchana

7.1 Introduction

At the end of 2019, Africa, with its about 1.3 billion people scattered in 54 countries, had experienced since 2000 a relatively strong growth due mainly to growth in the export proceeds from commodities, services, and manufacturing, although the continent continued to host most of the world's poor.

In addition to traditional trade partners such as the European Union and the United States, China and India have increasingly become important trade partners.[2] However, total trade from Africa to the rest of the world averaged US$ 760 billion in current prices in the period 2015–17. Africa exports about 85% of its trade and about 15% is regional trade.[3] Although since 2005, Africa's intraregional trade has been on the rise, African countries were more embedded in the global value chain (albeit through commodity exports) than in the regional value chain (see Figure 7.1).

The African Continental Free Trade Agreement (AfCFTA) aims at accelerating growth in intraregional trade. Under this agreement, goods and services are allowed to move in and out of participants' countries without duties fees, with the condition that the local content is at least 30%. The AfCFTA is expected to boost the continent's economy by strengthening intraregional trade and supply chains.[4] Free trade is expected to help many countries move away from mainly exporting raw materials to building manufacturing capacity. It will also reinforce Africa's negotiating position on the international stage.

The AfCFTA is part of the long-term goal of the African Union (AU) and as soon as all countries have ratified it and the free trade area starts working smoothly, the AU will start the process of moving into a customs union that will entail the removal of tariff barriers between all African countries' members, together with the acceptance of a common (unified) external tariff against non-members. So far, the AfCFTA team has worked more to ensure that the relevant protocols under which the area will operate are completed. It focused on what goods would be subject to the agreement, the tariff regime, etc. Policymakers have focused on setting the stage for a typical free trade agreement with various protocols. Specifically, six main protocols have been adopted with many annexes. These protocols are on i) trade in goods; ii) trade in services; iii) rules and procedures on the settlement of

DOI: 10.4324/9781003456568-7

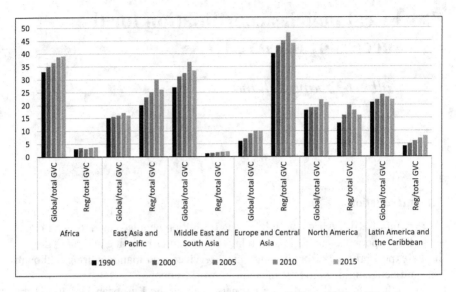

Figure 7.1 GVC activities increased globally and regionally from 1990 to 2015.

Source: Author computation from WDR 2020 data.

disputes; iv) competition policy; v) investment; and vi) intellectual property rights. The protocol on trade in goods focused on trade tariffs which will have an impact on fiscal policy. The agreement also makes the case that its ultimate objective is to move toward a customs union in the medium term.

The Covid-19 crisis has shown that allowing the free movement of goods, services, capital, and people across the entire continent is key to keeping African countries on track for all to achieve mid-income status by 2030 and high middle-income status by 2063. The AfCFTA is therefore a necessary first step in this direction. Although necessary there is no guarantee that this step will be a success so as to provide the momentum to launch the next steps toward this strategic goal. Among other necessary conditions of success for the AfCFTA are fiscal and monetary policies relevant at each step of the integration process.

However, no protocol has specifically looked at the conditions under which this agreement should be successful. In fact, although African countries have gradually been moving out of using tariffs as a key source of government revenues, customs tariffs remain an important component of government revenues for a number of countries.

This chapter explores the relevant fiscal policies necessary to achieve success at this stage of the agreement as well as the reforms that are needed to move the agreement to the custom-union stage and further. We use the economic integration analytical framework and empirical evidence based on the experience of the evolution of other free trade agreements.

Our findings suggest that the implementation of the AfCFTA could lead to a slight reduction of government revenues in the very short term, which will be more than fully compensated in the medium term. Moreover, to strengthen integration and expand African firms' participation in the continental value chain, a reduction in the rate of income and profit tax would be needed. This should be compensated for by the enlargement of the tax base, the strengthening of fiscal administration, and the increase of indirect taxes and property taxes. Efforts should be made immediately to harmonize external tariffs for all African countries to avoid a downward tax competition and foster greater cooperation.

The AfCFTA will not be successful if it does not yield fruits on growth, job, and economic inclusion. There is therefore a need to mobilize enough revenue to provide public investment in connectivity infrastructure, and social spending in education, health, and social protection. Revenue mobilization efforts should focus more on the increase of indirect taxes and the tax base. These efforts should be adapted to the country's participation level in the continental and global value chain.

The remainder of the chapter is organized as follows. Section 2 presents the analytical framework based on the continental value chain. Section 3 analyses the findings from this framework. Section 4 analyses the integration journey of three examples of the free trade agreement journey with a focus on fiscal policy reforms. Section 5 presents policy recommendations.

7.2 Analytical framework

The chapter adapts the Global Value Chain (GVC) framework to the Continental Value Chain (CVC), taking into account how countries are integrated into the continental and the global value chain. A comparative analysis based on the historical perspective of a group of countries that have embarked on the journey of economic integration complements the methodology and analysis. It focuses on how fiscal policies should be set at this point in the process. This methodology is consistent with the overreaching goal (ultimately achieving the continent's Political Union) of the African Union that mandated the AfCFTA. Economic integration has seven stages, from preferential Trade Area to Political Union (see Figure 7.2); the AfCFTA, which is a free trade agreement, is in its second stage.

Using the CVC, the AfCFTA success depends on firms/enterprises getting involved in CVC; (see Figure 7.3). Firms will be the engine of the AfCFTA, but they will need drivers to make this happen. These drivers are the right set of policies needed to leverage the geography, the endowments, the institutions, and the market size for development. Also, the type of social policies that are needed to bring about poverty reduction, growth, and jobs. In fact, as the AfCFTA becomes a reality, some workers will gain, but others could lose in some locations, countries, sectors, and occupations. Financial assistance, which is especially important in middle-income countries, will help workers adapt to changing production patterns and distribution that the AfCFTA will bring about. Also, adjustment policies could include facilitating labor mobility and equipping workers to find new jobs, unemployment benefits, and active labor market programs. The AfCFTA

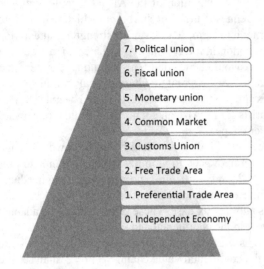

Figure 7.2 Stages of integration.

Source: Balassa, Bela, 2013.

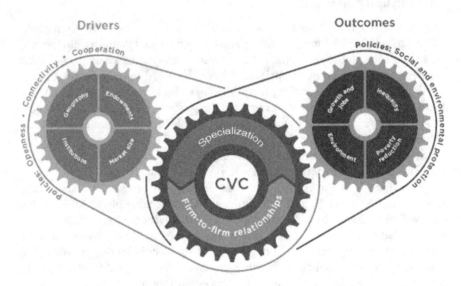

Figure 7.3 CVC interactions between firms typically involve durable relationships.

Source: Author adaptation from WDR 2020.

secretariat could also establish and monitor appropriate labor standards; exporting good prices should reflect both their economic and socio-environmental costs.

The type of a country's G/CVC linkages is based on the country's extent of backward G/CVC participation, measured as the portion of imports embodied in manufacturing exports as a percentage of a country's total exports, combined with the country's sector specialization of domestic value-added in exports and engagement in innovation. Countries in the commodities group have a small share of manufacturing exports and limited backward CVC integration. Their share of commodity exports can be low, medium, or high. Countries specialized in limited manufacturing CVCs engage in some manufacturing exports, often alongside commodities exports, and exhibit medium backward CVC integration. Countries specialized in advanced manufacturing and services CVCs have a high share of manufacturing and business services exports and high backward GVC integration. Countries specialized in innovative CVC activities spend a large share of GDP on research and development, receive a large share of GDP from intellectual property, and exhibit high backward CVC integration.

The chapter uses a comparative analysis of free trade and macroeconomic policy lessons from three successful economic areas (ASEAN, EU and ECOWAS) and their implication for Africa.

7.3 Analysis of findings from regional value chain and economic integration process

The participation of African countries in the global value chain is mainly through commodities. In fact, the majority of African countries (about 60%) are involved in commodities. Only 25% are classified as being mostly involved in limited manufacturing (see Figure 7.4). Noticeably no country is in innovative manufacturing. The integration in the continental value chain provides a different picture (see Figure 7.5). Most countries are involved in limited commodities in their intra-continental trade, followed by limited manufacturing; almost no country is classified as a high commodity exporter. Therefore, policies to pursue the regional value chain should be tailored to those that are relevant for limited commodities and limited manufacturing.

The chapter looks at fiscal policies to support the buildup of the continental value chain, focusing on those that are relevant for limited commodities and to limited manufacturing countries. Tariffs are part of fiscal policy as it affects government revenue. As such it always leads to a necessary reorientation of fiscal policy.

Table 7.1 shows fiscal and monetary policies relevant to each country, depending on its place in the continental value chain (CVC). Policies to make endowment a driver of CVC are related to i) profit taxes, ii) foreign currency regulation to attract FDI; iii) interest rate, capital/reserve requirement policy on financial institutions to improve access to finance; and iv) the labor cost regulation that could have fiscal

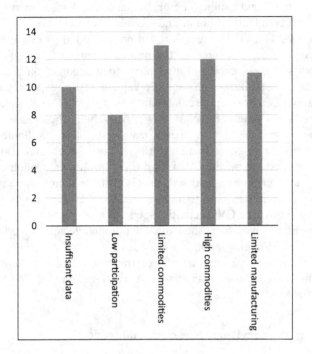

Figure 7.4 Number of countries by their type in the GVC.

Source: Authors computation from WDR 2020 data.

implications. For example, labor tax, and retirement mandatory saving rates are all fiscal in nature. Regarding the market size, reducing or eliminating tariffs on goods is the most important type of fiscal policy to be used. In contrast, exchange rate policy can be a tool to improve competitiveness to expand access to the regional market. Regarding geography, likely fiscal policies are related to public investment in logistic, road, and ICT infrastructures. keeping an adequate macroeconomic framework is paramount.

7.3.1 Fiscal, monetary, and financial policies to spur trade and growth[5]

Macroeconomic stability. Many African countries have weak underlying economic fundamentals—such as the significant fiscal deficit (-4.2% of GDP on average 2011–19 for the entire continent) and low domestic saving. With Covid-19, there has been further erosion in other indicators and greater volatility in the exchange rate and reserves. African countries' fiscal deficits have primarily reflected high levels of current expenditure rather than capital expenditure and a low rate of revenue collection; the average tax revenue to GDP is 13.6%, the weakest of any region in the world. Moreover, these countries also post a significant current account deficit

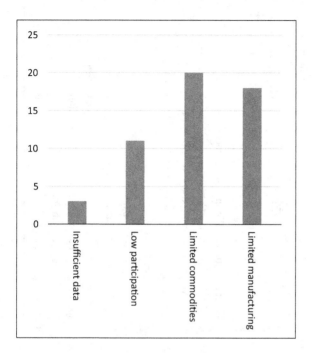

Figure 7.5 Number of countries by their type in the CVC.

Source: Authors computation from Pralac WDR 2019 data.

(-6.7% of GDP on average 2011–19) due to larger imports than exports. Hence, reducing current account deficits over time will minimize risks from other factors that bear on the assessment of sustainability by financial markets. African countries participating in the AfCFTA should pay attention to risks associated with current account deficits, especially in the context of the mobility of international capital within the continent.

Given that many African countries export mostly commodities, fiscal adjustments in Africa in the past had to contend with the declining importance of commodities revenues. This has required tax reform efforts, the strict prioritization of expenditures, and the provision of a greater role to the private sector in infrastructure development.

Endowments. Attracting more FDI will be critical to achieving the AfCFTA growth objective. Governments will then face pressure to reduce the profit tax rate and reduce labor tax (reform labor and retirement taxation to reduce labor costs) to reduce labor costs to bring in more regional FDI in countries specialized in limited manufacturing in the CVC.[6] However, income and profit taxation is the second-largest source of government revenue; it accounts for 27% of the government revenues in 2011–19 (see Figure 7.6), or about 5% of GDP. Its ratio to GDP is slightly low compared to other regions. For countries specializing in limited

Table 7.1 Relevant fiscal, monetary, and financial policies by CVC participation

	Low participation	Limited Commodities	Limited manufacturing
Fiscal and monetary policies to spur trade and growth			
Macroeconomic	Macroeconomic stability	Adequate macroeconomic framework.	
Endowments			
FDI	Profit taxation	Mining taxation	Profit taxation
		Currency exchange flexibility	
Finance	Capital requirement		Stock markets development
Labor costs	—	Exchange rate policy	Labor and retirement taxation
Market size and connectivity			
Access to inputs		Tariff reduction or elimination on goods	
Markets access		Exchange rate policy harmonization	
Infrastructure		Public investment in connectivity infrastructure	
		Fiscal incentive to the private to invest in connectivity infrastructure	
Social protection and fiscal policies to achieve development outcomes			
Govt revenue			
Growth and jobs	Public investment	Indirect taxation	
Inequality		Income and property taxation	
Spending			
Growth and jobs	Public investment		Social spending
Inequality	Social spending in education, health, social protection	—	
	—	Targeted subsidies	
Poverty reduction	Social spending in education, health, social protection	Social spending in education, health, social protection	

Source: Author.

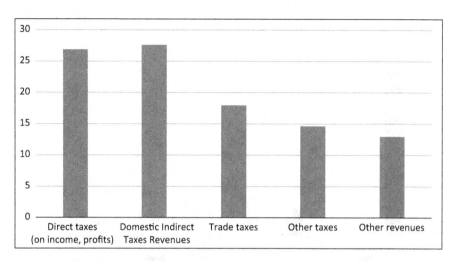

Figure 7.6 Share or total revenue, 2011–19.

Source: World Development Indicators.

commodities, the pressure will be about providing attractive but fair mining taxation. The transparency of mining taxation will be key, and the AfCFTA could help set a continental mining taxation code. In addition, tax policies and administrations mostly focus on the formal sector and official source of income. Governments should expand the tax base and strengthen tax administration to ensure that any eventual reduction in tax rate does not lead to a sharp reduction in revenue.

Given that private firms should be the engine of the AfCFTA, monetary policy reform must lead to greater domestic financing of the private sector. Currently, the banking sector financing of the private sector remains weak. In fact, the credit to the private sector represents 23.5% on average between 2011–19. Only Mauritius, South Africa, Tunisia, Morocco, Cabo Verde, and Namibia have a ratio greater than 50%, while seven-country has this ratio lower than 10%. A reform of capital requirement could support an increase of financing to the private sector. However, the key reform should be identifying each private-sector firm's right level of risk to price financial assets instrument accordingly. Providing incentives to build credible continental risk assessment agencies that will keep track of the risk exposure of firms in Africa will be paramount.

While strengthening the banking sector will be key for limited commodities countries, stock markets will be instrumental for countries specialized in limited manufacturing within the CVC. African stock markets will be critical to AfCFTA success, given bidirectional causality between FDI and stock market development indicators (Soumaré and Tchana Tchana, 2015). In Africa, the stock market is in its developmental phase; the number of listings at stock exchanges on the African continent increases, and the importance of stock exchanges for equity issues is growing.

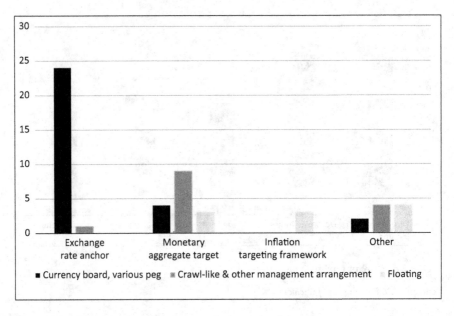

Figure 7.7 Africa–Number of country exchange rate regime.

Source: Author computation from IMF 2020.

The main stock market is the Johannesburg Stock Exchange (JSE), accounting for about 64% of Africa's market capitalization. In total, by the end of 2020, there were 29 stock exchanges in Africa, representing 38 nations' capital markets. The Egyptian Exchange (EGX), the Casablanca Stock Exchange of Morocco, the Nigerian Stock Exchange, the Namibian Stock Exchange (NSX), Zimbabwe Stock Exchange are the other significant stock markets. The continent also has two regional stock exchanges: i) the *Bourse Régionale des Valeurs Mobilières* (BRVM, Abidjan, Cote d'Ivoire) for UEMOA; and the *Bourse des Valeurs Mobilières de l'Afrique Centrale* (BVMAC, Libreville, Gabon) for CEMAC.

Exchange rate convertibility and flexibility will be key to improving labor cost competitiveness and attracting additional FDI. The multitude of monetary policy arrangements (see Figure 7.7) requires using a range of monetary policy instruments and operations to achieve the inflation objective, to fluidify and reduce the financial cost of trade between participant countries. Policy interest rates are binding for monetary operations in only a few countries, while some countries move away from hard targets on reserve money. These differences reflect a range of underlying factors: i) the extent of donor funding; ii) financial depth and development; iii) fiscal dominance. Although central bank financing of national budgets is generally subject to defined limits in African countries, exceptional financing instances arise, usually when efforts to fund budgets using market-based instruments result in excessive interest costs.

Market size and connectivity. At the core of the AfCFTA is reducing or eliminating tariffs on all goods (or some goods). In 2011–19, these tariffs accounted for about 18% of the total government revenues. Given that interregional trade accounts for about one-fifth of the Africa region global trade and assuming that the AfCFTA will reduce these tariffs by 50%, it means that a typical African country will lose only about 1.8% of its total revenue as the result of this reform at the beginning of a full elimination (of the current 6.1% tariff rate, see African Union, 2020) will lead to 3.6% reduction of revenue. Overall, it will not be challenging to find another source of revenue to fill this loss. However, it would be significant for countries with most of their trade within the African region, such as South Africa, Botswana, Zambia, Namibia, and Mozambique, countries with important intra-Africa trade. For these countries, there is a need to increase indirect taxes, such as the VAT, to find an alternative.[7]

While waiting for the customs union, the AfCFTA should start the dialogue on external trade tariffs and norm harmonization to reduce tax arbitrage. A case that has gained attention in recent years has been Nigeria's fear that Benin could export used cars with low tariffs and dump Nigeria's nascent car industry. It is important that even without the customs union, the AfCFTA secretariat works to propose harmonized external tariffs. The AfCFTA secretariat should also guide how countries can sign a free trade agreement with other entities so that they are not incompatible with fiscal and monetary policies.[8]

The 54 countries participating in the AfCFTA have about 41 different currencies, many non-convertibles. Moreover, monetary policy regimes and practices differ across African countries. The exchange rate regime is classified as floating in only ten countries (Madagascar, Seychelles, Zimbabwe, Ghana, South Africa, Uganda, Mauritius, Mozambique, Zambia, and Somalia) (see Table 7.5). The majority of countries have their currency pegs to Euro, US Dollar, or South African Rand. Under a currency peg, the institutional challenges are greatly reduced because of the elimination of monetary independence. Under this regime, national central banks' operating responsibilities are limited, and the need for harmonized or coordinated activities reduced. By contrast, under current exchange rate flexibility, central banks face the challenge of operating an independent monetary policy.

To seize the full potential of the AfCFTA, the continent should step up its investment in connectivity infrastructure (see Simbanegavi and Gwatidzo's chapter in this book). Public investment in connectivity infrastructure has been lower than 10% of total spending in recent years. Each country should increase investment in roads, railways, and ICT to expand connectivity infrastructure; a focus should be given to transborder infrastructure to ensure that the continent is fully connected by road and railway from east to west and from the north to the south (see Bougna's chapter in this book). Public investment will not be enough, and governments should provide fiscal incentives to the private sector to invest in connectivity infrastructure. This incentive could be a tax holiday or tax credit corresponding to a proportion of investment in connectivity infrastructure.

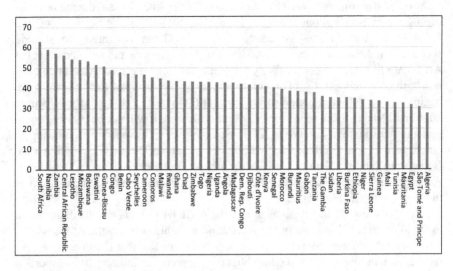

Figure 7.8 Africa–Gini coefficient.

Source: World Bank, Development Research Group.

7.3.2 Social protection and fiscal policies to achieve the outcomes

Increasing government revenues. Like any major reform, the AfCFTA will likely lead to winners and losers within countries and between countries. Fiscal policies will be needed to correct some of the negative impacts of the reform. Most importantly, the government should increase its sources of income to be in a position to act. An increase in government revenue should come primarily from indirect taxation, the efficiency of tax administration, and better taxation of commodities for net-commodities exporters of commodities. An increase in indirect taxes will have less effect on job creation. Governments should seek to improve revenues from royalties and ensure that production-sharing agreements are as advantageous as possible. Between 2011–19, other taxes accounted for only about 14% of total revenue, about 3% of GDP. There is room to improve this, given that the continent has substantial endowment with natural resources.

Efforts should be made to arrive at the right level of income tax for redistribution purposes; however, this could impact investment, so this should be done cautiously. Some harmonization level is needed. Meanwhile, property taxation remains at an embryonic level in many African countries. The issue is not mainly about the tax rate; it is mostly about easy and affordable land and property registration processes and an acceptable tax rate that does not incentivize taxpayers to avoid paying taxes. This is a source of income for states and municipalities. It is also an instrument to launch land markets and financing sources.

It is worth mentioning that the overall impact on import tariffs revenue is expected to be positive in the AfCFTA scenario at the continental level. Simulations by the World Bank (2020) show that although tariffs decline, the increase in the volume of imports would lead to higher tariff revenue collection with an increase of 3% at the continental level compared to the baseline in 2035. Faster economic growth leading to a higher level of economic activity is likely to increase the total revenue from other taxes.

Increase investment and social spending. Africa allocates about 70% of the budget to current spending. Specifically, 29% goes to wages and salaries, 15% to the purchase of goods and services, and 14% is transfers from the government to individuals or local government. Capital expenditure accounted for only about 30% (7.3% of GDP). Most of the capital spending goes to buildings, schools, and hospitals. In 2019, Africa spent on average 8.4% of its GDP on education and health, representing about 40% of the total spending, although appreciably it could be improved. However, to reduce poverty, African countries must keep public investment at an adequate level to increase long-term growth way above demographic growth. The increase in public revenue should be adequately shifted to investment spending. Moving progressively capital spending at about 40% of spending and 10% of GDP will be critical.

Africa is the continent with a higher level of inequality. Nine (9) African countries have a Gini higher than 50, and 28 African countries are among the 50 countries with a higher Gini coefficient (see Figure 7.8). Moreover, Africa is the region with most of the poorest countries. Dependence on commodities is one of the rationales behind this issue. To be successful, African countries should step up their spending in social sectors such as education, health, and social protection. Investment in human capital is key to allowing economic transformation and improving social outcomes. A targeted subsidies program should be created or strengthened in countries rich in natural resources. Well-targeted programs such as conditional cash transfers could be used to ensure population acceptance of resource extraction and provide the incentive to build up human capital critical for economic diversification.

7.4 Lessons from other development zones

7.4.1 Association of Southeast Asian Nations (ASEAN)[9]

The ASEAN was created on 8 August 1967 by Indonesia, Malaysia, the Philippines, Singapore, and Thailand, with the ASEAN Declaration. The region accounts for about 8.5% of the world's population and a rapidly growing world output share. In 1992 it enacted its free trade agreement.

The economic achievements of the countries in this region over the past five decades have been impressive (see Table 7.2). As a result of strong, sustained economic growth since 1970, Singapore and Brunei Darussalam have joined the ranks of the rich industrial countries, while Malaysia and Thailand have seen their real

Table 7.2 ASEAN member states: Selected key macroeconomic indicators, 2018

Country	Growth rate of GDP at constant prices (%)	GDP per capita (US$)	Total trade		Y-o-y change in FDI inflows (%)
			Ratio to GDP (%)	Y-o-y change (%)	
Brunei Darussalam	0.1	31,086.8	79.1	23.7	9.5
Cambodia	7.5	1,643.1	57.9	-44.2	13.6
Indonesia	5.2	4,135.6	37	18.3	6.8
Lao PDR	6.3	2,534.9	62.9	13.1	-22.2
Malaysia	4.7	11,414.2	129.7	12.7	-13.2
Myanmar	6.8	1,407.8	46.6	8.6	-11.2
Philippines	6.2	3,485.1	53.3	3.7	-4.4
Singapore	3.1	65,233.3	215	11.7	2.5
Thailand	4.1	7,806.7	85.7	-5.8	64.7
Vietnam	7.1	2,715.3	199.1	13	9.9
ASEAN	**5.2**	**4,818.8**	**93.8**	**8.7**	**5.3**

Source: ASEAN Macro-economic Database, ASEAN Merchandise Trade Statistics Database, ASEAN Foreign Direct Investment Statistics Database (compiled/computed from data submission, publications and/or websites of ASEAN Member States' national statistics offices, central banks and relevant government agencies, and from international sources).

per capita incomes rise sharply to join the club of high middle-income countries. Indonesia, the Philippines, has seen its growth rate rise closer to that of the other countries in the region. In much of the region, this rapid growth has also been accompanied by dramatic reductions in poverty.

An outstanding feature of the region's economic success has been exceptionally high saving and investment rates that have shown increasing disparity with the rest of the world. The strong and rising saving performance has reflected contributions from both the private and the public sectors. In addition, these countries have been able to tap successfully additional foreign savings to complement their already formidable domestic effort. Although countries vary considerably concerning starting conditions, natural endowments, and individual experiences, there is broad acceptance of the key policy settings contributing to the region's strong economic fundamentals. First, fiscal and monetary policies oriented toward macro-stability have helped keep inflation low and external imbalances under control. Second, the strategy was market-friendly and outward-oriented, with liberal external regimes that maintained strong competitive positions. Third, careful government interventions in several areas--such as the antipoverty programs--unleashed a powerful virtuous circle of government spending (especially on education and health), productivity, and growth that helped ensure the economic and political sustainability of the reform process in these countries. Fourth, these countries' willingness to adjust policies flexibly and quickly in response to changing economic circumstances and challenges allowed a rapid transformation of the economic structure while maintaining intact strong macroeconomic fundamentals.

7.4.2 European Economic Community (EEC)

The EEC aimed to lay the foundations of an ever-closer union among the peoples of Europe. Calling for balanced economic growth, this was to be accomplished through: i) the establishment of a customs union with a common external tariff; ii) common policies for agriculture, transport, and trade, including standardization; and iii) enlargement of the EEC to the rest of Europe. For the customs union, the treaty provided a 10% reduction in customs duties and up to 20% of global import quotas. Progress on the customs union proceeded much faster than the twelve years planned. The Single European Act was signed in 1986. It dealt with the reform of institutions, the extension of powers, foreign policy cooperation, and the single market. The act was followed by the Maastricht Treaty, agreed on 10 December 1991 and coming into force in 1993, establishing the European Union and paving the way for the European Monetary Union.

The EEC's most important achievement has been its customs union. It was completed in 1968 when each of the six members abolished tariffs and quotas on goods from the other five member countries and adopted a common external tariff on goods from the rest of the world. The customs union has propelled the growth of intra-community trade from less than 40% to over 60% of the participating countries' total trade. Undoubtedly, the completion of the customs union and, later, the single market program's implementation stimulated cross-border trade and investment and contributed to economic growth.

7.4.3 Economic Community of West African States (ECOWAS)

The ECOWAS is a regional political and economic union of fifteen countries located in West Africa. The union was established in 1975 to promote economic integration. A revised version of the treaty was signed in 1993 with the stated goal of achieving "collective self-sufficiency" for its member states by creating a single large trade bloc through building a full economic and trading union.

ECOWAS is one of the most integrated African regional blocks. Among its achievements, the UEMOA has successfully implemented macroeconomic convergence criteria and an effective surveillance mechanism. It has adopted a customs union and common external tariff and has combined indirect taxation regulations, in addition to initiating regional structural and sectoral policies. ECOWAS and UEMOA have developed a common plan of action on trade liberalization and macroeconomic policy convergence. The organizations have also agreed on common rules of origin to enhance trade, and ECOWAS has agreed to adopt UEMOA's customs declaration forms and compensation mechanisms. In realization of the need to raise funds for the sustenance of the community projects and programs, ECOWAS established the community levy. The levy of a 0.5% tax imposed on goods from the non-ECOWAS member states is also used in financing the ECOWAS Commission and Community institutions' activities.

7.5 Conclusion—Fiscal policy road map for economic convergence in Africa

Findings and experiences from successful free trade areas suggest that the AfCFTA needs some tax harmonization to avoid tax arbitrage, leading countries to compete in reaching the lower tax level to attract companies and FDI. Such a move will be detrimental to free trade and the evolution of the regulation process and there is a need to avoid Benin-Nigeria-type issues. Hence, the AfCFTA secretariat should start preparing a protocol on tax harmonization.[10] This fiscal protocol should be given priority to facilitate a steady reduction of the extent of fiscal dominance. The possible use of fiscal rules should be assessed, including enforcement mechanisms, considering institutional capacity constraints and individual reform plans.

The AfCFTA implementation should focus on direct tax rates such as profits taxes to agree on a tax rate range and tax base while accounting for the degree of integration in the continental value chain. Specifically, for countries classified as limited commodities, efforts should be made to establish and harmonize mining/commodities taxation. African policymakers could contribute to sustainability by ensuring that policies are transparent, implementation is consistent, and trade and investment policies foster openness. As for the property tax, a bracket should be set.

Improvements in tax administration and tax collection systems could make a strong contribution. The still low ratio of tax revenue to GDP in Africa, considerably below that in many other countries, is a testimony that more efficient tax administration is an important channel for raising public savings.

Regarding public expenditure, policymakers should carefully weigh important competing claims for additional spending on physical and human infrastructure rather than other activities. There is a need to develop stricter criteria to evaluate the returns on public sector investment and foster a more private-sector-friendly environment.

A continental policy for public investment in connectivity infrastructure should be prepared and adopted. The continent lacks the road, railway, energy, and telecommunication infrastructure needed to expand intra-Africa trade significantly (see Bougna's chapter in this book). Each government will have to significantly increase the share of public investment in infrastructure from less than 3% of GDP to at least 5% in the medium term. Public investment should be complemented by private sector participation in connectivity investments. It is critical to agree on a continental transparent and fair framework to incentivize private financial participation in infrastructure. Increasing the economic return of infrastructure by a rigorous selection of infrastructure projects and improving its efficiency will be key for private sector participation. The AfCFTA team should help to improve coordination in the provision of regional infrastructure; priority should be given in coming years to the continental road corridors already identified by the African Union.

Each African country should expand social and environmental protection fiscal and monetary policies to achieve a better outcome in growth and jobs and reduce inequality and poverty. Therefore, efforts should be made to increase capital spending to improve the quality and quantity of health, education, and social protection services. The almost 8% of GDP allocated to these sectors is a good start; the AfCFTA secretariat could set an ambitious but reachable target to push countries toward further integration. A continental directive about targeting subsidies to avoid unfair competition should be adopted for countries rich in natural resources.

The ASEAN experience shows that it is critical to achieve and maintain an adequate macroeconomic framework. It means that the AfCFTA should prepare a directive to agree on some convergence criterion regarding inflation, fiscal, and current account deficits. It could learn from the ECOWAS experience. In any case, this means that each country would have to increase the share of public revenue to GDP. Only two plausible avenues are left: the increase of indirect tax rate and base and the increase of tax administration efficiency to improve collection efficiency. A directive of the AfCFTA could be useful in this regard.

Notes

1 The views and opinions expressed in this paper are those of the authors and do not necessarily reflect the views or positions of their employers or institutions.
2 12.5 % of Africa's exports are to China, and 4 % are to India, which accounts for 5 % of China's imports and 8 % of India's.
3 The only other region with a higher export dependence on the rest of the world is Oceania.
4 It would boost regional trade by 15–25 % in the medium term, according to the International Monetary Fund.
5 Identified monetary policies will be analyzed in Chapter 8.
6 According to WDI, between 2011–19, Africa FDI represented 2.1% of GDP, compared to 2.6% of GDP at the global level. This was way below the 3.5% for Europe and central Asia and 3.8% for Latin America and Caribbean.
7 In 2018 intra-African exports represented 15% of Africa's world exports. South Africa is the main intra-Africa exporter and importer; 34% of intra-Africa exports are from South Africa while South Africa imports 20% of intra-Africa imports. Other main intra-African exporters include Nigeria (9%), Egypt (6%), Ivory Coast (4%), and Zimbabwe (4%). Apart from South Africa, the other main intra-African importers are all located in southern Africa—Botswana, Zambia, Namibia, and Mozambique, accounting for a further 24% of intra-Africa imports. Eswatini, Zimbabwe, Togo, Gambia, and Uganda are the only countries with intra-Africa exports more significantly than exports to the rest of the world.
8 Benin shares an approximately 800 km north–south border with Nigeria. The economic relationship between these two countries is quite unbalanced and asymmetric, with Nigeria exerting more influence on Benin than vice versa. Nigeria's economic power comes from its features, including a large population of around 190 million, massive oil wealth, and cultural diversity. Whereas Benin, being geographically small, generates substantial income and employment from its formal and informal trade with its neighbors, particularly Nigeria. Benin has adopted low-tariff policies to serve as a trading hub, importing goods and re-exporting them legally and illegally to Nigeria. In August 2019, Nigeria closed its land borders to all goods to protect its domestic market from tonnes of re-imported rice and frozen poultry unloaded in Benin and then sent onwards to Lagos.

This measure goes against all commercial and freedom of movement treaties signed under the ECOWAS and has important economic consequences. Although Nigeria has reopened its border with Benin for free trade of goods, it remains that those actions have to be conducted by both Benin and Nigeria governments to offset the negative impacts of the local market failures. At the forefront of such action, the coordination of macroeconomic and trade policies between these two countries stands as the major challenge to undertake. These policies include the re-enforced security at the border and harmonized trade policies with ECOWAS' other members.

9 An economic union comprising ten member states in Southeast Asia promotes intergovernmental cooperation and facilitates economic, political, security, military, educational, and sociocultural integration among its members and other countries in Asia.

10 Tax competition could be counterbalanced with calling to tax agglomeration rents that lock in firms in denser locations. Fiscal dominance raises the issue of the independence of central banks/monetary policies. Fiscal rules are about commitment to policies to ensure credibility and predictability of the macroeconomic environment. They will all impact the success of the AfCFTA through different channels that need to be properly identified.

References

African Union. 2020. "African Continental Free Trade Area Questions & Answers", African Union, Compiled by the African Trade Policy Centre (ATPC), of the Economic Commission for Africa (ECA), in association with the African Union Commission.

Balassa, Bela. 2013. *The Theory of Economic Integration (Routledge Revivals)*. London: Routledge.

Schiereck, Dick, Andreas Freytag, Maximilian Grimm, Wolfgang H. Bretschneider. 2018. Public corporations in Africa: A continental survey on stock exchanges and capital markets performance. Jena Economic Research Papers, No. 2018-013, Friedrich Schiller University Jena, Jena.

Soumaré, Issouf and Fulbert Tchana Tchana. 2015. "Causality Between FDI and Financial Market Development: Evidence from Emerging Markets", The World Bank Economic Review, 29(suppl_1): S205–S216. https://doi.org/10.1093/wber/lhv015

World Bank, 2020. "The African Continental Free Trade Area: Economic and Distributional Effects". © Washington, DC: World Bank. http://hdl.handle.net/10986/34139 License: CC BY 3.0 IGO.

Appendix

Table 7.3 Typology of African countries in the GVC

Low participation	Limited commodities	High commodities	Limited manufacturing
Senegal	Egypt	Algeria	Morocco
Sierra-Leonne	Mauritania	Libya	Tunisia
Guinea Bissau	Mali	Guinea	Ethiopia
Benin	Burkina	Nigeria	Kenya
Niger	Cote d'Ivoire	Gabon	Tanzania
Zambia	Ghana	Congo	Namibia
Botswana	Chad	Congo DR	South Africa
Eritrea	RCA	Angola	Lesotho
	Somalia	Uganda	eSwatini
	Mozambique	Madagascar	Sao Tome & Principe
	Togo	Malawi	Mauritius
	Burundi	Cameroon	
	Rwanda		

Source: Author based on WDR 2020 computation.

Note: Countries not appearing in the table do not have data to compute the index.

Table 7.4 Typology of African countries in the CVC

Insufficient data	Low participation	Limited commodities	Limited manufacturing
Zimbabwe	Benin	Burundi	Morocco
Sudan	Sierra-Leonne	Rwanda	Tunisia
South Sudan	Guinea Bissau	Mauritania	Ethiopia
	Botswana	Mali	Kenya
	Eritrea	Burkina Faso	Tanzania
	Madagascar	Chad	Namibia
	Libya	RCA	South Africa
	Gabon	Somalia	Lesotho
	Congo	Mozambique	eSwatini
	Angola	Togo	Sao Tome & Principe
	Cabo Verde	Guinea	Mauritius
		Uganda	Cameroon
		Malawi	Cote d'Ivoire
		Niger	Ghana
		Congo DR	Senegal
		Algeria	Egypt
		Zambia	Djibouti
		Nigeria	Comoros
		The Gambia	
		Equatorial Guinea	

Source: Authors computation from Pralac WDR 2019 data.

Table 7.5 Exchange rate arrangement

	Exchange rate anchor				Monetary aggregate target	Inflation targeting framework	Other
	USD	**EU**	**Composite**	**RAND**			
Currency board	Djibouti						
Conventional peg		Cabo Verde Comoros São Tomé and Príncipe Senegal Togo Benin Burkina Faso Côte d'Ivoire Guinea Bissau Mali Niger Cameroon CAR Chad Congo, Rep Equatorial Guinea Gabon	Libya	Eswatini Lesotho Namibia	Guinea Malawi Nigeria		
Stabilized arrangement			Morocco		Congo, DR		Egypt Sudan
Crawling peg Crawl-like arrangement	Liberia		Botswana		Algeria Burundi Ethiopia Rwanda Tanzania		Mauritania South Sudan Tunisia

Other managed arrangement	Angola Sierra Leone	Kenya
Floating	The Gambia Madagascar Seychelles Zimbabwe	Ghana South Africa Uganda	Mauritius Mozambique Zambia Somalia
Free floating		

Source: IMF 2020.

Table 7.6 African stock market capitalization

#	Economy	Region	2011	2012	2013	2015	2017	% of Total
1	South Africa	South	845.6	998.3	970.5	735.9	1038.6	63.9
2	Namibia	South	137.9	144.2	136.9	88.9	97.5	9.0
3	Nigeria	West	43.1	57.8	82.8	49.9	28.6	7.5
4	Morocco	North	60.2	52.8	54.8	45.9	58.5	3.6
5	Egypt	North	51.7	60.1	54.3	55.2	35.7	3.6
6	Botswana	South	54.7	53.0	54.1	46.0	18.6	3.6
7	Ghana	West	28.5	30.5	28.2	18.9	11.3	1.9
8	Kenya	East	10.3	15.9	20.6	25.0	18.5	1.4
9	Tanzania	East	7.4	8.4	14.8	9.5	9.0	1.0
10	Malawi	East	16.4	10.6	13.0	11.3	13.3	0.9
11	BRVM	West	7.0	8.1	10.5	15.0	12.1	0.7
12	Zambia	South	9.4	9.4	10.2	5.8	11.2	0.7
13	Mauritius	East	7.7	7.1	8.5	7.2	10.5	0.6
14	Tunisia	North	9.6	8.9	8.5	—	—	0.6
15	Uganda	East	4.1	5.9	8.3	9.6	5.7	0.6
16	Zimbabwe	South	3.7	4.0	5.4	2.7	3.8	0.4
17	Other	Multiple	5.7	5.3	5.6	—	—	0.4
	Total	All Africa	1303.0	1480.3	1518.4	1126.8	1372.9	100.0

Source: Schiereck et al. 2018.

8 Monetary policy harmonization for AfCFTA[1]

*Constant Lonkeng Ngouana and
Fulbert Tchana Tchana*

8.1 Introduction

The choice of an exchange rate regime is one of the most consequential economic policy decisions that countries must take. It is intrinsically related to (and cannot be dissociated from) the choice of monetary policy regimes, given that the value of a currency reflects a host of factors, including the stance of monetary policy. While it is widely acknowledged that the exchange rate can play a critical macro stabilization role when it is allowed to adjust in response to shocks (see, e.g., IMF, 2020; Adler and Tovar, 2014; and Hove, Touna-Mama, and Tchana-Tchana, 2015), there is in principle no good or bad monetary policy/exchange rate regime per se. Some countries have indeed successfully maintained a fixed exchange rate—on their own or together with other countries as part of a currency union—to import credibility from a strong anchor country while others have successfully relied on a flexible exchange rate to manage their macroeconomy. In that sense, there is no exchange rate/monetary policy regime that is unconditionally right for all countries at all times.

In this context, the question of a common currency for African countries (i.e., a fixed exchange rate among member countries) presents tradeoffs, reflecting the role of a currency as a means of exchange and broader macroeconomic considerations. On the one hand, by limiting transaction costs, a common currency could foster greater economic integration in Africa (e.g., through increased intra-Africa trade and capital flows). On the other hand, however, individual African nations would de facto surrender autonomous monetary policy to a supranational central bank, foregoing a precious macro stabilization tool at the individual country level, thereby shifting the burden to fiscal policy. Which of these two pros and cons factors dominates in practice is a non-trivial yet highly relevant policy question.

Robert Mundell pioneered the idea of the so-called optimal currency area (OCA, henceforth) in the early 1960s, identifying a set of pre-requisites for a group of countries seeking to adopt a common currency (see also McKinnon, 1963; Kenen, 1969; and Mundell, 1973). These include labor mobility, business cycle synchronicity, capital openness with price and wage flexibility, and risk sharing among member countries (see Box 1).

DOI: 10.4324/9781003456568-8

How does this translate to AfCFTA? Would African nations need to "check all the boxes" before adopting their contemplated common currency, or could they learn and adapt by doing? Put more simply, would the benefits of economic integration from a common currency outweigh the cost of giving up autonomous monetary policy for African nations? One would need a fully-fledged welfare analysis, e.g., based on a multi-country general equilibrium model, to provide a satisfactory answer to this question. It is also understood that the implications of the currency union need not be the same for all member countries—after all, AfCFTA is made of an heterogenous group of countries, from oil exporters to oil importers, from tourist-intensive to mostly agriculture-based, from sub-Saharan Africa to North Africa, with vastly different economic structure and exposure to shocks.

We adopt a quantitative approach in this chapter, exploring conditions for a common currency in Africa, using some stylized facts on business cycle synchronicity and estimated trade benefits of a common currency. We found that given differential macroeconomic fundamentals across the continent, there would be merit in defining a set of ex-ante convergence criteria. Those ex-post criteria should be simple and easy to measure and complemented with clearly defined corrective mechanisms to ensure credibility and avoid moral hazard. The adoption of a common currency could proceed gradually by sub-regional blocs, before moving to a more ambitious and complex continental undertaking. While waiting to fulfill the necessary criteria, the AfCFTA team should immediately start the harmonization of monetary policies to improve the convertibility of various currencies. Various efforts that have started in the six regions on monetary convergence should continue. To avoid some of the challenges that ECOWAS has faced in its journey toward a single currency, all regions could adopt the European Union strategy consisting of working together with the central bank of the most important economy in the region to anchor their monetary convergence. For example, ECOWAS could follow the Nigeria Central Bank's policy while SADC could follow the South Africa Reserve Bank.

The remainder of the chapter is organized as follows. Section 2 reviews the theory of optimal currency area. In Section 3, we estimate the trade benefits of sharing a common currency and contrast the case of the CEMAC and the WAEMU, two longstanding monetary unions on the continent. Section 4 explores convergence criteria. Section 5 analyses the integration journey of three examples of the free trade agreement journey with a focus on monetary policy reforms. Section 6 presents policy recommendations and conclusions.

8.2 Optimal currency area

In a setup in which a country—a potential member of a currency union—is subject to asymmetric shocks that could undermine the real economy, Mundell (1961) argues that a regime with floating exchange rates would be better if the shocks are too large and cannot be contained. This is because the supranational central bank is not equipped to accommodate the circumstances of an individual country at each point in time in the normal conduct of monetary policy. It influences monetary conditions based on the "average" economy in the union (one-size-fits-all). Against this background, four main criteria have traditionally been put forward for a successful currency union, including the mobility of labor and capital and risk sharing (Box 8.1).

To these traditional criteria, and very relevant for AfCFTA, Kenen (1969) argues that a group of countries with diversified domestic production is more likely to constitute an optimum currency area than a group whose member countries' production structures are highly specialized. He went as far as suggesting that product diversification may be more relevant than labor mobility for OCA. In fact, if a country is not diversified, and, let's say, produces only a single export product, its income falls whenever a negative demand shock hits its exports, absent a flexible exchange rate. The macro adjustment indeed takes the form of reduced wages and prices or increased unemployment under a fixed exchange rate regime. In contrast, in a diversified economy with uncorrelated sectoral shocks, a negative shock in a

---

Box 8.1 Traditional criteria for the optimal currency area

The following four criteria have traditionally been referred to for a successful currency union (optimal currency area):

Labor mobility across the region. When labor can move freely, countries negatively affected by a shock will see an outward movement of unemployed persons towards countries with better economic conditions, including lower unemployment (assuming asymmetric shocks). Several factors can affect labor mobility, including institutional (work permit), physical distance, as well as cultural barriers (e.g., language). Labor mobility would endogenously lessen the negative impact of an asymmetric shock in the source country, reducing the need to rely on independent monetary policy as a stabilization tool, and thereby increasing the net benefit of joining a currency union.

Capital openness, and price and wage flexibility across the region. This allows market forces to balance supply and demand. However, wages are often rigid downward, or take time to adjust, leading to price distortions.

Risk sharing mechanism. This includes automatic fiscal transfers to countries at a disadvantage (e.g., through taxation redistribution). It is one of the most politically palatable and often faces resistance from taxpayers in better-off countries.

Business cycle synchronicity. This captures the extent to which real GDP growth is correlated among member countries. When business cycles are correlated, the central bank can optimally use the interest rate tool to contain inflation pressures during economic expansions or stimulate economic activity during recessions. In contrast, optimal monetary policy may differ across countries when business cycles are asynchronous, weakening the case for a supranational central bank.

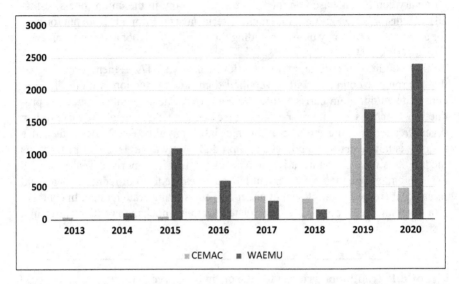

Figure 8.1 Security issuances on the regional bond market (in billions of XAF).

Source: BEAC and BCEAO.

specific export sector/industry might be offset by a positive shock in another sector, neutralizing the negative shock and keeping income stable. In fact, the terms of trade of a well-diversified economy are not as volatile as those of a single-product economy (see Figure 8.1). This implies that sufficiently diversified economies can more easily trade their national currency (or autonomous monetary policy) for better integration with other countries of a currency union.

8.3 Estimating the trade benefits of sharing a common currency

Estimates of the trade effect of a currency union varied markedly—some authors find little to no effect (see, e.g., Frankel and Wei, 1993) while others find very large effects. Using a gravity model, Rose et al. (2000) finds that two countries sharing the same currency trade three times as much as they would with different currencies. The so-called "rose effect" triggered a vast array of research using increasingly sophisticated econometric methods and larger datasets.

One major criticism of existing trade elasticities based on the gravity model is the omitted variable problem. To the extent that differences are likely larger in a large set of countries, we zoom in on the ECOWAS, a group of 15 countries, part of the same economic community. ECOWAS provides a nice natural experiment in the sense that half of the countries in the union share a common currency while the other half doesn't. Those countries are also different in their language and colonial ties. These introduce an additional source of variation that allows us to isolate the net impact of currency. Moreover, the adoption of the currency is relatively exogenous compared to endogenously formed currency unions—they were formed based on colonial ties. This is an extra source of variation. We exploit the natural experiment whereby eight of the fifteen member countries of the ECOWAS share a common currency (the CFA franc) to estimate the impact of a common currency on bilateral trade. More specifically, we estimate the following gravity equation using bilateral trade flows for the panel of 15 ECOWAS countries from 1960 to 2019.

$$Y_{o,d,t} = \alpha + \theta_{o,d} + \delta_t + \beta_1 X_{o,t} + \beta_1 X_{d,t} + \gamma CC_{o,d,t} + \varepsilon_{o,d,t}$$

Where $Y_{o,d,t}$ is the real log trade flow between county o(origin) and d(destination) in period t; X is a set of controls, including log real GDP, population, common language, and distance.[2] The dummy variable $CC_{o,d,t}$ takes the value 1 if the origin country, o, and the destination country, d, share a common currency in year d.

The estimate of our parameter of interest, γ, suggests that countries sharing a common currency in the ECOWAS (i.e., WAEMU countries) trade 60 percent more among each other than other pairs of countries in the ECOWAS, after controlling for other relevant trade factors. To put things in perspective, this is about the trade impetus from sharing a border, one of the most prominent determinants of bilateral trade.

Beyond trade benefits, a common currency could also increase capital flows. This is evidenced by the rapid expansion of the regional market for government securities in the CEMAC and WAEMU (Figure 8.1). This source of financing can be particularly important at times of global financial stress when other sources of financing dry out. For instance, governments in the CEMAC and WAEMU raised amounts equivalent respectively to US\$ 1 billion and US\$ 5 billion in securities of maturity of a year and more on their regional bond market in 2020.

8.4 Lessons from the European Economic Community and ECOWAS' journey toward monetary union

As presented in the previous chapter, the EEC aimed to lay the foundations of an ever-closer union among the peoples of Europe. The Maastricht Treaty in 1991 established the European Union and paved the way for the European Monetary Union.

The creation of the single currency reduced cross-border transaction costs for individuals and businesses alike and further stimulated trade and investment. During the transition from multiple currencies to a single currency, the currency of the largest economy (the deutschmark) has served as an anchor for a common monetary policy—the arrangement functions as an effective currency board. Tensions from diverging macroeconomic developments (growth, inflation, fiscal policies) and the Bundesbank's understandable focus on German economic developments led some countries to reconsider their commitment to the exchange rate mechanism until a common currency was adopted. The euro operates as a floating global reserve currency, with minimal intervention in support of the currency. Decentralized monetary policy operations require upfront harmonization and integration. In such an arrangement, monetary and exchange rate policies are decided centrally in existing currency unions. Still, they differ substantially in the degree of centralization of monetary policy and foreign exchange operations. The European System of Central Banks and European Central Bank statute explicitly stipulates those operations should be delegated to national central banks.

The EMU experience shows that harmonization in a floating currency regime is more demanding because, without an external anchor, macroeconomic stability relies on instruments and operations' effectiveness. An established track record in the use of common instruments and operations would help minimize uncertainty and reinforce credibility ahead of adopting a common currency. EMU harmonization involved intensive multiyear coordination. Twenty years elapsed between adopting an exchange rate mechanism and a full monetary union, with a strong regional institution to lead integration launched five years ahead of monetary union.

ECOWAS encompasses a monetary union and other countries with their own currencies. The West African Economic and Monetary Union (UEMOA), an eight, mainly French-speaking, states within the ECOWAS share a currency union; the XOF is pegged to the euro. The West African Monetary Zone (WAMZ), established in 2000, comprises six mainly English-speaking countries within ECOWAS that plan to adopt their own common currency.

Although ECOWAS is one of the most integrated African regional blocks; it has not been able to move toward a monetary union as desired since 2003. The bloc adopted a new road map and a new convergence pact that will cover the period between 2022–2026, and 2027 is the launch of the single currency to be named "eco," in 2021 after their failure to meet their most recent deadline. The concept of a single currency was first raised in ECOWAS in 2003. Its introduction, however, has been delayed multiple times before this year: in 2005, 2010, and 2014. The single currency project has faced several challenges such as the difficulty in anchoring the convergence process to the monetary policy of the main regional economy (Nigeria), mostly because the UEMOA central bank already exists and believes that given its experience in managing a monetary union and its relationship with the European central bank, it should have the leading role in this process. Other challenges included member states under economic pressure and struggling to pay their national debts, and political instability.

8.5 A case for convergence criteria, monetary and financial policy harmonization

Credibility is often referred to as the single most important asset for a central bank. The contemplated benefits of a common currency in Africa (e.g., reduced transaction costs) can only materialize if the common currency is widely accepted as a means of exchange. Instilling confidence in this currency in turn requires that it be backed by solid macroeconomic fundamentals, not only in selected member countries but in all member countries, given the risk of contagion. Considering that AfCFTA member countries are starting from very different macroeconomic fundamentals, and given the macro stabilization role of monetary policy, it becomes natural to consider setting convergence criteria for joining the currency union, or at the minimum, binding criteria while a member of the union. To be credible, criteria must be binding, embedding enforceable corrective mechanisms. Currency unions typically set convergence criteria to ensure the viability of the currency union. Those criteria are typically set on aggregates that can undermine the credibility of the supranational central bank to contain inflation and thereby guarantee the value of the currency.

The rate of inflation is a typical convergence criterion. The target should be set high enough to grease the wheel but low enough not to derail macroeconomic stability (for example, Kenya and Ghana target an inflation rate of 5+/–1% and 8 +/–2% respectively). The target could be adjusted over time as the continent succeeds in sustainably lowering inflation, balancing flexibility against credibility—changing the target too often may undermine credibility and des-anchor inflation expectations, a cornerstone of inflation control. One practical consideration would be how to assess the inflation convergence criterion for CEMAC and WAEMU member states whose track record on inflation control on their own has not been observed yet, considering that low inflation has essentially been imported from the hard peg to the euro. Other criteria have included fiscal aggregates such as the level of deficit. One consideration for AfCFTA would be whether to base this on headline fiscal balance or a measure of non-oil fiscal balance. The former measure would level the playing field between oil exporters and non-oil exporters, while the latter, by incentivizing a structural transformation in oil-producing countries would help address over time the challenge that the commodity cycle poses to the conduct of monetary policy at the continental level.

The level of public debt is a natural candidate for convergence criterion for several reasons. First, as a stock variable, it summarizes the fiscal position of a country and provides a rough indication of available fiscal space. Second, a high debt level would entail high interest costs, putting pressure on the overall balance and financing needs of the government. Third, it is independent of the type of fiscal balance that is chosen. Which quantitative limit should be put on public debt at the regional level is subject to empirical work. On the one hand, the anchor should be set low enough to avoid undue pressures on the budget for debt servicing, considering the debt management capacity on the continent. On the other hand, it should be set low enough to ensure that countries have enough fiscal space for counterfactual fiscal policy and to undertake critical development projects. Interestingly, debt levels have generally converged among African countries.

The latter would probably be better, given the virtuous circle with respect to diversification. And, while critical, both for economic development and for macro stability and business cycle synchronicity, economic diversification could be left to the discretion of individual countries. In fact, it is a tool for sub-nationals to limit the opportunity cost of giving up on their independent monetary policy. One alternative would be to start with sub-regional monetary unions as training wheels, to limit coordination issues. This would not only have the advantage of pooling together countries that are similar enough but would also allow for some "learning by doing," making subsequent aggregation at the continental level easier. This is supported by our finding that business cycle synchronicity is negatively correlated with distance in Africa (neighborhood effects), probably reflecting translation costs. However, beyond this average result, the business cycle of one country may be more correlated to a distant country's than a neighbor's.

While waiting for convergence criteria to be achieved, AfCFTA should focus on reducing the cost of financial transactions implying many currencies by seeking to establish a mechanism that will reduce intermediation and the use of non-continental currencies as reserves. There is a need to review the feasibility of alternative policy frameworks, such as nominal income targets and inflation targets. Policy credibility would be enhanced by greater transparency in monetary policy decisions.

Concerted efforts should be given to expanding the reach of existing stock markets to consolidate them into viable and liquid marketplaces. Several stock markets could take the lead in some given sector and region. The leading companies could be allowed to list on many markets to raise funds for their development. The expansion of the stock market capitalization will support the development of the private sector in general and their contribution to connectivity infrastructure.

The regulatory framework should be gradually adapted to internationally recognized and agreed-upon practices. This includes capital account regimes, capital market regulations, and prudential frameworks for financial activities that consider the evolving nature of the work in this area. Statistics should be upgraded under common definitions. This is especially important for measures of inflation, chiefly on the headline and core inflation.

Harmonizing national monetary policy frameworks should come after the vast majority of countries have achieved macroeconomic frameworks that keep inflation low. Differences across African countries in the degree of exchange rate flexibility, how monetary instruments are used, the weight given to monetary aggregates, and the role of policy interest rates in monetary operations are substantial. The time-table for strengthening the monetary policy's effectiveness, harmonizing legal frameworks, and developing common monetary policy practices and instruments should be consistent with the starting date for the monetary union.

8.6 Conclusion

This chapter explores conditions for a common currency in Africa, using some stylized facts on business cycle synchronicity and estimated trade benefits of a common currency. It presents updated estimates suggesting that a common currency fosters trade, all else equal. It also finds that the degree of business cycle synchronicity is still low in Africa, e.g., with divergence between oil exporters and non-oil exporters. It argues that the latter evidence suggests that economic diversification would be key for the success of a common currency initiative in Africa. In fact, specialization by a country in a single export product that is not common to other countries (e.g., crude oil) could lead to diverging terms of trade, in which case the one-size-fits-all monetary policy moves by the supranational central bank could amply the negative shock in the specialized country. Increased labor mobility on the continent (currently relatively weak) and risk-sharing mechanisms would also be needed to improve the chance of success of the currency union. This should be interpreted with caution because a common currency may also, by opening markets for new products, foster economic integration among African nations. Likewise, financial integration could help finance investment opportunities that would not be possible otherwise.

Given differential macroeconomic fundamentals across the continent, there would be merit in defining a set of ex-ante convergence criteria (i.e., before a country can join the union) and/or ex-post criteria (for countries already in the union). Those ex-post criteria should be simple and easy to measure and complemented with clearly defined corrective mechanisms to ensure credibility and avoid moral hazard. The adoption of a common currency could proceed gradually by sub-regional blocs, before moving to a more ambitious and complex continental undertaking. While we examine potential gains in intra-trade (or increased economic integration more broadly) from a common currency separately from the cost of giving away autonomous monetary policy, the two dimensions need not be independent. In fact, by strengthening economic integration, a common currency could endogenously increase business cycle synchronicity and lessen the cost of centralized monetary policy. This could operate through a channel whereby increased demand in one African country leads to higher import demand for the goods produced in other African nations. The question of a common currency for African nations is a complex and multi-faceted one that includes both political and socio-economic dimensions; it can hardly be settled in an essay of this nature. In any case, an eventual move to a common currency in Africa should be examined thoroughly and paced very carefully as the cost of getting it wrong could far exceed the benefit of getting it right.

Notes

1 The views and opinions expressed in this paper are those of the authors and do not necessarily reflect the views or positions of their employers or institutions.
2 We run a similar regression replacing common language with colonial origin—both cannot enter the equation jointly, given that they are strongly correlated among ECOWAS countries.

References

Adler, G. and C. E. Tovar, 2014, "Foreign Exchange Interventions and their Impact on Exchange Rate Levels," *Monetaria, Centro de Estudios Monetarios Latinoamericanos, CEMLA* (1) (January), pp. 1–48.
Frankel, J. and S.-J. Wei, 1993, Emerging Currency Blocs, No. 4335, NBER Working Papers, National Bureau of Economic Research, Inc.

Hove, S., A. Touna Mama, and F. Tchana-Tchana, 2015, "Monetary Policy and Commodity Terms of Trade Shocks in Emerging Market Economies," *Economic Modelling, Elsevier*, Vol. 49(C), pp. 53–71.

IMF Policy Paper, October 8, 2020. "Toward an Integrated Policy Framework."

Kenen, P., 1969, "The Theory of Optimum Currency Areas: An Eclectic View," in Mundell and Swoboda (eds.), *Monetary Problems in the International Economy*, University of Chicago Press, Chicago.

McKinnon, R. I., 1963, "Optimum Currency Areas," *The American Economic Review*, Vol. 53, pp. 717–725.

Mundell, R. A., 1961, "A Theory of Optimum Currency Areas," *American Economic Review*, Vol. 51 (4), pp. 657–665.

Mundell, R. A., 1973, "The Monetary Consequences of Jacques Rueff: Review Article," *The Journal of Business, University of Chicago Press*, Vol. 46(3), pp. 384–395, July.

Rose, A. K., B. Lockwood, and D. Quah, 2000. "One Money, One Market: The Effect of Common Currencies on Trade." *Economic Policy*, Vol. 15(30), pp. 9–45. www.jstor.org/stable/1344722

9 Transport policies for a successful AfCFTA[1]

Théophile Bougna

9.1 Introduction

Economic growth through trade solutions cannot be thought of without considering transport infrastructure, one of the mechanisms through which effective trade occurs. There is empirical evidence that trade costs related to infrastructure quality are strongly correlated with both total trade volume and gross domestic product (Limao and Venables, 2001; Edmonds and Fujimura, 2008; Banik and Gilbert, 2010). Likewise, there is evidence that decreasing direct and indirect trade costs by 1% can result in an average of a 0.25–0.4% increase in GDP (OECD, 2009). Access to transport infrastructure is therefore an important policy concern, affecting workers, farmers who rely on accessing markets and input suppliers, women and children for access to basic socio-economic infrastructure like schools, health centers, and markets. Reliable transport networks attract foreign investments and improve trade efficiency. Without good infrastructure, the private market is limited to domestic and local affairs. The aim of this chapter is to explore current gaps in trans-African transport development and consider the prospects of transport as a key enabler for a successful implementation of the AfCFTA.

Transport infrastructure can be broken down into hard and soft infrastructure. Hard transport infrastructure includes roads, bridges, airports, railroads, ports, and practically any physical aspect of transport. Soft transport infrastructure is related to transport efficiency, as well as trade efficiency more generally. This includes digitization related to logistical efficiencies, monetary and time costs associated with transportation, and efficiency at customs, with regards to total number of mandatory documentation and the time costs of procedures. In this chapter, we focus on hard infrastructure by analyzing roads, railways and ports prospects for better intra-African trade. Transport can only be beneficial if it is being used. There is a new shift in global transport infrastructure goals with more focus on access, affordability, and sustainability to larger portions of the population, and in particular marginalized groups that tend to be excluded from access to transport services.

"The world is not yet flat; transportation costs still matter" (see Behrens et al., 2018). This assertion is so true for African countries where high transportation costs, due to the poor state of infrastructure, the lack of adequate infrastructure, as well as the importance of tariff and non-tariff barriers undermine African countries'

DOI: 10.4324/9781003456568-9

ability to trade efficiently. The average daily rate of travel has increased over time, due to both decreased costs of transport and improved connectivity and the growth of international travel. The transport sector is just one example of how inequality has deepened under economic growth. In the UK, the top 5% of income earners travel five times further than the bottom 5%, and only 9% of public expenditure is allocated to bus services, in which the poor make nearly 4 times as many trips as the rich; car ownership, commutes to work, and city parking costs are other factors that create economic barriers to the poor.

In Africa, urban transport is characterized as highly fragmented and underfunded; as states face rapid urbanization, low public transport fares and insufficient subsidies, transport infrastructure is decreasingly able to keep up with demands (Kumar and Barrett, 2008). This has invariably opened a gap for unreliable, informal transport to overtake the market. Poor populations in Africa experience high costs of travel, both in terms of time burden due to road congestion and unreliable routes, as well as the price. Using data on 14 major African cities, Kumar and Barrett (2008) show that the average family can afford no more than one daily round trip by bus, and for the poorest households even the most basic standard of mobility is impossible to afford. There are society-level costs associated with increased levels of transportation as well; Banister (2019) lists the consequences of increased transport volume as the staggering number of road deaths (1.2 million globally), safety concerns, congestion, community severance, as well as climate change, local pollution, health effects, and reduction of open spaces, all of which derive from increased reliance on transport. It is important to address these shortcomings with the construction of new infrastructure.

The narrative around access to transport in the context of a world with rising inequalities has also pushed Multilateral Development Banks (MDBs) towards commitments to transport infrastructure development in middle and lower-income countries. Africa is one of the last regions to remain without a comprehensive and continental-wide transport system. Despite being home to the most daunting transport and development challenges, countries in South East Asia managed to develop some of the most innovative solutions to their national and regional transport needs through their recent transnational transport development effort which includes investment in railways, ports, highways, and airports.[2]

African countries are not sufficiently investing in connectivity infrastructure, which significantly and negatively hampers their regional trade prospects. There is therefore an urgent need for a massive and strategic investment to improve connectivity. Recent endeavors in Africa to close the transport infrastructure gap include programs such as the Belt and Road Initiative (BRI) by China, and the Program for Infrastructure Development in Africa (PIDA), a joint effort between the African Development Bank (AfDB), and the UN Economics Commission for Africa.

Despite the fixed nature of transport infrastructure, transport is surprisingly adaptive to consumer needs and changing environmental conditions, at least in OECD countries. In recent years, there has been a shift in discourse towards the ways in which transport must adjust to meet tightening emissions goals. The Paris Agreement signed in 2016 offers an implementable response to the current climate crisis to avoid worst-case scenarios. In the height of the climate crisis, dialogue around the decarbonization of transport has become a pressing concern; due to reliance on oil-based fuels, international goals to reduce greenhouse gas (GHG) emissions are particularly challenging for transportation infrastructure. Global emissions have increased by 2.5% annually between 2010 and 2015, and over the past fifty years, the transport sector has experienced the fastest emissions growth (Dhakal et al., 2022). Transportation is unquestionably one of the largest hurdles in effectively avoiding the worst-case scenarios of climate change, with 55% of the world's total liquid fuels dedicated to this industry (IEA, 2019). Experts argue for decarbonization of transport, not just to avoid the worst of climate change but also to adjust to the depletion of high-quality oil sources. Conventional GHG mitigation strategies in the transportation sector focus on vehicle technology efficiency gains and fuel switching, primarily for personal vehicles. The switch to mass transit is also a viable solution.

Overall, transport transformation away from combustibles is considered a high-cost and difficult endeavor and should be implemented gradually given the high heterogeneity of countries. Carrara and Longden (2017) find that freight transportation may only expect to shift away from oil-based combustion by the middle of the century. Nieto et al. (2020) note that there is much uncertainty in the process of decarbonization, which depends largely on both lifestyle changes and the increased availability and sustainability of currently uncertain technologies, such as carbon capture and sequestration, hydrogen, fuel cells, etc. The authors mentioned that although these seem like viable alternatives to combustion-based fuels, there remains uncertainty about the present bio-fuel options, as they are responsible for indirect land use change whose emissions are of the same magnitude as emissions of fossil fuels. In particular, key mineral reserves such as lithium, copper and magnesium are limited, making wide-scale use of electric vehicles unfeasible without severe battery recycling policies.

With increasing global interconnectedness and foreign investment strategies, developing countries are now turning to the process of establishing both national and transnational road networks, a critical component of efficient trade. Historically, Africa has lacked a consistent and large enough source of financing to build transport infrastructure and complete the vision of an interconnected continent. However, China, one of Africa's biggest trade partners (Initiative, 2019) signed a partnership agreement in 2015, known as the Forum on China-Africa Cooperation (FOCAC), with the African Union (AU), to cooperate on major infrastructure network development and industrialization transnationally in Africa. The goal of this accord is to close the continent's infrastructure deficiency gap and facilitate African regional infrastructure development through the physical integration of Africa and the joint development of transnational infrastructure projects.[3]

A successful AfCFTA requires effective, efficient, and sustainable transport policies that encompass forward-looking strategies and interventions at both national and sub-national levels. This chapter points towards four essential pillars for the continent's economic transformation through a continental efficient transport network. The continent should first tackle its infrastructure gap by resolving inefficiencies, attracting private financing, and effectively implementing private-public partnerships (PPPs) in developing regional transport infrastructure. Second, the continent should prioritize the development of a new generation of intermodal and competitive transport systems which will contribute to unleashing efficiencies, overcoming frictions, promoting foster trade and regional integration, and fostering the continent's economic transformation. Third, policymakers should prioritize the completion of the trans-African highways to complete the continent integration.

The rest of the chapter is organized as follows: Section 9.2 discusses the continental transport infrastructure gap and the current programs and partnerships aiming at addressing this gap. Section 9.3 discusses the state of the current transport infrastructure distinguishing between roads, railways and ports. Section 9.4 assesses whether the current state of Africa's transport infrastructure can boost the AfCFTA, and Section 9.5 concludes with a set of policy recommendations.

9.2 The continental transport infrastructure gap

9.2.1 State of the transport infrastructure gap in Africa and challenges

Over the last two decades, Africa's infrastructure investment has remained at around 3.5% of the GDP per annum. In order to close its infrastructure gaps, the continent needs to raise this share to 4.5% (Woetzel et al., 2017). The G-20 Global Infrastructure Outlook, 2017 report revised the total infrastructure investment requirement for Africa to US\$ 4.3 trillion by 2040 or US\$174 billion per year (see Figure 9.1). The report has estimated that currently around 38% of infrastructure investments in Africa have been directed towards the electricity sector, with 20% going to water and 27% to transport. The report has estimated a 39% infrastructure investment gap with more focus on energy and transport (83%). This corresponds to a yearly 1.7% of GDP investment. As can be seen in Figure 9.2, Africa needs to invest more in its energy (0.24% yearly gap), roads (0.8%), ICT (0.3%), and water (0.25%) sub-sectors.

The benefits of closing the infrastructure gap are huge and most would come from closing the gap in the transport sector. It is estimated that closing the infrastructure quantity and quality gap relative to the best performers in the world has the potential to increase the growth of GDP per capita by 2.6% per year (Calderon et al., 2019). In the World Bank report on African regional integration, Brenton and Isik (2012) cite limitations of physical infrastructure as one of the major limiting factors in the path towards continental trade integration, thus impeding economic growth and development. Likewise, Vhumbunu (2016) notes that integrating trans-national transportation systems in Africa is a first-order priority because of its land cover area of approximately 30 million km^2, and the fact that around 40% of its countries are small and landlocked.

The sovereign fragmentation of Africa remains a critical hindrance to trans-national infrastructure development. According to Klopp and Makajuma (2014), the historical fragmentation of Africa by colonial powers has had profound impacts on the ability of countries to coordinate transnational infrastructure development.

Figure 9.1 Africa infrastructure gap and investment forecasts: 2007–2040.

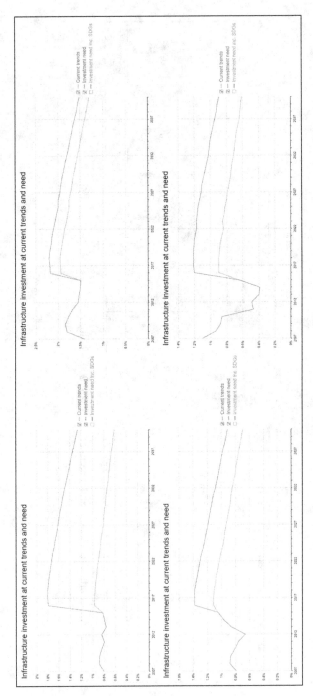

Figure 9.2 Infrastructure forecasts for roads, water, ICT and energy sub-sectors.

Source: Global Infrastructure Outlook. Note: Top and Bottom left (roads and water resp.); Top and Bottom right (Energy and ict resp.). The Forecast use an average annual GDP growth rate of 4.2%. SDG Disclaimer–Includes the additional investment needed for countries that have not yet met the SDGs).

In reality, countries remain isolated from one another and there exists a large infrastructure gap, which is still observable today. This is due to many reasons including the different institutions, language, and political systems stemming from colonization. Governance has also served to impede infrastructure development in the context of Africa; institutional bottlenecks, such as administration, bribes and other rent-seeking activities by officials, and general inefficiencies across borders increase the cost of large-scale transportation projects (Klopp and Makajuma, 2014).

Overall, the large need for transport infrastructure in Africa requires significant financing. Multilateral development banks such as the World Bank, the African Union, and the African Development Bank promote continental interconnection and movement of people across Africa, through the construction of transportation infrastructure. One reason for the lack of adequate investment in infrastructure and connectivity is that Africa's development banks remain undercapitalized, and trade finance for African SMEs is limited.[4]

Additionally, private-public partnerships (PPP) are largely underutilized in the context of transport infrastructure in Africa; these PPPs offer much promise to bridge transport investment gaps and have been highly utilized with relative success in regions such as Latin America and South Asia as shown in Figure 9.3 (World Bank Africa Pulse, 2019). In contrast, the World Bank finds that Sub-Saharan Africa has a relatively high ratio of cancelled or distressed projects. Where multilateral coordination has failed to coordinate trans-continental projects, PPPs have great potential to fill these financing gaps and provide third-party leadership and coordination. Morocco is an example of a country where PPPs were successfully used to contribute to filling the infrastructure gap.

Despite the promise that PPPs offer financially constrained countries, they do require a substantial level of investor confidence and patience. Consider the case of Abidjan, the largest city of Côte d'Ivoire, with one of the fastest-growing populations in the world (Figure 9.4). With a rapidly expanding urban population, demand for transport infrastructure has heightened more than ever before. The city relied on two bridges which connect the north to the south, as well as connecting northern landlocked countries to the country's ports and airways. In response to the increasing strain on existing infrastructure, the government committed to construct a third bridge, funded through the West African Public Private Partnership (PPP), with the bidding process starting in 1998 (Achi, 2014). Due to a 10-year civil conflict and subsequent political instability, private investors backed away from the project. At the end of the conflict, the cost of construction increased steeply due to the national destruction of supply chains, forcing the government to finance 28% of the project's total cost (€75 million).

9.2.2 Existing programs and partnerships

There is a need for, and availability of, funding, coupled with a large pipeline of potential projects, but not enough money is being spent on African infrastructure. Despite this situation and the existing gap, infrastructure investment in Africa has been increasing steadily over recent years. This includes major continental

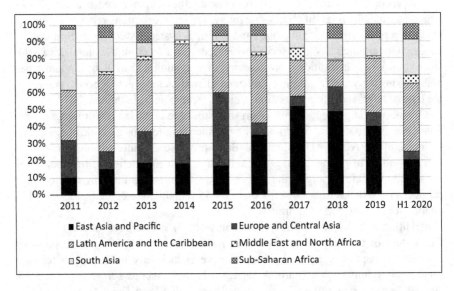

Figure 9.3 Regional share of investment commitments in infrastructure projects with private participation.

Source: World Bank, 2020.

Utilizing private public partnerships (PPPs) for reliable transport infrastructure delivery	
Successful strategies	Mistakes to avoid
I. Utilize locally sourced labour and materials as much as possible II. Include maintenance plans in contracts to ensure sustainable infrastructure development III. Multinational cooperation on regional projects and improving logistical efficienies through digitalization IV. Coordinate industrial policy with project needs to ensure adequate supply of construction materials	I. Overlook sustainability considerations and fail to incorporate climate resistant technology II. Impose costly user fees and tolls in an attempt to quickly recuperate investment costs III. Focus on unilateral projects rather than regional ones

Figure 9.4 How to navigate a successful PPP?

initiatives such as the Programme for Infrastructure Development in Africa (PIDA), which aimed at mobilizing resources to transform Africa through modern infrastructure. However, Africa's track record in moving projects to financial close is poor: 80% of infrastructure projects fail at the feasibility and business-plan stage. This is what the McKinsey Global Institute called the "Africa's infrastructure paradox". In 2019, the African Transport Network Projects totaled US$ 430.3 billion investment value, with a focus on roads, railways and bridges. This includes 448 large-scale transport projects (roads, rail and bridges) across Africa at all 8 stages of development from announcement to execution. More than half (52.4%) of the total project pipeline by value is being publicly driven by African governments allocating funds for constructing new roads and repairing existing ones, whereas 33.3% of the total project pipeline is funded by various joint financing arrangements between the public and private sector. Despite the COVID-19 challenges, Africa received US$ 1.8 billion across seven projects, marking a three-percent increase in investment levels from the first half-year of 2019. Private infrastructure investment in IDA countries (countries with gross net income (GNI) per capita below the threshold of US$ 1,175) remained high despite the COVID-19 crisis.

9.2.2.1 The Program for Infrastructure Development in Africa (PIDA)

PPPs remain an underutilized tool to finance and operationally support the integration of African road networks. However, programs are beginning to emerge in order to help address this gap. The Program for Infrastructure Development in Africa (PIDA) is a continental initiative aimed at tackling the infrastructure deficits in Africa by 2040, a joint effort by the AU Commission, in partnership with the United Nations Economic Commission for Africa, African Development Bank and the NEPAD Planning and Coordinating Agency. Through the proposed funding of both public and private sources, the overall goal of PIDA is to promote socio-economic development and poverty reduction in Africa, through improved access to integrated regional and continental infrastructure networks and services and the overall reduction of the continent-wide infrastructure deficit.

The PIDA is the African Union's strategic framework for regional and continental infrastructure development. It provides a common framework for African stakeholders to build the infrastructure necessary to integrate the continent physically, economically, and socially. The PIDA offers a sought-after opportunity to boost intra-African trade, create new jobs for Africa's growing population, improve overall socio-economic development on the continent, and provide the requisite infrastructure and environment to facilitate the implementation of the AfCFTA. In terms of its implementation, while progress is being made, there remain notable hurdles, such as lack of financing, lack of capacity for project preparation, and the limited involvement of the private sector in infrastructure projects financing through PPPs. However, if PIDA is to attract private investment sources, there is an urgent need for countries to guarantee competitive markets, clear legislation, enforcement of commercial law and overall transparency, or in other words, good governance.

9.2.2.2 China's contribution to African transport: The Belt and Road Initiative

The Belt and Road Initiative (BRI) is a global infrastructure development strategy adopted by the Chinese government in 2013 to invest in nearly 70 countries and

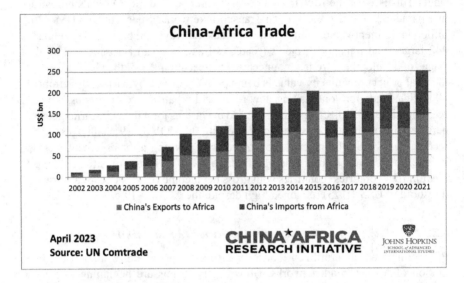

Figure 9.5 China-Africa trade relations.

Source: China Africa Research Initiative.

international organizations, including several African countries (Figure 9.5). The project centers around bridging the infrastructure gap faced by many developing regions; the initial focus for the BRI has gone towards infrastructure investment, education, construction, railway and highway, automobile, real estate, power grid, and iron and steel (Ding et al., 2016). The project is indeed large in nature; in 2015, Chinese companies made approximately US$ 100 billion of direct investment in foreign countries, about 15% of which went into the "Belt & Road" countries (Huang, 2016).

Nigeria and Egypt are the two largest recipients of the BRI initiative among African countries, receiving US$ 23.2 billion and US$ 15.3 billion in 2014–2018, respectively (Scissors, 2020). BRI is also intended to benefit the Chinese economy by strengthening ties and interdependence with new markets; Huang (2016) estimates that new investment associated with the Belt & Road Initiative alone could have raised Chinese GDP by 0.25% in 2015.

Despite this promising outlook for foreign direct investment in African infrastructure projects, experts are dubious that China can single-handedly fund such ambitious projects; Derek Scissors (2020), AEI China economist and creator of the China Global Investment Tracker made a statement in June of 2019 that although the BRI appears to be expanding, it is only the case that more countries are joining the BRI, but the true extent of BRI activities is shrinking. He also argues that financing is likely to tighten over time rather than loosen, and subsequently China will refocus on countries it views as the most profitable to invest in, which would likely be oil-rich countries, leaving many African landlocked countries that desperately need infrastructure development in the dark.

Huang (2016) argues that the success of the BRI will hinge on the following two risk factors: First, the BRI lacks a formal coordination mechanism, and thus will rely on bilateral communication with high variance depending on the country. Second, he also points to clashing political regimes, financial sustainability, and trade balances as layers that may hamper infrastructure growth. For example, China remains with excess steel production to the tune of 300–400 million tons, after exports. Some experts fear that opening trade between China and steel-producing countries would lower prices and harm their economies. While the BRI offers a promising vision to close the infrastructure gap, conditional on continued funding and multilateral coordination on regional projects; it is important to note that data on China aid flows are much less transparent than from traditional donors and more Chinese projects are similarly associated with higher trade network imbalances (Graff, 2019).

Under the current conditions of insufficient financing for transport infrastructure, and governance failures, the emphasis of PPPs, if well implemented must play a pivotal role in the development of African transport infrastructure in the coming years. However, the complex nature of infrastructure projects requires upfront investments to reinforce countries' capacities in implementing successful PPPs. For PPPs to be successfully and effectively implemented, African governments need to put in place strong legal, institutional, accountability, and reporting frameworks to limit rent-seeking and properly manage fiscal risks.

9.2.3 The balance of political economy and infrastructure development in Africa

In the scramble to develop transport for their immense infrastructure needs, African countries depend mostly on external financing sources. Foreign investors come with very different goals: high rates of returns from private investment groups, or lasting regional involvement in economic affairs for example. These countries have to find the right balance between obtaining the necessary funding to close the African infrastructure gap and maintaining autonomous decision-making power over economic affairs. This will be a key factor in producing efficient and effective transport investments for a successful AfCFTA. Two important elements surround the politics in the economics of infrastructure development in Africa.

First, in large parts of Africa, infrastructure investments are facilitated through international lending. Many of these projects failed to deliver on their promises. The many "white elephants" projects across the continent are the testimony of a failed infrastructure development strategy. The extensive use of foreign funding coupled with the exclusive reliance on foreign contractors and consultants undermined the promise of big infrastructure projects to deliver on local economic development prospects. There was minimal use of domestic resources, higher levels of input imports, and very little technological transfer. The construction sector is a growth escalator in developing countries, as such, investment decisions should encompass strategies to leverage job creation and economic transformation in Africa.

Second, foreign private investment firms have different incentives while investing in African infrastructure. Some managed to establish long-term relationships with governments leading to potential corruption, inefficiency in service delivery, and very limited technological transfer in the sector. Without strong institutions, and proper accountability systems, this allows them to collude and deliver poor-quality infrastructures at higher costs. Investment malpractices in the infrastructure sector have been reported in several countries including Cameroon, and Liberia, resulting in discontent among local populations (The Oakland Institute, 2011).

There is a need to design transparent and fair systems in African infrastructure development. Such systems ensure the enforcement of sustainable development procedures and fair compensation practices when local populations are employed for work or when their land is used. Besides these elements, it is important to recognize that a big part of the infrastructure gap in Sub-Saharan Africa is connected to its inherent inefficiencies, the young domestic construction sectors where domestic firms and contractors never really had the chance to compete with larger foreign firms. The rise of technological and engineering schools in Africa should be an opportunity for governments and the private sector to work toward the creation of a large pool of competitive domestic firms to build African infrastructures.

9.3 Current state of transport infrastructure in Africa

To have a precise understanding of the African transport infrastructure gap, let's first consider what the optimal state of infrastructure would look like. Ideally, countries should have multiple and connected transport infrastructure types depending on their topography and geography. Railway lines, roads, airports, and ports are the four sub-sectors that should be embraced during transport development, and if a country is landlocked, it should commit much more to increasing road and rail infrastructures.

To give a brief comparison, the average road density (measured by km of road per 1000 km^2) of European countries is 321.56, while the average road density of Africa is only 81.5 (World Road Statistics, 2020). Railway lines are also underutilized in Africa; the average railway density across Africa is 3 million traffic units per route-km, which is comparable to European countries' statistics. However, these trends are carried by North African countries such as Morocco, Egypt, and Algeria. Sub-Saharan railways have traffic densities of just more than a million and many are averaging less than 300,000, presenting a large barrier to effective transportation (Bullock, 2009). While we should not expect African infrastructure to catch up to Europe in the next 10 years, it provides a good example of what road and railway densities look like among relatively small, well-connected countries. If nothing else, trans-African infrastructure projects should aim to improve connecting Africa and bridge the infrastructure inequalities between North Africa and Sub-Saharan Africa.

In most African countries, roads dominate the transport sector. It covers about 80–90% of passenger and freight traffic. According to Porter (2014), one of the main changes to African infrastructure in the past few decades has been the decline of rail transport services in many regions, primarily West Africa, due to the ease and flexibility that road construction offers, thus resulting in a recent expansion of motorized road transport services. For individual travel, the motorcycle-taxi is now changing the means of rural and urban transport services in many parts of Africa, due to the introduction of cheap motorcycles from China and India. The World Bank has estimated that about US$ 200 billion of trade in Africa is carried by the region's trunk road network, comprising strategic trading corridors that link deep seaports to economic hinterlands.

Africa relies heavily on its road network despite the notable gap in road infrastructure. What is the cost of this missing infrastructure? In the absence of a developed highway network to facilitate trade across Africa, deficient infrastructure lowers economic productivity across Africa by 40% and causes traffic deaths. Additionally, while it takes 19 days to ship a container from Singapore to Kenya, 20 more days are required to send those goods by truck from Mombasa and Nairobi via a single-lane road.

Transport infrastructure development in Africa faces a unique challenge, which is rapid urbanization. Okoye et al. (2019) and Jedwab and Moradi (2016) have shown that increased urbanization is an expected outcome when transport infrastructure is built in previously disconnected regions. However, there is little incentive for existing transport providers to expand their services or develop in new regions. Unsurprisingly, competition requires demand, which is closely linked to population density and wealth (Porter, 2014). Unfortunately, it tends to be the landlocked areas with low population density that have the most dire, unmet transport needs, and therefore perpetually lack the infrastructure development necessary to see improved connectivity and increased standards of living. Porter finds that in remote areas of Africa, chronic poverty is more the norm than the exception, and even if transport services are available to these communities, fares are often too costly for people to access.

While the need for transport infrastructure is dire, especially in Sub-Saharan Africa, unilateral project funding is constrained by fiscal budgeting, which can be dampened by government investment inefficiencies in project section and management as well as corruption. It can also be constrained by private investments, which can be inconsistent and result in a lot of inefficiencies and unfinished projects. Scaling up infrastructure at the regional level remains a critical fiscal issue that must be addressed to achieve transnational transport networks, which would utilize cost-sharing on regional infrastructure projects. At its current state, African countries have struggled to cooperate, and countries need to work more on solving these coordination failures.

The lack of transport providers and financing is not the only explanation for the gap in transport infrastructure across the continent: geography also acts as an important deterrent to transport development. The rugged and wild nature of the terrain, especially in East Africa, poses extreme challenges for transport infrastructure development efforts. In larger countries such as Sudan, Ethiopia, and Kenya, this problem is aggravated by the sheer magnitude of their geographic area. For example, Proinvest (2005) finds that in 2006, only 20% of Ethiopia's vast land area of 1.1 million square kilometers was located within a 10 km range of an all-weather road, indicating that much of the land remains unconnected to export ports and that rural areas in the region are not easily accessible, especially during rainy seasons (Njoh, 2012). Going forward, and in order to have a successful AfCFTA, policymakers must consider how to alleviate the above constraints that have previously inhibited infrastructure development.

Climate change has become increasingly impactful to decision-making procedures around the globe. With regards to transport infrastructure development, climate change adds another dimension of planning, which must be accounted for to avoid catastrophe. For instance, Mozambique was hit by Cyclone Eloise in 2019, destroying its port city Beira. Unfortunately, the complete destruction of the port may have been avoided had developers designed infrastructure durable to predictable types of natural disaster events. Moving forward with the AfCFTA, engineers must design climate-resistant infrastructure to see a successful and sustainable investment strategy.

9.3.1 Road sub-sector and its importance to trade and economic growth

Envisioned in 1971 by the United Nations Economic Commission for Africa (UNECA), the Trans-African Highway (TAH) is a network of nine highways that would span a total of 60,000 km (37,282 mi) across the continent. The TAH network trans-continental road projects are developed by UNECA; the AfDB and the AU with the participation of regional international communities. Consisting of nine (9) major routes, three (3) of which run north to south, these highways are designed to connect the whole continent. Road construction on the east-to-west routes is mostly completed, except for TAH 5 and TAH 6, which are 80% completed, and TAH 8 which is incomplete due to instability in the DRC. Of the north-to-south routes, TAH 3, seen in purple in Figure 9.6, has the most missing links of all the highway routes, which consists only of paved roads in Libya, Cameroon, Angola, Namibia, and South Africa.

The development of the North African Highway runs 5,600 km from Morocco through to Egypt. Another major project is the US$ 6.56 billion East-West Highway in Algeria, one of the world's largest public construction projects, which is part of Algeria's highway expansion program and connects with neighboring North African nations Tunisia and Morocco and forms part of the North African Highway. The new six-lane highway with a total length of 1,216 km runs from the Tunisian border in the east of Algeria to the Moroccan border in the west and will link Algeria's large cities including Algiers, Setif, Constantine and Oran, while passing through Libya, Tunisia, Algeria, Morocco, and Mauritania. Other African nations are also carrying out ambitious highway projects to improve links, including Kenya, where a major road sub-sector improvement program is being implemented focusing on rehabilitating and constructing new national roads to link the country with its neighbors and beyond.

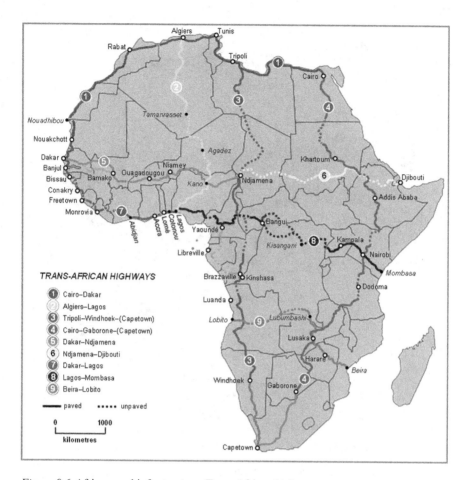

Figure 9.6 African road infrastructure: Trans-African highways.

9.3.2 Africa road infrastructure and economic development prospects

To understand the importance of accessibility of transport infrastructure on economic development, we examine the relationship between transport infrastructure and country-level gross domestic product and trade openness in Africa. Using road data from the Global Roads Inventory Dataset (GRIP) which contains road data on road density between 1997–2014, we approximate the accessibility to road infrastructure in a given country (Figure 9.7). The road density raster layers (road length per unit of area) are produced at a resolution of 5 arcminutes, which is approximately at the 8 km x 8 km pixel level. The data distinguishes between road types: highways, primary roads, secondary roads, tertiary roads, and local roads. We combine the GRIP roads data with data on total land area, which is a

Figure 9.7 Global Road Inventory Project Road Density, Africa (2018).

Source: GRIP (Global Roads Inventory Project)–2018.

time-invariant characteristic measured in squared kilometers, provided by World Bank Data. Additionally, we merge this data with country-level GDP per capita, obtained from The World Bank World Development Indicators Data, and trade openness data, obtained from Our World in Data (ourworldindata.org). Both GDP and Trade Openness data are collected as a panel to cover the same span as the GRIP dataset.[5]

Road density is defined by the concentration of roads in a geographic area. In the GRIP data, density is disaggregated to the 5-arcminute level. We aggregate road density to the country level and use this to estimate the impact of transport access on economic outcomes. We create the following variables to estimate road density: first Total Roads, which counts the total number of roads of any type contained within a country. Total Highways counts the total number of highways for a given country. Total Paved Roads follows the same aggregation but for any road that is paved with cement. Total Open Roads counts total roads in a country that are open to public use. Next, we create two variables, Above Median Total Road Count and Above Median Total Highway Count, which are binary variables equal to one if a country has above median counts of total roads and highways, respectively. Finally, the variables Ratio of Total Roads to Total Land Area, and Total Highways to Total Land Area divide the road count by the land area size to control for country size. Table 9.1 provides descriptive statistics for the data contained in our analysis.

Regression results based on a simple OLS model show positive and significant effects of transport accessibility, measured through road density on economic growth (see Table 9.2a in the Appendix). However, there are heterogeneous effects depending on the type of connection. For example, when looking at access to all road types, we find a positive effect however the magnitude is extremely close to zero. On the other hand, access to highways seems to matter much more, as shown by the significance and magnitude of the effect of total national highways, having above-median highways. These results are consistent with the economic literature, which emphasizes the importance of transport infrastructure to promote economic growth through increased efficiency in supply chains and thus increased trade. Highways seem to matter much more for the economy than secondary and tertiary roads, as they are able to accommodate higher traffic volume and are more important routes to connect cities and countries. In Table 9.2c, we control for the cost of trade, measured by the percentage of tariff for a given price of a good. When controlling for this, we find robustly positive effects of road infrastructure on GDP. Transport infrastructure is therefore a necessary condition of economic growth. In its absence, communities become disconnected, farmers have more difficulty selling their excess production, and cross-country trade becomes increasingly burdensome.

Looking at the effects of road density on GDP per capita, we find that the positive effects disappear when controlling for regional effects. Looking at the direction of regional effects, we see that higher GDP per capita and thus better economic activity is concentrated in the northern countries of Africa, which in this sample include Algeria, Egypt, Libya, Morocco, Sudan, and Tunisia (see Table 9.2b). Table 9.3a looks at the effects of road density on Trade Openness, which is measured by the percentage of exports plus imports divided by a country's total GDP. Surprisingly, when looking at the overall effect for all of Africa, we do not find a significant effect on trade openness, and in fact, when looking at Above Median Total Roads we see a negative effect, although small in magnitude. One potential explanation is that road density is in fact not a good proxy for access to road infrastructure or that it does not necessarily imply the existence of transnational highways, which are the requirement to see a positive impact on trade. This indeed would explain why we observe a positive effect on GDP per capita but not on Trade Openness and would impose a strong policy recommendation of prioritizing transnational transport infrastructure if countries want to boost not only GDP but also total trade volume. Going forward, it would be valuable to have data surrounding access to transnational highways which seem to be much more important to trade than the total number of roads if they only connect cities within a given country. This is an important consideration when looking at how to maximize the success of the new AfCFTA.

An analysis of the effects of road density on global connectivity measures, which come from the DHL Global Connectedness Index, tracking the depth and breadth of international trade, capital, information, and people flows. First, we examine global connectivity depth, which is the extent to which a country is connected to the world (for example in terms of trade, it would measure import plus export GDP over a country's total GDP) (see Table 9.4a). Next, we examine global connectivity breadth, which captures whether its international flows are spread out globally or are more narrowly focused (see Table 9.4b). The main result of interest from this analysis is that highway density, more than anything else, has a positive impact on connectivity depth. This means countries are more likely to have more trading partners. Of course, having a diverse trade network ensures the robust economic health of a nation and is an important policy objective when considering transport infrastructure development.

9.3.3 The prospect of railroads in Africa

Aside from road networks, railroads are another very important transport medium to bolster trade and have great potential to increase agricultural land values. The AfDB report suggests that there are only six African countries with better railroad infrastructure than the global average. Three of them are in North Africa (Morocco, Tunisia and Egypt), while the remaining three are from Southern Africa (Namibia, South Africa and Swaziland). Africa's total rail network size is 82,000 km, 84% of which is operational, with the remainder closed due to war damages, natural disasters, or general neglect and lack of maintenance and funding.

Despite being cheaper, faster, more reliable and less polluting, rail transport in Africa is struggling to generate enough revenue to fully cover operating, maintenance and capital expenditure costs. In its current state, the African railway network needs kilometers of new railways to be constructed or upgraded to improve the continent's integration and boost intra-African trade through the AfCFTA. Most of the railway lines in Africa were constructed by mining companies during colonization and suffer from inefficiencies and inadequacy which contribute to higher transportation costs.

The long-term economic benefit of the railroads depends on whether there are strong local increasing returns. Donaldson and Hornbeck (2016) estimated that had the U.S. railroad network expansion not happened between 1870 and 1890, the total value of U.S. agricultural land would have decreased by 60%, with limited potential for mitigating these losses through feasible extensions to the canal network or improvements to country roads. In a similar study, Okoye et al. (2019) examine the historical expansion of railroad networks in Nigeria; the authors find that railway development sharply increased economic development in the short term, especially in landlocked areas with low prior access to ports of export, which mainly consists of the northern parts of Nigeria.

Astonishingly, these effects on economic development persist today, despite most colonial-era railroads no longer functioning. Another interesting result is that railways did not have significant impacts in the south of Nigeria, where prior access to ports of export was high, and consequently railways were adopted at much lower rates due to the higher cost than already existing means of transportation. These results mirror the estimates of Jedwab and Moradi (2016), who find that in Ghana, colonial railways contributed to decreased trade costs and boosted the cultivation of cocoa in railroad areas, which subsequently resulted in increased settlement in these locations and thus sped up the process of urbanization into these regions. Similar results were found for Kenya where colonial railroads causally determined the location of European settlers, which in turn decided the location of the main cities of the country at independence.

In terms of economic and strategic prospects, railroad investments can produce economic change by reducing trade costs and integrating markets. For example, Ethiopia relies on Djibouti's ports for 90% of its foreign trade. However, since the old railroad (built by France in the 1910s) collapsed in 2009 after decades of decline, Ethiopia's billions of dollars of imports and exports from products like fuel, coffee, and livestock have had to travel by truck. This was a three-to-four-day journey along rutted and dusty roads. The new Addis Ababa–Djibouti railway was inaugurated in 2018, it provides landlocked Ethiopia with access to the sea and links Ethiopia's capital city Addis Ababa with Djibouti and its Port of Doraleh (759 km). This new rail line cut the trip to 12 hours compared to 3–4 days. Another example is the West African mineral railway line, a 1,286 km line connecting the interior of Senegal and Mali with Dakar Port. The traffic has ceased since March 2018 and its revitalization is a strategic priority for both Senegal and Malian Governments. They recognized the importance of having a competitive railway system in terms of socio-economic development, transport mode balance, and regional integration. In addition, building and improving African railways can help save planet Earth from environmental calamity and save the global economy. Under the new European Green Deal, railways are currently seen as vital to making Europe a carbon-neutral economy by 2050.[6]

9.3.4 Ports and intermodal facilities in Africa

Africa has a total coastline of 30,725 km, with around 90 major ports and a number of small ports providing services for fishing and tourism. The continent is also endowed with a number of rivers and lakes that have great potential (inexpensive, energy-efficient, and environment-friendly). The African port situation is characterized by a large number of small ports, each with a capacity of less than 1 million TEUs (20-foot equivalent unit) (Figure 9.8). Apart from northern African countries and South Africa, the vast majority of ports across the continent are generally patchy, and in need of improvement and development.

With the AfCFTA agreement, countries need to embark on major regional maritime projects to better reap the expected benefit from increased trade between countries. There is evidence that exports can drive economic growth and economic

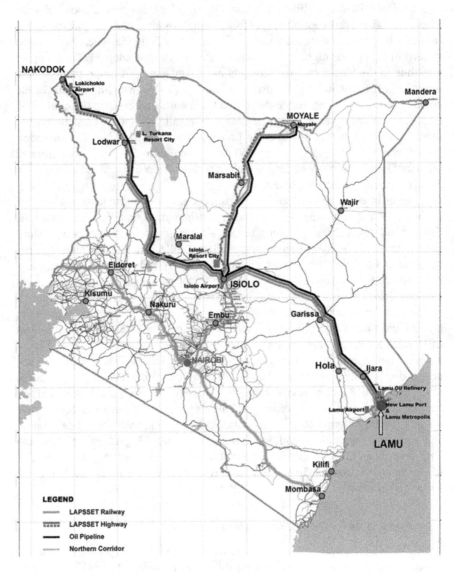

Figure 9.8 Lamu Port in Kenya.

Source: AfDB, Port Development in Africa, 2010.

development. Higher domestic transportation costs act as a strong constraint to exports from Africa.

Any policy aiming at lowering domestic transport costs in African countries can contribute to improving the prospect of exports. The continent lacks natural ports and there is therefore a call to build dry ports (or inland terminals) closer to exporters and importers. The potential of Africa's shipping sector is huge; 90% of the continent's imports and exports are transported by sea. In its Integrated Maritime Strategy paper, the African Union called the shipping industry "a new frontier for the continent's renaissance". However, until very recently, countries were not investing enough in port terminal infrastructure development. In a 2018 report, PricewaterhouseCoopers (PwC) argued that Africa should take advantage of the economic potential of its ports and shipping sector to realize its growth ambitions. Their analysis shows that a 25% improvement in port performance could increase GDP by 2%.

There is a regained interest in the maritime sector as African governments are pursuing ambitious port expansion projects. The African port sector has attracted more than $15 billion in private investment, and public funding brings the total to US$ 85 billion. Togo invested US$ 380 million head start investment by Terminal Investment Limited to expand the Lomé container port to handle post-Panamax vessels and act as a transshipment hub. Nigeria is investing US$ 1.5 billion in the Lekki port which is expected to open for operations in 2023. This port aims to be a transshipment hub for West Africa. It is designed to receive vessels with a capacity exceeding 18,000 TEU. Côte d'Ivoire invested US$ 930 million for the expansion of the Abidjan port to improve its cargo handling capacity. In Kenya, the $3 billion Kenya Ports Authority investment program envisages that Mombasa Port will have an annual capacity to handle 110 million tons of cargo by 2040. Morocco Tanger Med 2 1.3 billion investment contributed to tripling the port's capacity from 3 m to 9 m TEU. This extension allowed the port to become Africa's leading container port, surpassing Port Said (Egypt) and Durban (South Africa).

9.3.4.1 Africa should invest in a port project with regional potential: Example of Kenya's Lamu port

The Lamu port is part of a bigger US$ 24 billion project known as LAPSSET (Lamu Port South Sudan-Ethiopia Transport Corridor) that includes not only a giant seaport to relieve Mombasa, but also roads, a 1,500 km railway, fiber-optic lines, an airport, and a refinery (Figure 9.9). This port is set to be opened in June 2021 and will specialize in handling containers and oil cargo between the East African hinterland and the rest of the world. It will also enable Kenya to become a gateway of choice for Ethiopia, South Sudan and Somalia.

9.3.5 Air transport infrastructure in Africa

Air traffic seems like an obvious solution to connect landlocked countries with the rest of the world. However, air transport infrastructure is much more expensive than other modes such as roads and rail. Subsequently, it is highly underutilized as a tool for trade and transport in Africa; with respect to passenger traffic, in 2018, 213.7 million passengers were processed at African airports, which accounts for only 2.4% of global passenger traffic. Additionally, domestic passengers represented only 32.7% of the total passenger movements in Africa. Cargo traffic

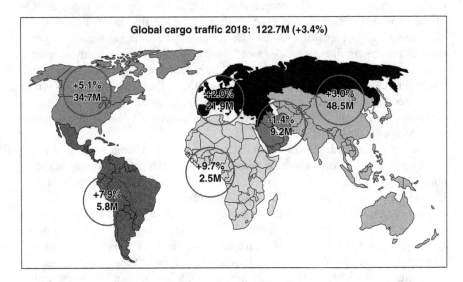

Figure 9.9 Global air cargo traffic by region, 2018.

Source: Airports Council International, 2021.

by air does not fare much better, representing only 2% of global cargo traffic volume. However, cargo traffic growth by air increased by 9.7% across Africa, representing the highest growth rate across the globe (IATA, 2019; IRF, 2020).

Recognizing the large gap in air transport infrastructure in Africa compared to other developing regions such as the ASEAN and LATAM, an important AfCFTA objective should be to invest more in strategic airport development, with specific emphasis on Sub-Saharan countries and landlocked countries (Figure 9.10). In fact, if a country is unable to access ports, it must be able to utilize all other modes of transport to boost connectivity.

One African country that has reaped the benefits of air transport infrastructure development is Ethiopia; according to the International Air Transport Association (IATA), if it stays on track, Ethiopia's sustained prioritization of air transport, connectivity and tourism as a strategic asset would support an extra 900,000 jobs and US\$ 9.3 billion of GDP by 2037. Currently, air transport and the foreign tourists that it brings by air supports 5.7% of the nation's GDP, equating to US\$ 4.2 billion, and approximately 1.1 million jobs. Other African leaders should follow suit in the prioritization of air traffic infrastructure to increase connectivity with the globe and expand out of primarily regional trading. When continental airlines have access to a country's airports, the country is attracting more fiscal international entities to engage in trade. Country pairs with good airport infrastructure trade more than twice as much, everything else being equal. Africa's intercontinental traffic relies on the three major hubs of Johannesburg, Nairobi, and Addis Ababa. There is a need to develop and increase the network in West and Central Africa. Moving

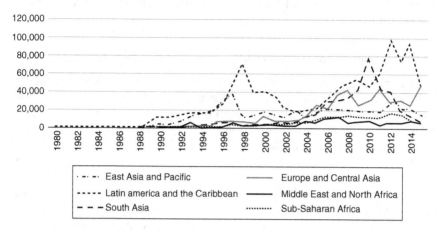

Figure 9.10 Trends in PPIs worldwide.

Source: World Banks PPIs Database, 2016. Data in millions of US$.

forward, investments in the sector should also aim at reducing the cost of traveling by air within Africa, which is considerably more expensive per mile flown than intercontinental travel.

9.4 Can the current state of Africa's transport infrastructure boost the AfCFTA?

Looking at the current state of continental transport infrastructure, Africa is a fragmented continent; not in the sense that countries strive towards a different future, but rather they are physically disconnected due to limitations in the transport network. For example, of the trans-African highways, which are the only network in place to connect the whole of Africa, many links are incomplete, especially when looking at the north-south routes. Given this shortcoming, trade could not thrive under the AfCFTA, despite everyone's best intentions, simply due to the high time costs of transporting goods.

However, given the heightened interest by China in financing African infrastructure projects, both through the BRI and the FOCAC, as well as the new trans-African joint agreement, PIDA, aimed at closing the continental infrastructure gap, there is indeed hope that in the next ten years, the state of infrastructure in Africa may comfortably sustain the transport load generated through the increased trade stemming from the AfCFTA. It is, however, conditional on the concentrated effort of these agreements to complete projects on time through proper financing and strong regional and bilateral coordination. In addition to China and other MDBs interested in financing the prospect of African development, there must be a strong commitment from African leaders to secure more funding for African infrastructure development. Solving inefficiencies in the sector, boosting initiatives like

PIDA, and strengthening PPPs become a necessity to effectively finance Africa's infrastructure development.

9.4.1 What would the optimal state of infrastructure in Africa look like?

Tilman Graff (2019) assesses the efficiency of transport networks for every country in Africa and simulates the optimal road system for every African country. His analysis shows that Africa would gain 1.1% of total welfare from better organizing its national road systems. The paper also shows that past transport investments have not targeted the regions identified as most in need of additional investment, and colonial infrastructure projects significantly skew trade networks towards a suboptimal equilibrium.

Also hinging on the success of African transport integration, Latin America heavily relied on foreign financing to close its infrastructure gap. China played a large role in the progression of such projects. Since 2005, between China's Development Bank and the China Export-Import Bank, China has provided more than US$ 125 billion in loan commitments to Latin American (LATAM) countries, and in 2015, financing to LATAM countries from China's Policy Bank surpassed World Bank and Inter-American Development Bank contributions combined (Myers and Wise, 2016). Interestingly, the amount of Chinese involvement in a given project tended to be dynamic, according to Bersch and Koivumaeki (2019), who find that where countries have strong institutions, Chinese companies played a role as would other foreign bodies involved in infrastructure development, but in Latin American countries with weak infrastructure institutions, China played a much more all-encompassing role in terms of financing, management, and bilateral coordination.

In addition to the Chinese input that has proven invaluable in the context of LATAM infrastructure development, private participation in infrastructure (PPI) has been another important aspect that has contributed to the success of projects. Using case studies from LATAM and the Caribbean, Tei and Ferrari (2018) find that the success of transport infrastructure projects depends not only on the size of the investment but also on being associated with a regional organization as well as the involvement of private companies. Figure 9.11 highlights the growing importance of PPIs globally; as shown in the graph, Latin America and the Caribbean account for the majority of the Projects involving PPI, followed by South Asia and East Asia, respectively. Within LATAM, the majority of the funding through PPIs went to Brazil and Mexico, which together registered 60% of the total financing value (Tei and Ferrari, 2018).

Similar to the context of Latin America, the ASEAN has also fallen under China's BRI funding scheme.[7] China's commitment to ASEAN countries began when Chinese President Xi Jinping raised the initiative of jointly building the 21st-Century Maritime Silk Road with ASEAN countries in 2013 which launched the BRI initiative. Although most trade in the ASEAN occurs by sea, the BRI also included the development of land infrastructure. The Maritime Silk Road Initiative and the Asian Infrastructure Investment Bank (AIIB) have concentrated on the construction of physical transport infrastructure; in Indonesia, the joint effort has planned to build 24 new ports, 15 airports, 18 special economic zones, and thousands of kilometers of railway. As Okoye et al. (2019) mentioned in the context of Nigeria with railways, regions tend to under-develop transport infrastructure when other, more affordable options are available. In the case of Nigeria, coastal cities opted for seaports and roads rather than railways. The same trend is observed in ASEAN countries.

China and Indonesia have also signed a US$ 6 billion high-speed rail project, and China has agreed to provide US$ 50 billion in loans for these projects, including railway, electric power, and metallurgy. Success has come from this recent push in transport investment. The Chinese high-speed railway industry is expanding into Indonesia, and at the same time, China-Laos railway cooperation has progressed rapidly (Jianren, 2016). In the midst of a global pandemic, which puts a steep cost on human contact, there have been increased digitalization efforts of soft transport infrastructure such as logistics services, in ASEAN countries; according to the Master Plan on ASEAN connectivity, effort is now being put into reducing supply chain costs via logistical efficiencies and digitalization. This result has come about by commitment from all countries to coordinate legal standards and border processes (Secretariat, 2016).

To achieve harmonious development of transport infrastructure, African leaders must link their industrial policy to transport policy. This will ensure an adequate supply of construction materials so that project timelines are kept on track and supply chains are kept as local as possible. One success story of this has been Dangote Cement in Nigeria.

Aliko Dangote founded his own cement company in response to increasing infrastructure projects in his home country, despite an absence of suppliers due to perceived national instability and corruption. Now, he is worth over US$ 25 billion, making him one of the richest people globally. His company's core business strategy has been to "provide local, value-added products and services that meet the basic needs of the populace through the construction and operation of large-scale manufacturing facilities in Nigeria and across Africa" (Akinyoade and Uche, 2016). In fact, the cost of cement shortages is extremely high, which would have to be imported externally from Turkey. To avoid this cost, countries must coordinate industrial production with new transport goals. Having seen much success from his locally sourced business operations, African leaders should promote and incentivize domestic-based materials suppliers to be involved in future AfCFTA projects.

To build a successful infrastructure development program that meets its trade forthcoming growth, African leaders should mobilize and unleash domestic and regional private financing. They should also learn from what worked well for LATAM and ASEAN countries, which rely heavily on external financing sources such as PPPs and FDI involvement. On the other side of the same argument, foreign leaders should consider the value of such an investment; resources and land in Africa largely remain underutilized due to poor infrastructure. An investment in multi-modal regional transport projects has the potential to yield extremely favorable terms once trade can soar.

9.4.2 Toward an integrated transport policy for a successful AfCFTA

The continent is heterogeneous in terms of the countries' and sub-regions' transport systems and endowments, therefore a "one-size-fits-all" approach to transport policy is complicated or impossible to realize. While some countries face geographic hurdles whether it be rugged terrain, extremely large areas to reach, or sparse population settlements, other countries such as the DRC and Sudan lack proper infrastructure due to instability. With every country facing its constraints and barriers, it is important to emphasize overarching coordination mechanisms to ensure that all needs are met, and each project is being kept up to speed. This can be implemented through government will and the already existing programs, such as the PIDA or BRI. There is an urgent need to coordinate infrastructure investments towards an efficient spatial equilibrium that will unleash countries' potential to trade. This will require solving regional coordination failure, implementing national and regional regulations reforms, identifying the continent's missing links, and promoting regional and intermodal transport infrastructure projects.

9.5 Conclusion and policy recommendations

The following set of policy recommendations is intended to inform policymakers on what should be done in the transport sector for the AfCFTA to achieve its maximum potential and improve the livelihood of Africans. These recommendations are guided by the successes of South East Asia and Latin American countries, as well as evidence and current shortcomings from existing African transport.

First, inefficiencies should be resolved, and private financing and private-public partnerships should be effectively implemented throughout the process of Africa's regional transport infrastructure network development. When traditional financing sources cannot meet project needs, PPPs are a crucial source of funding, which can help alleviate budget constraints for governments and banks and offer a joint project with less associated risk to private firms. This strategy, which is conditional on sound legal and institutional settings, has picked up a lot of steam in transport infrastructure projects in Latin America and Southeast Asia but remains underutilized in Africa.

Second, there is an urgent need to design a broader intermodal and competitive transport system that will contribute to the regional integration and socio-economic development of the continent. This will encompass the prioritization and improvement of connectivity in disconnected and landlocked countries. Realistically, there is a large list of road and rail networks that are planned to be built in the coming years which cannot all be completed in one round. To maximize the marginal benefit of a given country/community to access a highway network, PIDA and BRI programs should plan on reaching the most isolated countries first. Second-order priorities should be connecting major routes, increasing volume capacity, and maintenance.

Third, Africa should be creative in finding innovative solutions for its infrastructure development. Africa should solve inefficiencies in infrastructure projects and look beyond aid for infrastructure financing and governments. Other support institutions should consider financially and economically feasible alternative financing solutions. Two examples include the creation of an African Infrastructure Investment Trust Fund and the implementation of Toll-Operate-Transfer (TOT) initiatives. In the first solution, African governments can rely upon liquidity from pension funds and private equity firms where they can lend to government entities managing roads and highways. Second, if well-designed and managed Toll-Operate-Transfer (TOT) can provide more funds to build more continental highways in Africa, especially in a context where the private sector is hesitant to invest in Africa infrastructure. The idea is to help monetize publicly funded and commercially operational national and regional highway projects. Third, regional savings can also be mobilized to finance the continent's infrastructure development.

Fourth, based on the evidence we have gathered from the analysis of the relationship between road, economic growth, and trade openness, programs should emphasize the construction of trans-African highways to complement and connect within-country highways.

While both are important for the total output of a country (GDP), only transnational highways seem to matter to boost trade. Additionally, there should be a focus on completing the north-to-south trans-African highways routes on highways that are the least completed. To realize the full integration of the continent, policymakers should prioritize the completion of the trans-African highways. Additionally, there should be a renewed focus on existing programs like PIDA to work on increasing program completion rates rather than embarking on too many new projects at once, thus resulting in high rates of cancelled or distressed projects.

Fifth, Africa should improve its institutional capacity in project conceptualization and management. There is a need for a continental entity in charge of overseeing and providing expertise to various regional infrastructure projects, at different stages from project identification, feasibility studies, environmental and social impact assessment, and reporting. Additionally, leaders should take care to draft climate-resistant requirement standards in their contracts with developers to avoid future destruction of transport infrastructure. Sustainability is an often overlooked but increasingly important component of infrastructure development. In this sense, African leaders should take ownership to ensure sustainability standards are being met in all projects, even those financed by foreign entities such as the BRI.

Finally, policymakers should increase the collaboration and experience sharing with Latin America and Southeast Asia regions, which relied heavily on external financing, in particular Chinese loans and investments, as well as the extensive use of PPPs. Prospecting outside of Africa will be a crucial step in expanding financing capacity for African infrastructure projects. Rather than only looking for government or MDBs assistance, policymakers should explore private-public partnerships, which if well executed can offer an alternative source of funding.

In addition to the above considerations, due to the state of the world under the global pandemic, any policy solution should have digital procedures embedded into it. This should include but not be limited to digital procurement and bidding procedures, monitoring and log-keeping, and the improvement of logistics services.

There is hope and optimism that the African transport infrastructure gap can be reduced and reach a level where it needs to be to support the boosted trade stemming from the AfCFTA and contribute to the continent's economic transformation. Conditional on the continued coordination between African countries under the leadership of programs such as PIDA, along with external financing and other private economic and strategic partners, Africa could reasonably expect and work toward the building of a more integrated and intermodal transport network at the service of its intra-trade ambition over the next decade.

Notes

1 The views and opinions expressed in this paper are those of the authors and do not necessarily reflect the views or positions of their employers or institutions.
2 China has built hundreds of kilometers of high-quality mass transit (metro and bus rapid transit). Indonesia was one of the first cities in Asia to implement a bus rapid transit system, TransJakarta, in 2004.
3 Chinese involvement in transport infrastructure development in Africa began with the Tanzania-Zambia Railway (TAZARA), a railway project constructed between 1968 and 1976 to link the Zambian town Kapiri-Mposhi and Tanzanian port of Dar es Salaam. Since then, the nature of Chinese involvement in transport infrastructure has focused on larger scale development, such as the regional or continental level. By the end of 2009, China succeeded in financing the construction of over 500 infrastructure projects in Africa (Vhumbunu, 2016).
4 For example, East African Development Bank only has assets of US$ 390 million.
5 Note that there is not an observation for each country/year, rather data from GRIP is sparsely collected over a long period, and often a country only has two data points totals.
6 That's the aim of the European Green Deal, the initiative adopted on 13 December 2020, and introduced by Ursula von der Leyen, the new President of the European Commission. The draft of policy initiatives includes proposals for a radical shift from road to rail for both goods and passenger transport, as a fundamental weapon in the war against greenhouse gas emissions.
7 ASEAN countries include Cambodia, Thailand, Myanmar, Philippines, Malaysia, Laos, Vietnam, Singapore, and Indonesia.

References

Achi, P. (2014). Abidjan builds bridge to support country's rapid growth. World Finance.
Akinyoade, A. and Uche, C. U. (2016). *Dangote cement: An African success story?* Leiden Univerity Research Paper 131. Available at https://hdl.handle.net/1887/38674
Banik, N. and Gilbert, J. (2010). Regional integration and trade costs in south Asia. Trade Facilitation and Regional Cooperation in Asia, p. 123.
Banister, D. (2019). Transport for all. *Transport Reviews*, 39:289–292.
Behrens, K., Brown, W. M., and Bougna, T. (2018). The world is not yet flat: Transport costs matter! *The Review of Economics and Statistics*, 100(4):712–724.

Bersch, K. and Koivumaeki, R.-I. (2019). Making inroads: Infrastructure, state capacity, and Chinese dominance in Latin American development. *Studies in Comparative International Development*, 54(3):323–345.

Brenton, P. and Isik, G. (2012). *De-fragmenting Africa: Deepening regional trade integration in goods and services*. Washington D.C.: World Bank Publications.

Bullock, R. (2009). Off track: Sub-Saharan African railways. Africa Infrastructure Country Diagnostic Background Paper, 17.

Calderon, C., Kambou, G., Korman, V., Kubota, M., and Cantu Canales, C. (2019). Africa's Pulse, No. 19, April 2019: An Analysis of Issues Shaping Africa's Economic Future. The World Bank.

Carrara, S. and Longden, T. (2017). Freight futures: The potential impact of road freight on climate policy. *Transportation Research Part D: Transport and Environment*, 55:359–372.

Dhakal, S., Minx, J.C., Toth, F.L., Abdel-Aziz, A., Figueroa Meza, M.J., Hubacek, K., Jonckheere, I.G.C., Kim, Y.-G., Nemet, G.F., Pachauri, G.F., Tan, X.C. and Wiedmann, T. (2022). *Emissions Trends and Drivers*. Cambridge University Press, Cambridge, UK and New York. doi: 10.1017/9781009157926.004

Ding Yani, Huang Mengting, and Huang Rong, (2016). *A Data-Based Explanation of One Belt One Road*. Beijing: The Commercial Press.

Donaldson, D. and Hornbeck, R. (2016). Railroads and American economic growth: A "market access" approach. *The Quarterly Journal of Economics*, 131(2):799–858.

Edmonds, C. and Fujimura, M. (2008). Road infrastructure and regional economic integration: evidence from the Mekong. *Infrastructure and Trade in Asia*, 143:172.

Graff, T. (2019). Spatial Inefficiencies in Africa's Trade Network. NBER Working Paper #25951.

Huang, Y. (2016). Understanding china's belt & road initiative: motivation, framework and assessment. *China Economic Review*, 40:314–321.

IEA, I. (2019). World energy statistics and balances, IEA. Initiative, C. A. R. (2019). China Africa trade. International, A. C. (2019). Air Traffic Statistics.

Jedwab, R. and Moradi, A. (2016). The permanent effects of transportation revolutions in poor countries: evidence from Africa. *Review of Economics and Statistics*, 98(2):268–284.

Jianren, L. (2016). The 21st century maritime silk road and China-Asean industry cooperation. *International Journal of China Studies*, 7(3):375.

Klopp, J. and Makajuma, G. (2014). Transportation infrastructure integration in east Africa in a historical context. Linking Networks: The Formation of Common Standards and Visions for Infrastructure Development, pp. 115–36.

Kumar, A. and Barrett, F. (2008). Stuck in traffic: Urban transport in Africa. AICD Background Paper, 1.

The Oakland Institute (2011). Understanding Land Investment Deals in Africa: Sierra Leone. Country Report. Oakland, California.

Limao, N. and Venables, A. J. (2001). Infrastructure, geographical disadvantage, transport costs, and trade. *The World Bank Economic Review*, 15(3):451–479.

Myers, M. and Wise, C. (2016). *The political economy of China-Latin America relations in the new millennium: Brave new world*. New York: Taylor & Francis.

Nieto, J., Carpintero, Ó., Miguel, L. J., and de Blas, I. (2020). Macroeconomic modelling under energy constraints: Global low carbon transition scenarios. *Energy Policy*, 137:111090.

Njoh, A. J. (2012). Impact of transportation infrastructure on development in east Africa and the Indian ocean region. *Journal of Urban Planning and Development*, 138(1):1–9.

OECD "Regional Trade and Investment: Trends, Issues and ESCAP Responses. Note by the Secretariat, ESCAP, Sixty-fifth Session, 23–29 April 2009, Bangkok. E/ESCAP/65/2".

Okoye, D., Pongou, R., and Yokossi, T. (2019). New technology, better economy? The heterogeneous impact of colonial railroads in Nigeria. *Journal of Development Economics*, 140:320–354.

Porter, G. (2014). Transport services and their impact on poverty and growth in rural Sub-Saharan Africa: A review of recent research and future research needs. *Transport Reviews*, 34(1):25–45.

Proinvest (2005). https://thetimesofafrica.com/proinvest-africa-2018/.

Scissors, D. (2020). China global investment tracker. American Enterprise Institute. www.finance.senate.gov/imo/media/doc/Derek%20Scissors%20-%20BRI%20Testimony.pdf.

Secretariat, A. (2016). Master plan on Asean connectivity, 2025. Jakarta, ASEAN Secretariat.

Tei, A. and Ferrari, C. (2018). Ppis and transport infrastructure: Evidence from Latin America and the Caribbean. *Journal of Transport Geography*, 71:204–212.

The International Air Transport Association (IATA). (2019). The importance of air transport to Ethiopia. Available at www.iata.org/en/iata-repository/publications/economic-reports/ethiopia--value-of-aviation/

The International Road Federation: https://worldroadstatistics.org/orld Road Statistics. IRF World Road Statistics (2020).Vhumbunu, C. H. (2016). Enabling African regional infrastructure renaissance through the China-Africa partnership: A trans-continental appraisal. *International Journal of China Studies*, 7(3):271.

Woetzel, J., Garemo, N., Mischke, J., Kamra, P., and Palter, R. (2017). Bridging infrastructure gaps: Has the world made progress. McKinsey & Company, 5.

World Bank Africa Pulse. (2019). https://documents1.worldbank.org/curated/en/348741492463112162/pdf/114375-REVISED-4-18-PMWB-AfricasPulse-Spring2017-vol15-ENGLISH-FINAL-web.pdf

World Bank. 2020. https://documents1.worldbank.org/curated/en/348741492463112162/pdf/114375-REVISED-4-18-PMWB-AfricasPulse-Spring2017-vol15-ENGLISH-FINAL-web.pdf

Appendix

Table 9.1 Summary statistics by region, African road density

	Central Region	Eastern Region	Northern Region	Southern Region	Western Region
Total Roads	9913.357	8193.074	30748.71	42720	12966.3
	3.493826	3.728996	2.667225	1.19609	4.205272
Above Median	.5	.4444444	.4285714	.5	.5925926
	3.605551	4.560702	3.122499	1.732051	6.149649
GDP per capita	3823.341	1590.822	10810.66	7371.957	2189.701
	3.573591	9.743896	4.842021	2.948157	8.81405
Trade_openness	83.22452	60.17886	71.44207	93.38614	61.06865
	8.064271	9.781988	7.625507	4.282053	16.43451
Perc. highway	.0001376	.0000166	.0035329	.00532	.000549
	1.463422	1.437218	2.355374	1.33144	1.588612
Perc. paved	.0332604	.0770087	.0225431	.0547928	.0827323
	2.180798	1.957984	3.453688	3.195417	2.000662
Open roads	1	1	.923092	1	.9259259
	.	.	12.97944	.	18.02776
Total land_area (Sq. Km)	896837.9	631809.1	1203930	819957.5	593787.8
	4.689268	10.87418	5.477937	2.941295	6.427473
Ratio of total road to Land	.014499	.0589238	.0456481	.0373726	.0557431
	2.674768	1.642367	1.909511	1.304221	4.589307
Ratio of total highway to land	2.10e-10	4.70e-11	5.40e-09	4.39e-09	1.22e-09
	1.279491	1.213104	2.761327	1.33144	2.081432
N	14	27	14	4	27

Source: Author computation based on GRID and WDI databases.

Table 9.2a The effect of road density on GDP per capita

Total Roads	0.048**					
	0.021					
Total Highways		549352.400***				
		162503.551				
Above Median Total Roads			-298.794			
			1136.312			
Above Median Total Highways				2924.356**		
				1288.633		
Ratio of Total Roads to Land Area					-1983.611	
					4835.111	
Ratio of Total Highways to Land Area						3.742e+11***
						1.323e+11
N	83	83	83	83	83	83

Source: Author computation based on GRID and WDI databases.

Table 9.2b The effect of road density on GDP per capita, including regional fixed effects

	(1)	(2)	(3)	(4)	(5)	(6)
Total Roads	0.008 0.018					
Total Highways		157424.358 152632.948				
Above Median Total Roads			15.828 894.199			
Above Median Total Highways				-69.802 1132.505		
Ratio of Total Roads to Land Area					-639.400 3802.794	
Ration of Total Highways to Total Land Area						9.530e+09 1.23e+11
North Region	0.000	0.000	0.000	0.000	0.000	0.000
South Region	-2213.4 1353.4	-2213.789 1345.104	-2231.200 1356.286	-2236.674 1355.883	-2201.252 1366.701	-2231.023 1354.325
East Region	6829.0 1565.3	6452.832*** 1597.990	6988.452*** 1523.371	7017.236*** 1597.513	7007.238* 1526.358	6937.880*** 1650.294
West Region	3299.3 2354.8	2732.787 2401.452	3548.617 2283.047	3573.546 2318.547	3563.242 2284.289	3508.822 2340.006
Central Region	-1656.8 1325.8	-1698.398 1318.660	-1635.106 1328.811	-1628.100 1329.241	-1607.269 1335.232	-1643.251 1331.967
N	85	85	85	85	85	85

Source: Author computation based on GRID and WDI databases.

Table 9.2c The effect of road density on GDP per capita, controlling for costs of trade

	dir2	dir3	dir4	dir5	dir6
Total Roads	0.024*** 0.001				
Total Highways	242252.957*** 6526.056				
Above Median Total Roads		792.762*** 46.095			
Above Median Total Highways			894.985*** 56.846		
Ratio of Total Roads to Land Area				962.237*** 204.109	
Ratio of Total Highways to Land Area					7.673e+10*** 5.446e+09
Observations	14284	14284	14284	14083	14083

Source: Author computation based on GRID and WDI databases.

Table 9.3a The effects of road density on trade openness

	dir11 b/se	dir22 b/se	dir33 b/se	dir44 b/se	dir55 b/se
Total Roads	0.0 0.0				
Total Highways		-904.224*** 1062.007			
Above Median Total Roads			-16.704** 6.663		
Above Median Total Highways				-8.994*** 8.086	
Ratio of total roads to Land area					-35.283 29.513
Ratio of total highways to Land area					1.60E+08 8.52E+08
Observations	85	85	85	85	85

Source: Author computation based on GRID and WDI databases.

Table 9.3b The effects of road density on trade openness, controlling for costs of trade

	dir11 b/se	dir22 b/se	dir33 b/se	dir44 b/se	dir55 b/se
Total Roads	-0.000*** 0.000				
Total Highways		-1645.901*** 1062.007			
Above Median Total Roads			-10.466*** 63.437		
Above Median Total Highways				-12.757*** 0.534	
Ratio of total road to Land area					-10.259*** 1.955
Trade Costs	-0.009*** 0.001	-0.009*** 0.001	-0.008*** 0.001	-0.008*** 0.001	-0.009*** 0.001
Observations	14284	14284	14284	14284	14083

Source: Author computation based on GRID and WDI databases.

Table 9.4a Global connectedness depth score—total cross-border flow to relevant domestic activities

	Dependent	dir2	dir3	dir4	dir5	dir6
Total Roads	-0.000*** 0.000					
Total Highways		-734.016*** 6.854				
Above Median Total Roads			-4.559*** 0.099			
Above Median Total Highways				-5.751*** 0.068		
Ratio of Total Roads to Land Area					-2.449***	
Ratio of Total Highways to Land Area						-2.242e+08*** 7152434.974
Observations	23166	23166	23166	23166	23166	23166

Source: Author computation based on GRID and WDI databases.

Table 9.4b Global connectedness breadth score—total cross-border flow to relevant domestic activities

	b/se	b/se	b/se	b/se	b/se
Total Roads	0.000*** 0.000				
Total Highways		654.326*** 11.531			
Above Median Total Roads			-1.283*** 0.152		
Above Median Total Highways				7.468*** 0.103	
Ratio of Total Roads to Land Area					-11.703*** 0.245
Ratio of Total Highways to Land Area					5.698e+08*** 10048194.64
Observations	23166	23166	23166	23166	23166	23166

Source: Author computation based on GRID and WDI databases.

10 Industrialize Africa by leveraging on its natural resources

The AfCFTA to be a game changer[1]

Komi Tsowou

10.1 Introduction

Africa's structural transformation through industrialization is a necessary condition to achieve inclusive development and create much-needed jobs. The contribution of industrialization to inclusive development stems from its ability to shift resources, including labour and capital, from low to high productivity and value-added activities. This shift can help create decent and productive jobs to sustain livelihoods for African citizens (AfDB et al., 2017; ECA, 2015). Yet, most of the continent's resource-rich countries continue to depend heavily on commodities exports, with limited, if not any value added (Tsowou and Ajambo, 2020; UNECA, 2015; UNECA, 2017). Economic diversification will be critical for Africa to achieve the goals contained in the AU's Agenda 2063 and the UN Agenda 2030.

Africa's industrialization ambition cannot however be fully achieved without integrated markets. The fragmentation of African economies and many tariffs and non-tariffs barriers reduce the scope for economies of scale. This has impeded the competitiveness of African industrialists (UNECA, 2015; Tsowou and Ajambo, 2020). In recognition of the industrialization potential of integrated African markets, the African leaders signed in 2018 the Agreement Establishing the African Continental Free Trade Area (AfCFTA). The scope of the agreement goes beyond the traditional free trade area, covering not only trade in goods but also trade in services, investment, intellectual property rights, competition policy and e-commerce. The overarching goal of the AfCFTA is to create a unified continental market for goods and services, facilitated by the movement of persons. It further intends to "promote industrial development through diversification and regional value chain development, agricultural development and food security."[2] The design of the agreement reflects an explicit willingness of Africans to enable trade and investment to support inclusive industrialization.

This chapter aims to make the case for a well-implemented AfCFTA that contributes to spurring industrialization in Africa's leveraging on its abundant resources, and thus reducing dependence to the unprocessed commodities exports. It demonstrates that African markets exist for "Made in Africa" products and there is a huge potential to supply those markets with value-added products processed from natural resources of the continent. Reaping the benefits of the AfCFTA starts with putting the agreement

DOI: 10.4324/9781003456568-10

into national perspective through the "domestication" of its provisions. Integrated African markets create economies of scale required to add value to the continent's natural resources, preferably through well-established RVCs. Deliberate efforts are needed to establish RVCs around production hubs, mainly in resource-rich countries with strong comparative advantages. In the meantime, other countries can position themselves on the various segments of the chains. These require goods to be moved efficiently and thus, the importance of the AfCFTA state parties to fully adhere to and implement the agreement. Building competitive economies in resource-rich countries and others, while providing industrialists with necessary incentives and resources including labour and finance will be very instrumental to achieving the *industrialize Africa*'s ambition of the AfCFTA.

The chapter is organized as follows. Section 10.2 provides an overview of commodities dependence and their implications for African economies. Section 10.3 discusses the theoretical framework of industrialization and trade liberalization schemes. Section 10.4 discusses enabling factors to make the AfCFTA work for Africa's industrialization agenda. The last section concludes by highlighting the key priority actions.

10.2 The imperative for African economies to add value to their natural resources

10.2.1 Commodities dependence in Africa: An overview

Africa continues to depend heavily on natural resources exports. Over the period 2000–2019, Africa's ratio of commodity dependence, expressed as commodities exports[3] as a percentage of total merchandise exports (in value terms), annually exceeded 70%. Central and Western Africa seem to be the regions with the highest dependence on commodities exports, outpacing the average values for the continent (Figure 10.1). The situation is underpinned by resource-rich countries' limited capacity to promote value addition. Wherever this has been recorded, most of the values are created in the low rungs of the value chains (UNECA, 2015). Table 10.1 in the annex provides a list of African countries with their main resource's endowment, ranging from energy commodities (crude oil and natural gas), minerals ores and metals to agricultural and forestry products.

There has been in recent years efforts to promote value added in some resource-rich countries. Gabon, for example, has one of the largest high-grade manganese deposits (10% of global deposit and 4th) in the world which has been extracted since the 1960s and traded toward international markets, mainly under unprocessed form. However, from 2014, one of the country's main mining companies started processing two value-added manganese products: silicomanganese and manganese metal. Similarly, the country banned the export of unprocessed timber in 2010 and has seen the emergence of wood processing activities in recent years (Tsowou, 2018). Yet, the bulk of wood businesses are contracted in the primary and secondary wood processing (from sawing and rotary cutting to manufacturing of profiles, parquet and plies). Other examples of value-added activities across the

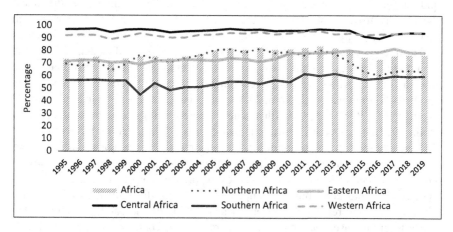

Figure 10.1 Commodities exports as percentage of total merchandise exports in Africa and its regions, 2000–2019.

Source: Author based on data from UNCTADStat (accessed in December 2020).

continent include textile and high-tech industries in Egypt; apparel and footwear products in Ethiopia; automobile manufacturing in South Africa; diamond processing in Botswana and agricultural food industries in many countries.

Despite these success stories, limited integration of markets has not allowed businesses to maximize the full potential of industrial activities so far. The overall contribution of manufacturing value added to Africa's GDP remained between 9 and 12% over the period 1995–2016 (Tsowou and Ajambo, 2020). Businesses face several constraints that undermine their competitiveness. Key constraints include high tariffs on goods, especially among countries that are not a member of the same regional FTA, and burdensome non-tariffs barriers (UNECA, 2015; UNECA, 2020; Okafor and Aniche, 2017). These impediments are expected to be addressed through the AfCFTA as discussed later.

10.2.2 Commodities dependence and African countries' vulnerabilities to shocks

Excessive dependence of African economies on low value-added segments of natural resources increases their vulnerability to the vagaries in international commodities markets, often featuring high price volatility (UNCTAD, 2013). In addition, the vulnerability of African economies to remote markets has been exacerbated in recent months by trade restrictions emanating from the COVID-19 pandemic, putting millions of livelihoods at risk (UNECA, 2020).

Both the existing literature and empirical evidence suggest that commodity dependence can be detrimental to growth and development through the "resource curse" phenomenon (UNCTAD, 2013). Some of the main underlying factors include macroeconomic instability induced by volatilities in commodities prices and the secular negative terms of trade as per the Prebisch-Singer hypothesis and the Dutch Disease phenomenon (appreciation of currencies of a resource-rich country due to large inflows of foreign currency in its commodity sector, which undermine the competitiveness of other economic sectors in the country). Volatile commodities prices and induced instability in macroeconomic performance are often associated with lower socio-economic outcomes in resource-rich developing countries (Carmignani and Avom, 2010). The secular deterioration in terms of trade and its instability impedes growth and development in those countries (Nkurunziza et al., 2017). The Dutch Disease phenomenon is underpinned by large inflows of foreign currency in the commodities sector or increases in commodities export prices. The resulting relative appreciation of domestic currencies, while making imports cheaper, makes non-commodities exports such as manufactures less competitive. This has contributed to impeding economic diversification (i.e. vertical diversification) in resource-rich countries (Frankel, 2011). Additional factors that frustrate broad-based development in resource-rich countries include social and political instability and conflicts arising from internal fights to control resource rents in a context of limited transparency and widespread mismanagement. These conflicts contribute to destructing productive resources and disrupting businesses (Berman et al., 2017; Caselli and Tesei, 2016; Nkurunziza et al., 2017).

African economies' overreliance on commodities notwithstanding, a closer look at the trade structure of the continent suggests that it trades more value-added content with itself. Based on 2000–2019 data, intra-regional trade flows for groups of products—total of all merchandise, primary commodities, manufactured goods—reveals that Africa trades more manufactured products with itself (Figure 10.2). Therefore, more integrated African markets including through the AfCFTA can provide a push to the development of the manufacturing sector. This is also evidenced by several empirical studies as discussed in the next section.

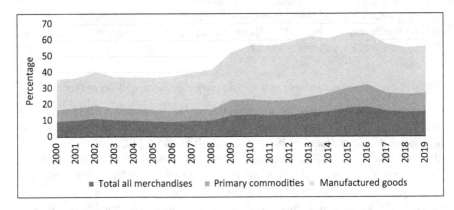

Figure 10.2 Intra-African exports as percentage of total exports of product groups—all merchandise, primary commodities, manufactured goods, 2000–2019.

Source: Author based on data from UNCTADStat (accessed in June 2020).

10.3 Industrialization and trade liberalization: Theoretical underpinning and empirical evidence

10.3.1 Theoretical underpinning

The literature on trade liberalization posits two sets of effects, namely, static and dynamic effects (Figure 10.3). The static effects of free trade area (FTA) introduced in the seminal work of Viner (1950) revolve around two key concepts—trade creation and trade diversion. On one side, trade creation refers to the positive trade performance resulting from a FTA, underpinned by the removal of trade barriers and increased competition. Subsequently, countries under FTAs enjoy greater efficiency, expanded economic outcomes and increased trade through an improved allocation of resources (including factors of production). On the other side, trade diversion is related to trade flows diverted from third parties to a FTA to countries within a FTA. This could however be detrimental if the diversion is made from a more-efficient third trade partner in favor of a higher-cost producing country. The negative effect of trade diversion could be exacerbated by adjustment costs arising from the implementation of a FTA, generally in the short run (Saygili et al., 2018). These costs result from the reallocation of resources and can materialize in the form of tariff revenue losses and shrinking sectors that can temporarily contribute to higher levels of unemployment.

Beyond Viner's theory on the trade creation impact of FTAs, the benefits of free trade are often underpinned by the gains accrued to producing firms in accessing larger sources of resources and to consumers from expanded access to markets for final products. In the context of a FTA, producers are expected to gain from access to lower-cost inputs and intermediate goods from other countries within the FTA and have access to larger regional and continental markets to sell their outputs

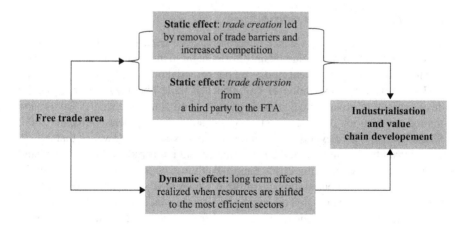

Figure 10.3 Conceptual framework of FTA effect on industrialization.

(Estevadeordal and Taylor, 2013; UNECA et al., 2010). Meanwhile, consumers are also better placed to enjoy cheaper products from countries within the Free Trade Area. These assumptions are expected to also hold in the AfCFTA context. Furthermore, the AfCFTA is expected to address challenges associated with multiple and overlapping trade agreements among African countries and between these countries and their international trading partners (Saygili et al., 2018).

The second set of effects of trade liberalization, which is dynamic effects, occur over the long run and can potentially offset adverse short-term effects. The dynamic effects are fully realized when resources are shifted to the most efficient sectors where countries' comparative and competitive advantages lie, following the implementation of a FTA (UNECA, AU, AfDB, 2010, Saygili et al., 2018).

Several channels underpin the dynamic effects. Expanded markets through trade liberalizing reforms provide increased incentives for investment, especially foreign direct investment (UNECA, 2018) and the transfer of technology (Bustos, 2011). In the African context, the fragmentation of economies poses serious impediments to industrial investments that often require large economies of scale to be profitable. The AfCFTA is expected to partially address this challenge through integrated African markets and the establishment of common rules for investment. Furthermore, market integration creates a favourable environment for competition that can contribute to increased productivity growth of firms (Melitz and Ottaviano, 2008). The productivity gain may also result from better access to imported inputs and intermediary goods that lower the cost of processed goods and better positions firms to innovate by combining varieties of inputs (Broda et al., 2006). Moreover, increased intra-regional trade can stimulate regional growth hubs capable of generating externalities to other economies. An interesting success story in this regard is the development of RVCs in Southern Africa around the South African automotive industry, which has created opportunities for suppliers of car components such as leather seats, fabrics and wires in Botswana, Lesotho, Namibia and eSwatini (Markowitz, 2016).

10.3.2 Empirical evidence: A review

This section reviews the evidence underpinning the impact of trade liberalization on industrialization and value chain development. This review is not exhaustive and instead focusses on recent studies on the potential implications of the AfCFTA.

The empirical investigation of the impact of trade liberalization on industrial development, or broadly on economic growth, is mixed. Some studies have found limited contribution of trade openness to industrial development (Debande, 2006; Shafaeddin, 2012). Several other empirical studies suggest however that a FTA can contribute to scaling up trade performance and industrial activities (Amiti and Konings, 2007; Shafaeddin, 2012; Santos-Paulino, 2002). In recent years, empirical works on the potential impacts of the AfCFTA have started to emerge. Mevel and Karingi (2012) simulated the impact of a continental free trade area agreement through the removal of trade tariffs among African economies. The authors found trade creation effects exceed trade diversion effects. Under the scenario with the

AfCFTA in place, intra-African trade was estimated to increase by 52 percent, compared with a baseline scenario without the agreement in place (in 2022). Africa's industrial exports were projected to display the highest gains, expanding by nearly 53 percent. Both unskilled and skilled workers were found to benefit from increased real wages, with expected shifts in employment from agricultural to non-agricultural sectors. The gains from the AfCFTA were found to be even higher if trade liberalization was accompanied by trade facilitation measures. Chauvin et al. (2016) model the likely effects of the AfCFTA on African economies running the following four scenarios incrementally, all implemented starting in 2017 in a linear phase-out period of 10 years: i) elimination of tariffs for agricultural goods, ii) elimination of tariffs on manufactured goods, iii) 50% reduction in non-tariff measures (NTMs) and, iv) 30% reduction in transaction costs associated with time. The authors found very limited short-run impacts of the AfCFTA in the first year after implementation. The long-run impacts on trade, growth and welfare gains were found to be larger and more positive in all scenarios, but with variations across countries.

Saygili et al. (2018) investigate the short-term and long-term impacts of the AfCFTA implementation on economies. They found some short-term adjustment costs related to skills upgrading and temporary unemployment, and lower wages in declining sectors in the private sector. For the public sector, lower tariffs revenues were identified as a concern. Yet, the authors found positive impacts in the long run, with the largest employment growth rates found in the manufacturing industry, followed by some services including construction and transportation, and agricultural subsectors. These findings corroborate the expectations placed on the AfCFTA to be a driver of Africa's structural transformation and industrialization. The World Bank (2020) found the AfCFTA to spur value added to Africa's resources while creating new opportunities for manufacturers and workers. The bank estimated the agreement could boost Africa's total exports by 29%, intra-continental trade by more than 81% and Africa exports to the rest of the world by 19%, with most of the gains accrued to the manufacturing sector.

10.4 Promoting value addition to natural resources under the AfCFTA

10.4.1 *AfCFTA to streamline cross-border trade and promote value addition through Rules of Origin (RoO)*

An effectively implemented AfCFTA is expected to allow a wide range of goods to be traded duty free. The modalities of tariffs liberalization under the agreement require that 97% of tariff lines will be fully liberalized. This shall support the production and trade of goods in Africa at a time tariffs barriers have impeded their competitiveness. Okafor and Aniche (2017) suggested that average tariffs on intra-African trade can be as high as 8.7% with only 15 countries importing or facing average protection rates lower than the continental average. In other words, African countries seem to be more protectionist; on average the whole continent with tariffs on intra-African trade of goods being as high as over 90% in some countries. In addition to the reduction of tariffs, the AfCFTA has also several provisions to remove non-tariffs barriers which constitute a significant share of cross-border trade costs across the continent. Non-duties related costs, in ad valorem equivalents of non-tariffs measures, in Africa can be as high as 14% for vegetables, 11.4% for beverages, 11.3% for machinery and 11.1% for optical and medical devices (UNCTAD, 2019). According to Gillson 2010, the South Africa-based food retailer Shoprite, spends up to US$ 5.8 million per year to adhere to trade rules and formalities including requirements to secure US$ 13.6 million in duty savings under regional trade preferences. These hurdles are expected to be reduced with the AfCFTA through simplification of trade procedures, adoption of integrated border management processes, harmonization and simplification of customs and transit procedures, and harmonization of quality infrastructure systems, among others.

For the goods processed to enjoy the AfCFTA benefits, they must comply with the set of rules defined in the Agreement's Rules of Origin (RoO). The AfCFTA RoO is composed of laws, regulations and rules that determine if a product has been obtained or sufficiently processed in the area to enjoy preferential treatments, at least those induced by tariff preferences. The AfCFTA RoO rules are expected to serve as an instrument that contributes to boosting trade among African economies. The AfCFTA RoO adopts a hybrid approach combining a set of product-specific and general rules. The rules can therefore provide inputs (e.g. raw commodities or semi-finished goods) sourced from the area, with comparative advantages to support the development of RVCs. Live animals (HS code Chapter 01), meat and edible meat offal (HS code Chapter 02) and dairy products (HS code Chapter 04) for example, will be compliant with AfCFTA RoO only when they are fully obtained in the state parties. For some other products, specific RoO such as thresholds for originating or non-originating value content, change in tariff classification or specific manufacturing or processing operations requirements are to be decided. For example, refined petroleum oils can be considered as originating when they are processed in the AfCFTA state parties from originating crude oil or the foreign value content does not exceed a certain threshold (Tsowou and Davis, 2021). As noted earlier, the wealth of resources existing across Africa shall incentivize manufacturers to source much of their inputs from AfCFTA markets. UNCTAD (2019) provided evidence through case studies on the potential of RoO under the AfCFTA to support the development of RVCs in the following sectors: tea, cocoa and chocolate products, cotton textiles and apparel, beverages, cement and automotive industries.

Africa's top imports, mainly sourced from the rest of the world, include agro-processed products, manufacture of base metals, wood, textile and rubber products, refined petroleum oil and its by-products.[4] Most of these products could potentially be manufactured across the continent considering its resources endowment (see Table 10.1). According to the estimates by the World Bank (2020), the AfCFTA can significantly boost value added in the following sectors: agro-food processing, wood and paper products, textile and weaving apparel, chemicals rubbers and plastic products, petroleum and coal products. These potential benefits will be possible only if manufacturing intermediate or finished goods within the AfCFTA markets is cheaper than extra-AfCFTA markets. The expectation is that this could be achieved through the removal of tariffs and non-tariffs barriers. It is important to note that RVCs approach will be instrumental to "industrialize Africa", by tapping into the natural endowments of resource-rich countries (UNECA, 2015). A main contention here is that the limited size of internal markets of several resource-rich African countries would make it nearly impossible to achieve the level of economies of scale required to fully develop a vertically integrated value chain at a national level.

The AfCFTA RoO alone will not be enough to support value-added across the continent. Several complementary actions are needed to ensure production and trade and the emergence of RVCs within the integrated markets as discussed in the following section.

10.4.2 Coordinated policies and complementary efforts to realize Africa's industrialization ambition under the AfCFTA

The discussions so far suggest that the AfCFTA has the potential to support Africa's transformational industrialization agenda. Realizing the AfCFTA ambition will not however be automatic. It starts with the effective operationalization of the agreement, that is, domesticating its provisions through national laws and regulations. Deliberate efforts through complementary policies, including industrial and investment policies shall aim to increase efficiency in production and trade and attract investments in the value-added sector (UNECA et al., 2019).

The wide scope and cross-cutting nature of the agreement calls for the design of an appropriate range of integrated policies, for example, in the areas of trade, investment and industrialization. Trade policies are to be well aligned with industrial and investment policies while conflictual provisions shall be avoided. Integrated policies will be able to ensure that actions to support value addition in one sector do not conflict with other sectoral objectives. Such policy frameworks shall be built on mutually reinforcing interests and actions from different entities, under strong leadership and high-level coordination. These are key to creating synergies towards achieving common objectives. Coordination and actions at regional and continental levels under the AfCFTA scheme will be critical to synergize efforts and maximize industrial development opportunities, especially in resource-rich countries in a holistic manner. For example, Gabon has banned since 2010, exports of unprocessed wood to promote local value addition while its neighbouring countries in the Central African region have not adopted a similar policy. The situation undermines the competitiveness of local wood processors in Gabon. The latter have claimed to face higher costs compared with their competitors in Asia who have continued to source their logs from countries in the Central African region (Tsowou, 2018). This calls for better harmonization and coordination of strategies at regional levels to support Africa's industrialization efforts.

Scaling up high value-added industries requires skilled labour. Skills gaps and mismatches remain however prevalent across the continent. Yet, without adequate skills, industrial development cannot materialize under the AfCFTA. Chapter 11 of this book noted the need for several agricultural resource countries in Africa to upgrade medium and high skills for the agriculture sector to be transformative and integrate the high end of agri-food value chains. ACBF (2016) estimated the skills gap across the continent to amount to 4.3 million engineers and 1.6 million agricultural scientists and researchers. To harness AfCFTA-led industrial opportunities, tailoring national-level education to the needs of businesses, and specifically, Small and Medium Sized Enterprises which are the backbone of production and trade in Africa shall be a must. This certainly entails improving access of young people to high-quality technical and vocational education and training programs just as increasing primarily their participation rates at tertiary level education in science, technology, engineering and mathematics (STEMs).

Competitive economies cannot be built without efficient and well-sustained infrastructure assets (also see Chapter 8 of this book). The efficient movement of resources, goods and people needed to catalyze industrial production and trade require well-functioning and resilient infrastructure assets. Energy and water resources, transport assets and technologies are key elements of production and trade. Long-lasting infrastructure shortcomings in Africa are being currently addressed through several high-level programs and projects at both national, regional and continental levels. At the continental level, the Program for Infrastructure Development in Africa covers a range of transborder infrastructure projects. Examples of these include the North-South Corridor Program, the Abidjan-Lagos Highway Development Program, the Walvis Bay Corridor and the Africa Clean Energy Corridor. These continental and regional projects have national components that shall be prioritized by countries in the face of limited financial resources. Estimates by the AfDB (2018) for example suggest that the continent's infrastructure financing needs amount to US$ 130–170 billion a year, with a financing gap in the range of US$ 68–108 billion.

Regional and national integrated economic zones including industrial parks, special economic zones and technology parks with efficient infrastructure assets could also circumvent infrastructure deficits across Africa. Countries like Egypt, Ethiopia, Kenya, Gabon and South Africa—to cite a few—have set up well-integrated economic zones that are at present supporting the development of dynamic manufacturing sectors.[5] These zones yield gains in economies of scale in infrastructure and services provisions to businesses and contribute to maximizing economies of agglomeration of industrial activities, including experience and technology sharing. The zones not only help countries close infrastructure deficits for businesses, but they also offer spatial proximity of industries resulting in the transfer of knowledge, ideas and technologies, which remain vital for innovation and growth. Integrated economic zones also contribute to the creation of a pool of workers, inputs and suppliers, which allow firms to maximize the benefits of their comparative advantages while achieving greater productivity and efficiency (AfDB et al., 2016; AfDB et al., 2017). The establishment of economic zones across the continent shall however draw on lessons from past unsuccessful experiences. Their underperformance in the past resulted from limited linkages with the domestic economy, inconsistencies with countries' comparative advantages and inefficient location, crowding-out of private investors and limited policy coordination (AfDB et al., 2017). Those impediments should be tackled or prevented if current and upcoming economic zones are to unlock Africa's manufacturing potential.

Tapping into the valuable investment opportunities offered by larger integrated African markets also requires facilitating access to low-cost finance. According to the AfroChampions (2020), the continent's trade finance gap for the private sector is about US$ 91 billion annually. Governments need to set an enabling environment with clarity of regulatory framework, political stability, and strength of investor protection (including the rule of law). Whenever possible, tax incentives could be promoted to reduce the financial burdens on privately funded businesses and projects while harmonizing fiscal, monetary, and financial policies (see Chapter 7 of this book). If Africa continues to face higher constraints to finance, compared to other parts of the world (Beck and Cull, 2014), investing in intra-African production and trade will be a daunting task for private businesses. The challenge to access affordable finance is particularly worrisome for SMEs which constitute the backbone of production in Africa.

Finally, digitalization is imperative to maximize the opportunities for industrialization in Africa (Myovella et al., 2020; Njangang, and Nounamo, 2020). The fourth industrial revolution, especially the digital economy, is changing the ways goods are produced and traded. Factory automation and robotics, the Internet of Things and artificial intelligence have changed the nature of manufacturing. Adoption of technologies creates opportunities for Africa to reduce costs and increase efficiencies of industrial businesses and services. Promoting technologies will contribute to increasing the competitiveness of services at a time of increasing servicification of the manufacturing sector.

10.5 Conclusion and policy recommendations

This chapter suggests that the success of industrialization in Africa, including in resource-rich economies, partly depends on their ability to reap the benefits of the AfCFTA. The design of the agreement translates to a strong will of Africans to ensure that AfCFTA markets contribute to industrialization within the continent. Current trade structure analysis throughout the chapter implies that continental markets exist for AfCFTA products. Opportunities for investments range from agricultural food to mineral and metal processing. However, the expected benefits from trade liberalizing efforts, including fostering industrial development and value addition in resource-rich countries, will not come overnight. Concerted and deliberate efforts are needed to transform AfCFTA ambitions into reality.

10.5.1 Establishing RVCs through deliberate efforts, preferably around dominant resource-rich countries and ensuring coordinated policies

The establishment of RVCs will be of critical importance to spur Africa's industrialization ambition while leveraging on the endowments of resource-rich countries. The similarity in the trade structure of African countries suggests that most competitive economies need to become regional trade hubs while others will connect to the various segments of an AfCFTA-led RVC. For instance, several Central African countries are very rich in forest resources. They could jointly develop regional production and trade hubs in one or two countries for the establishment of wood-based value-added activities (for instance Gabon has now a well-established wood industry (see Tsowou, 2018) while other countries can position on upstream or downstream segments of the chains. Similarly, cocoa producers in Western and Central African countries can position themselves around the leading countries (i.e. Côte d'Ivoire and Ghana) to establish strong RVCs from cocoa to chocolate products and then supply larger AfCFTA markets. Establishing these RVCs requires alignment among policies (e.g. trade, industrial and investment policies). AfCFTA state parties should avoid instituting for instance national policies or any action that could frustrate intra-African trade. In this regard, it is crucial to prioritize regional over national interests; the latter often tends to incentivize the protection of domestic industries and therefore jeopardize regional integration efforts.

10.5.2 Ensuring AfCFTA state parties effectively implement the agreement

Interconnecting regional trade and production hubs and AfCFTA markets efficiently starts with the domestication of the agreement and effective implementation of its provisions. By the time the first trading under the AfCFTA started in January 2020, only a few countries including South Africa, Ghana, and Egypt had the required AfCFTA-related customs procedures in place, out of the 35 countries that ratified the agreement as of 15 January 2021. The political momentum that accompanied negotiations and ratification of the agreement shall be kept in its decisive implementation timeframe. Commitments to the progressive elimination of tariffs on intra-African trade and removal of non-tariffs barriers under the AfCFTA shall be translated into concrete actions within the agreed timeframe. Complementary policies ranging from trade, industrial development and investment among others need to be aligned and effectively implemented under strong leadership at national, regional, and continental levels. Unless the agreement is effectively domesticated by the AfCFTA member states, the establishment of RVCs leveraging on continental resources will not materialize.

Providing industrialists in resource-rich countries, especially in the production hubs, with required resources including low-cost finance and labour including engineers and scientists is a must. This certainly implies addressing current challenges related to skills mismatches and gaps that are still pervasive in Africa as discussed in the previous section. Governments and private sector leaders shall invest in high-quality technical and vocational education and training programs tailored to the needs of industries. They shall also promote and ease access of youth to tertiary-level education in STEM.

The establishment of regional production and trade hubs, especially in resource-rich countries requires very competitive economies. This can be achieved through massive investments in infrastructure and technologies. Prioritizing public and private partnerships could be the most viable option. Furthermore, governments shall prioritize bankable infrastructure projects that are aligned with national and regional industrial priorities. The promotion of regional special economic zones could also be a viable option while leveraging on competitive advantages of each regional partner. For example, in 2018, Burkina Faso, Côte d'Ivoire and Mali launched a cross-border special economic zone, composed of the regions of Sikasso (Mali), Bobo Dioulasso (Burkina Faso) and Korhogo (Côte d'Ivoire).

The implementation of these actions requires efforts from all stakeholders. These span from governments, the private sector including multinationals operating in Africa, the development banks (such as The World Bank, AfDB, Afreximbank), the regional economic commissions, the African Union, and other development partners such as UN agencies and programmes, and every single African citizen.

Notes

1 The views and opinions expressed in this paper are those of the authors and do not necessarily reflect the views or positions of their employers or institutions.
2 Agreement Establishing the African Continental Free Trade Area, Article 3 and Article 4 (Consolidated text of the Agreement, signed on 21 March 2018).
3 These include agricultural products, as well as oil, minerals, ores and metals.
4 Based on data from UNCTADStat (unctadstat.unctad.org).
5 At the time this chapter is drafted, uncertainty remained on how goods produced within special economic zones shall be treated under the AfCFTA. However, considering the importance of these zones in supporting industrialization and circumvent Africa's infrastructure challenges, it is desirable to make the goods benefits AfCFTA trade preferences, providing they are produced according to the rules and regulations prevailing under the Agreement.

Appendix

Table 10.1 African countries and their main resources endowment

Countries	Resources	Countries	Resources
Algeria	Petroleum oil and natural gas	Liberia	Iron ores, precious metals and natural rubber
Angola	Petroleum oil	Libya	Petroleum oil and natural gas
Benin	Cotton, timber and minerals ores	Madagascar	Spices, nickel and fishery products
Botswana	Diamonds and other minerals	Malawi	Tobacco, sugar and tea
Burkina Faso	Gold and cotton	Mali	Precious metals, cotton and live animals
Burundi	Gold, coffee and tea	Mauritania	Iron ore, fishery products and precious metals
Cabo Verde	Fishery products	Mauritius	Fishery products, sugar and pearls
Cameroon	Petroleum oil, forestry products and cocoa	Morocco	Fishery products, vegetables and phosphates and other minerals and ores

(Continued)

Table 10.1 (Continued)

Countries	Resources	Countries	Resources
Central African Republic	Cotton, precious stones, fruits and nuts	Mozambique	Aluminium and coal
Chad	Petroleum oil, gold and cotton	Namibia	Fishery and copper
Comoros	Fishery products	Niger	Uranium, thorium, petroleum and precious metals
Congo, Republic	Petroleum oil, copper, forestry products	Nigeria	Petroleum oil and natural gas
Côte d'Ivoire	Cocoa, petroleum oil, fruits and nuts	Rwanda	Base metals and coffee
Congo, Republic Democratic	Minerals and metals (cobalt, copper, diamonds, manganese, tin, tantalum, etc.)	Sao tome & Principe	Cocoa and fishery
Djibouti	Live animals and potential for minerals, gold, granite, limestone, etc.)	Senegal	Fishery products, phosphates, iron ore and deposits of petroleum oil
Egypt	Petroleum oil and precious metals	Seychelles	Fishery products and coconuts,
Equatorial Guinea	Petroleum oil and natural gas	Sierra Leone	Iron ore, mineral, ores and metals
Eritrea	Minerals and precious metals	Somalia	Live animals, oilseed and oleaginous fruits, reserves of minerals and metals
Eswatini	Forestry products and sugar	South Africa	Mineral, ores and metals (silver, platinum, iron ore, gold)
Ethiopia	Coffee, vegetables and oilseeds	Sudan	Gold and live animals
Gabon	Petroleum oil, forestry products and manganese	South Sudan	Petroleum oil
Gambia	Forestry products, fruits and nuts, fishery products	Togo	phosphate, marble, limestone
Ghana	Gold, petroleum oil, cocoa	Tunisia	Vegetable
Guinea	Minerals ores and metals (bauxite, iron ore, diamonds, gold), fruits and other agricultural food products	Uganda	Coffee, minerals and metals and fishery products

Table 10.1 (Continued)

Countries	Resources	Countries	Resources
Guinea-Bissau	Fruits and nuts, timber and minerals ores	Tanzania	precious metals, fruits and nuts, tobacco, phosphate,
Kenya	Tea, vegetables and minerals	Zambia	Copper, tobacco, maize
Lesotho	Precious stones and beverages	Zimbabwe	Tobacco, minerals and metals

Source: Author based on data from UNCTADstat and national-level consultations.

References

ACBF (2016). *African Critical Technical Skills: Key Capacity Dimensions Needed for the First 10 Years of Agenda 2063*. African Capacity Building Foundation, 2016. Harare, Zimbabwe.

AfDB, OECD and UNDP (2017). African Economic Outlook 2017: Entrepreneurship and Industrialization. Paris: OECD. Online at www.africaneconomicoutlook.org/en

AfDB (2018). African Economic Outlook 2018. African Development Bank. Abidjan, Cote d'Ivoire. Online at www.afdb.org/fileadmin/uploads/afdb/Documents/Publications/African_Economic_Outlook_2018_-_EN.pdf

AfroChampions (2020). AfCFTA year zero report. https://africanbusinessmagazine.com/wp-content/uploads/2020/05/AfCFTA_Year_Zero_Report_final2020April_AfroChampions_compressed.pdf

Amiti, M., and J. Konings. 2007. "Trade liberalization, intermediate inputs, and productivity: Evidence from Indonesia." The American Economic Review, *97*(5): 1611–1638.

Beck, Thorsten, and Robert Cull (2014). "SME finance in Africa." Journal of African Economies, *23*(5), 583–613.

Berman, Nicolas, Mathieu Couttenier, Dominic Rohner, and Mathias Thoenig (2017). "This Mine is Mine! How Minerals Fuel Conflicts in Africa. American Economic Review 107(6): 1564–1610.

Broda, C., J. Greenfield and D. Weinstein. (2006). "From Groundnuts to Globalization: A Structural Estimate of Trade and Growth." Working Paper No. 12512. Cambridge, MA: National Bureau of Economic Research.

Bustos, P. (2011). Trade liberalization, exports, and technology upgrading: Evidence on the impact of MERCOSUR on Argentinian firms. American economic review, *101*(1), 304–40.

Carmignani F and D Avom (2010). *The Social Development Effects of Primary Commodity Export Dependence*. Ecological Economics, *70*(2), 317–330.

Caselli, F., & Tesei, A. (2016). Resource windfalls, political regimes, and political stability. Review of Economics and Statistics, *98*(3), 573–590.

Chauvin, N., Ramos, P., & Porto, G. (2016). Trade, Growth, and Welfare Impacts of the CFTA in Africa. In *CSAE Conference 2017: Economic Development in Africa* (No. CONFERENCE-2017-040).

Debande, O. (2006). De-industrialisation. European Investment Bank Papers, *11*(1), 64–82.

Estevadeordal, A., and A. M. Taylor. 2013. "Is the Washington consensus dead? Growth, openness, and the great liberalization, 1970s–2000s." Review of Economics and Statistics *95*(5): 1669–1690.

Frankel, Jeffrey. The Natural Resource Curse: A Survey. University of Pennsylvania Press, 2011.

Gillson, Ian. (2010). Deepening regional integration to eliminate the fragmented goods market in Southern Africa.World Bank Africa Trade Policy Note 9.

Markowitz, C. (2016). Potential for Regional Value Chains in the Automotive Sector: Can SADC Learn from the Asean Experience. South African Institute for International Affairs Occasional paper 231. June.

Melitz, M. J., & Ottaviano, G. I. (2008). Market size, trade, and productivity. The review of economic studies, *75*(1), 295–316.

Mevel, S., & Karingi, S. (2012,). Deepening regional integration in Africa: A computable general equilibrium assessment of the establishment of a continental free trade area followed by a continental customs union. In 7th African Economic Conference, Kigali, Rwanda (Vol. 30).

Myovella, G., Karacuka, M., & Haucap, J. (2020). Digitalization and economic growth: A comparative analysis of Sub-Saharan Africa and OECD economies. Telecommunications Policy, *44*(2), 101856.

Njangang, H., & Nounamo, Y. (2020). Is information and communication technology a driver of industrialization process in African countries?. Economics Bulletin, *40*(4), 2654–2662.

Nkurunziza, J.D., Tsowou K., and Cazzaniga S. (2017). *Commodity Dependence and Human Development*. African Development Review, *29*(S1), 27–41.

Okafor, J and E, Aniche (2017) Deconstructing Neo-Functionalism In The Quest For a Paradigm Shift In African Integration: Post-Neo-Functionalism and The Prognostication of The Proposed Continental Free Trade Area in Africa IOSR Journal of Humanities and Social Science *22*(2):60–72

Santos-Paulino, A. U. (2002). Trade liberalisation and export performance in selected developing countries. Journal of Development Studies, *39*(1), 140–164.

Saygili, M., Peters, R., Knebel,C. (2018) African Continental Free Trade Area: Challenges and Opportunities of Tariff Reductions. UNCTAD Research Paper No. 15–UNCTAD/SER.RP/2017/15

Shafaeddin, M. S. (2012). Trade liberalization and economic reform in developing countries. The IMF, World Bank and Policy Reform, 155.

Tsowou (2018). The role of infrastructure in unlocking the potential for value addition to natural resources: evidence from Gabon. Human Sciences Research Council, 8th African Unity for Renaissance Conference, 23–25 May 2018. Pretoria, South Africa

Tsowou, K., & Ajambo, E. (2020). Sectoral Approaches to African Political Economy. In *The Palgrave Handbook of African Political Economy* (pp. 647–665). Palgrave Macmillan, Cham.

Tsowou, K., & Davis, J. (2021). Reaping the AfCFTA Potential Through Well-Functioning Rules of Origin. Journal of African Trade (Forthcoming). DOI https://doi.org/10.2991/jat.k.210428.001

UNCTAD. (2013). Commodities and Development Report 2012: Perennial Problems, New Challenges and Evolving Perspectives. United Nations Conference on Trade and Development. New York and Geneva.

UNCTAD (2019). Economic development in Africa report 2019: Made in Africa–rules of origin for enhanced intra-African trade. United Nations Conference on Trade and Development, United Nations. New York and Geneva. 2019.

UNECA (2015). *Economic Report on Africa 2015: Industrializing Through Trade*. United Nations Economic commission for Africa. Addis Ababa.

UNECA (2017). *Urbanisation and Industrialization for Africa's Transformation*. Economic Report on Africa. United Nations Economic Commission for Africa. Addis Ababa.

UNECA (2018). Drivers for boosting intra-African investment flows towards Africa's transformation. Addis Ababa. Addis Ababa: UNECA

UNECA (2020). COVID-19 in Africa: protecting lives and economies. Addis Ababa. United Nations Economic Commission for Africa https://hdl.handle.net/10855/43756

UNECA (United Nations Economic Commission for Africa), AU (African Union) and AfDB (African Development Bank). 2010. *Assessing Regional Integration in Africa IV: Enhancing Intra-African Trade*. Addis Ababa.

UNECA (United Nations Economic Commission for Africa), AU (African Union) and AfDB (African Development Bank). 2019. Africa regional integration index report 2019. Addis Ababa and Abidjan.

Viner, J. 1950. *The customs union issue*. New York: Carnegie Endowment for International Peace; London: Stevens & Sons.

World Bank (2020). The African Continental Free Trade Area: Economic and Distributional Effects. Washington, DC: World Bank. https://openknowledge.worldbank.org/handle/10986/34139

11 Upgrading skills for Africa's economic transformation[1]

Vincent Belinga and Kolobadia Ada Nayihouba

11.1 Introduction

The AfCFTA aims to create a single market, deepen the economic integration of the continent, enhance the competitiveness of member states within Africa and in the global market, and achieve sustainable and inclusive socio-economic development, gender equality, and structural transformations of its member states.

Several studies have simulated the potential benefits of the AfCFTA. For instance, a recent report from the World Bank (2020a) shows that the AfCFTA if implemented will boost growth in the continent, reduce poverty, and broaden economic inclusion. Especially, by 2035, the AfCFTA would increase Africa exports by US$ 560 billion mostly in manufacturing. This corresponds to an increase in real exports of 29% relative to business as usual while intracontinental exports would increase by 81%. In addition, the AfCFTA would boost Africa's income by US$ 450 billion by 2035 (a gain of 7%), lift 30 million people out of extreme poverty and 68 million out of moderate poverty (see Chapters 3 and 4 for more developments and references on the potential social and economic impact of the AfCFTA).

To achieve its economic objectives, especially boosting its manufacturing exports, participation of African firms at medium and higher levels of global value chains (GVCs) either at the global level or at the continental/regional level will be critical. A feature of today's international trade which rapidly became important since the 1990s is GVCs in which the production process is split into many stages of production located in different countries (within the same continent or across continents) that contribute efficiently to the final product. Information and communication technology (ICT), trade liberalization and lower transport costs have enabled firms and countries to fragment the production process into GVCs.

GVCs are powerful drivers of productivity, job creation and poverty reduction. According to the World Bank World Development Report (WDR, 2020), firms participating in GVCs in Ethiopia, for instance, are more than twice as productive as similar firms that participate in standard trade. More generally, a 1% increase in GVC participation is estimated to boost income per capita by more than 1%, or much more than the 0.2% income gain from standard trade (WDR, 2020). This

DOI: 10.4324/9781003456568-11

productivity gain is typically higher when countries transition out of exporting commodities into exporting basic manufactured products using imported inputs as has happened in countries like Bangladesh, Cambodia, and Vietnam (WDR, 2020). GVCs are also determinants of economic transformation in developing countries as they draw people out of less productive activities into more productive manufacturing and services activities. As GVCs uplift income and employment growth, participation in GVCs also reduces poverty. However, most countries in Africa still produce primarily commodities (Figure 11.1) for further processing in other countries, and a limited number of countries in Africa are engaged in the production of limited manufacturing with medium backward GVC.[2]

Several factors determine country participation in high backward GVC. The transition from limited manufacturing to more advanced manufacturing and services, and to innovative activities depends on factors such as skills or quality of human capital broadly speaking, connectivity, regulatory institutions among others. Skills are singularly relevant as higher value-added positions in GVCs require both high-level technical skills and adaptability as changing technologies rapidly reshape the kinds of skills needed (WDR, 2020).

Trade between African countries still suffers from several barriers including high protection rates, and infrastructure gaps among others. According to estimates from the United Nations Conference on Trade and Development (UNCTAD, 2015),

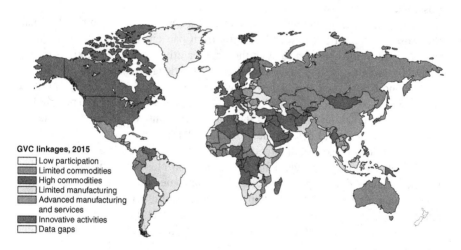

GVC linkages, 2015
- Low participation
- Limited commodities
- High commodities
- Limited manufacturing
- Advanced manufacturing and services
- Innovative activities
- Data gaps

Figure 11.1 Countries' participation in GVCs.

Note: The type of a country's GVC linkages is based on the country's extent of backward GVC participation, measured as the portion of imports embodied in manufacturing exports as a percentage of a country's total exports, combined with the country's sector specialization of domestic value added in exports and engagement in innovation.

Source: World Development Report 2020: Trading for Development in the Age of Global Value Chains. Washington, DC: World Bank.

an African firm exporting to markets outside the continent faces an average protection rate of 2.5%, while exporting the same good to an African market would face an average applied protection rate of 8.7%. Moreover, export costs to end market in Europe or in the US are very high in Africa: exporting a 20-feet container costs US$ 500 in China whereas it costs US$ 577 in Morocco, US$ 737 in Mauritius and US$ 2055 in Kenya (AfDB/OECD/UNDP, 2014). One of the key objectives of the AfCFTA is to progressively eliminate existing tariffs and non-tariffs barriers (NTBs) and refrain from introducing new ones to enhance and facilitate intra-Africa trade and create a continent-wide market. This is a major opportunity for Africa, especially for African firms to gradually integrate and deepen participation in high backward GVC within the continent where they produce and trade advanced manufacturing products and services. Skills will play an important role in such a transformation.

This chapter discusses skills needed for African economies' transformation using as an organizing framework the participation in high backward GVC with a focus on skills needed for high backward GVC integration in agribusiness, manufacturing and for two key service sectors critical for GVC integration, the digital economy and logistics. For each area, the chapter discusses its relevance for high-end GVC integration, skills requirements to integrate the GVC and the current skills supply and gaps. For the latter, the analysis builds on existing studies and existing data when available, with a greater focus on technical skills and touches upon foundational cognitive and behavioral skills whenever possible.

First, the chapter documents, based on existing analysis, that countries that make the most of economic and social benefits from participating in GVCs are those that invest in skills consistently with their comparative advantages. Skills enhance productivity gains as they make it easier for knowledge transfer and adoption of new technologies. Then, the analysis shows important gaps in the supply of critical technical and advanced skills (including STEM and ICT-related skills) required for backward participation in GVCs in the four areas of interest in several countries, with a certain degree of heterogeneity in the skills supply across countries. Going forward, African leaders both at country and at the AU levels should take a series of interrelated policy interventions to upgrade and close the existing skills gap. Policies should aim to improve access and outcomes of education and training systems, harmonize education systems, ensure recognition of academic credentials, and ease skilled workforce mobility across the continent through the implementation of the African passport and putting in place incentives to attract the skilled African diaspora.

The rest of Chapter 11 is organized as follows: Section 11.2 provides some stylized facts on the relationship between skills and GVCs participation; Sections 11.3, 11.4, 11.5, and 11.6 put forward the analysis in the four areas, namely agribusiness, manufacturing, digital economy, and logistics; Section 11.7 discusses some policy priorities; and Section 11.8 concludes. The use of backward GVC for the rest of the chapter mostly refers to GVC (C/GVC) within Africa.

11.2 Skills and participation in global value chains

Knowledge and skills that people accumulate over their lives enable them to realize their potential as productive members of society. Skills can help countries to get the most out of GVCs through various channels: they are essential to reap the productivity gains offered by participation in GVCs and ensure these gains transfer to a broad range of firms, including small ones, and thereby benefit the whole economy; they can protect workers against the potential negative impacts of GVCs in terms of job losses and lower job quality; skills are pivotal for countries to specialize in the most technologically advanced manufacturing industries and in complex business services that are expected to lead to innovation, higher productivity and job creation OECD (2017). Investigating the extent to which countries have been able to reap the benefits from GVC through the skills of their population in OECD countries along those channels, the report finds that skills have affected the global integration of countries differently with nevertheless a pattern of greater participation in GVC associated with skills improvement.

These findings are summarized in a scoreboard in Table 11.1. Between 2000 and 2015, countries like Korea and Poland, from different starting points, had increased their integration in GVC and specialization in technologically advanced industries, while improving the skills of their populations and achieving economic and social gains, thereby grasping the benefits of GVCs. Chile and Turkey meanwhile had substantially increased their participation in GVCs, developed the skills necessary to face GVC challenges, and boosted employment. But their skills were weakly aligned with the requirements of technologically advanced industries, partially explaining their low specialization in these industries. Germany and the USA had also sharply increased their participation in GVCs. Nonetheless, German population skills had supported the country's industry specialization pattern while this was less the case for the USA. Other countries, such as Greece and to some degree Belgium, were weakly integrated into GVCs, had not improved the skills of their populations much, and had not reaped the benefits of GVCs as a source of economic growth.

Several other studies analyzing the determinants of cross countries participation in the GVCs, including Ignatenko (2019) and Fernandes (2020), found that human capital along with other factors such as institution quality plays an important role in determining GVC participation. Notably, human capital endowment as well as skills distribution are determinants for a country's participation in the GVCs. A large part of the low-skilled labor force is competitive for labor-intensive sectors of the GVCs whereas a high share of skilled labor share facilitates the participation into the more sophisticated stages of the GVCs. Countries with well-developed levels of human capital are involved in activities with the highest values added (OECD, 2013). Yameogo and Jammeh (2019) estimated a fixed effect gravity model on 23 Sub-Saharan Africa countries to investigate the determinants of their participation in the GVCs. Their results show that Sub-Saharan Africa countries' GVC participation is strongly determined by skilled labor.

Table 11.1 Scoreboard on skills and global value chains

	Skills			Development of GVCs			Economic and Social Outcomes		
	A limited share of low-skilled people	Developing skills to face the challenges of GVCs	Skills to specialise in tech. advanced industries	Increasing participation in GVCs	Specialised in tech. advanced industries	Increasing specialisation in tech. advanced industries	Increasing productivity	Increasing employment	Improving social outcomes
Australia									
Austria									
Belgium									
Canada									
Chile									
Czech Republic									
Denmark									
Estonia									
Finland									
France									
Germany									
Greece									
Hungary									
Iceland									
Ireland									
Israel									
Italy									
Japan									
Korea									
Luxembourg									
Mexico									
Netherlands									
New Zealand									
Norway									
Poland									
Portugal									
Slovak Rep.									
Slovenia									
Spain									
Sweden									
Switzerland									
Turkey									
United Kingdom									
United States									

■ Top 25%   □ Around average   ■ Bottom 25%   □ Missing data

Note: the scoreboard puts together three blocks of information on countries' skills, participation in GVCs, and economic and social outcomes. It shows for each sub-category countries that perform in the top 25%, bottom 25%, and those around the OECD average. For instance, Finland is among the OECD countries that have the lowest share of low-skilled people, have not developed skills much to face the challenges of GVCs but have the skills to specialize in technologically advanced industries, and have not increased much their specialization in technologically advanced industries. It performs around the average for the other sub-categories.

Source: OECD Skills Outlook 2017: Skills and Global Value Chains, OECD Publishing, Paris.

Also, an analysis in Costa Rica and the Dominican Republic found that the different development paths of both countries over recent decades were primarily explained by the large differences in the investments each country made in human capital (WDR, 2020). Costa Rica's success in diversifying away from apparel to high-technology exports was supported by public social spending that averaged close to 20% of GDP in the 1980s and 1990s, therefore strengthening human capital. In the Dominican Republic, which battled to move away from low value-added apparel exports, public social spending during this time averaged just 5% of GDP, the lowest in Latin America countries.

Human capital accumulation through skills development happens over the life cycle. Workers need reliable qualifications and a strong mix of relevant skills. From early childhood to adult learning, education and training systems need to equip all learners with strong mixes of skills. This includes a mix of foundational cognitive skills (numeracy, literacy, problem-solving) and behavioral skills (interacting and communicating, self-organization, flexibility on the job, etc.), and technical skills (skills specialization) that provide workers the abilities and knowledge needed to perform specific tasks. While having a full landscape of existing skills is relevant to participating and making the most of GVCs, the discussion over the next sections will mostly focus on technical skills in the four identified areas—agribusiness, manufacturing, digital and logistics.

11.3 Skills for integration in the agribusiness value chains

11.3.1 Rationale: Why agribusiness GVC for the continent?

Africa is the continent with the fastest-growing population and this population growth is projected to continue to outpace that of the world for several decades (Figure 11.2). Africa's share of the world population is projected to increase from 17% in 2020 to about 40% in 2100. Half of this population will be aged 25–64. These projections suggest an expected growing demand for food products so the continent can feed its population.

Africa exports about US$ 35–45 billion of food products and imports about US$ 45–50 billion yearly where a high share of these imports is concentrated in a few countries. In Sub-Sahara Africa (SSA), only a few countries are responsible for the SSA trade food deficit. As pointed out by Louise Fox and Thomas S. Jayne,[3] oil and mineral exporters countries and FCV states are countries responsible for the trade deficit in food in SSA. While imports of food products in SSA have continued to rise in the last decades, exports of food products outside the SSA region also kept rising thanks to its higher rate of agricultural production growth than any other region of the world since 2000. Countries like Cote d'Ivoire, Ghana, and Kenya became agricultural export powerhouses, with a net agricultural trade surplus of more than US$ 5 billion per year. The share of African countries' food imports stemming from other countries in the continent is however very low, averaging about 20%. These developments suggest that Africa has the potential to feed its population by increasing its intra-trade of manufactured food products and to export to the rest of the world. The AfCFTA therefore offers such an opportunity through greater participation in high-end agribusiness value chains at regional or continental, levels (the rationale of agribusiness GVC is consistent with the first D, reaping the demographic premium, of the 3Ds framework—see Chapter 2 of this book for more developments on *Trade Patterns* and the demographic dividend).

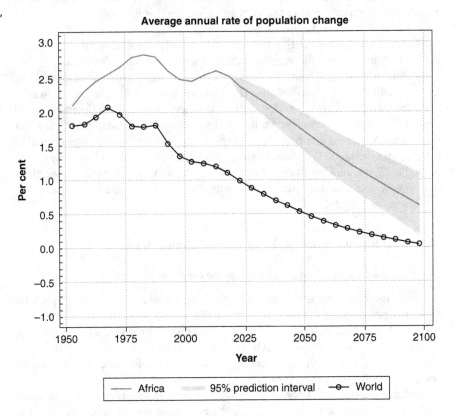

Figure 11.2 Trends and projections of Africa and world population growths.

Source: United Nations, Department of Economic and Social Affairs, Population Division. World Population Prospects 2019, Volume II: Demographic Profiles.

11.3.1.1 Skills requirements in the agribusiness value chains

The agribusiness value chains include upstream pre-production activities to down-stream post-production (Figure 11.3). The pre-production and production stages include research and development (R&D) aimed at improving the quality of seeds, appropriate techniques to increase productivity; provision of inputs; cultivating and harvesting. The post-production stage includes packing, processing, distribution, and marketing.

Each stage of the value chain requires a set of skills and capabilities acquired from formal education training (general or technical) but also from experience and practical training (see Table 11.2 as an illustration).[4] Agronomists involved in R&D require a high level of skills with a postgraduate degree, practical training and experience. The same institutional support which includes regulators and

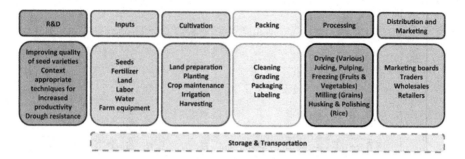

Figure 11.3 Simplified Agribusiness Global Value Chain.

Source: Bamber P. et al. (2014).

environmental specialists requires a high skill level with a minimum of a bachelor's degree. The other positions at each stage of the value chain require skills from medium-high level to low level with no formal education but with experience.

11.3.2 Current skills supply and gaps[5]

While agriculture contributes about 17% of the continent's GDP as of 2017, it still employs more than half of the workforce (51.1% in 2017) with wide disparities across the continent. Some countries like the Seychelles employ only about 4% of their workers in agriculture while other countries like Mali employ up to 63%. Labor productivity, measured by agriculture value added per worker is also widespread across the continent (Figure 11.4, left panel). But several countries are lagging in productivity compared to those at the top. While several factors like innovation, transfer of technology, physical capital, and arable land determine labor productivity, skills and human capital involved in the production process also determine the level of productivity. Skills development is crucial for agricultural transformation.

To have a transfer of technology that is effective, individuals need skills and competencies to effectively use the newly acquired technology. There is an inverse relationship between the share of employment in agriculture and productivity (Figure 11.4, right panel). Countries with a lower share of employment in agriculture tend to be more productive. On the contrary, countries with a higher share of employment have lower productivity. These countries' employment in agriculture is mostly concentrated in the production stage where the value added is very low and skills requirements are mostly manual. For instance, in Uganda, Burundi and Rwanda, most of the jobs in agriculture are concentrated in production roles or in the farm sector, and the development of the post-harvest segments of the value chain remains a priority and accounts for a relatively small proportion of employment in the agribusiness chain as well as the R&D stage of the chain (Bamber et al., 2014).

Table 11.2 Jobs and skills profiles for Agribusiness Value Chain

Position	Formal Education Requirements	Training/ Experience	Skill Level
R&D/Inputs			
Agronomists	Postgraduate degree	Experience and practical training	●
Extension Agents	Bachelor's degree in agronomy	Experience & Practical Training	●
Irrigation Technician	Technical education / Bachelor's degree	Training and Experience	◕
Soil Erosion Control Technician	Technical education/ Bachelor's degree	Experience/ technical training/ certification	◕
Nursery & Seed Multiplication Staff	May require high school diploma	Theoretical & Practical Training	◐
Transporter	Literacy and numeric skills	Experience	○
Producer	No formal education required but literacy and numeracy skills will help	Training and experience	○
Cereals/Root Crops Processing			
Operations Manager	Bachelor's degree	Training and experience	◕
Mobile Unit Operator (Root Processing)	Technical education	Training and experience	◕
Marketing/ Distributors (Root & Wheat Milling)	Technical education/ Certification	Marketing skills/ experience	◐
Warehouse Manager	Certified technical education	Technical training/ experience	◐
Collectors/ Aggregators	Literacy and numeracy skills	Training and experience	◕
Transporter	Literacy and numeracy skills	Training and experience	◐

(Continued)

Cold Storage, Packing and Processing Fruits and Vegetables

Cold Storage

Storage Unit Manager	Technical education /undergraduate degree	Training and experience
Operator/Technician	Literacy and numeracy skills	Training and experience
Packing		
Packer	Literacy and numeracy skills preferable	Training and experience
Processing		
Business Manager	Bachelor's degree	Training and experience
Quality Control Technician	Technical education/ Certification	Technical training/ experience
Aggregator/ Buying Agent	Literacy and numeracy skills	Technical training/ experience
Warehouse Manager	Technical education/ Certification	Technical training/ experience
Mechanics/ Machine Operator	Technical education	Technical training
Packer	Literacy and numeracy skills preferable	Training and experience
Distributor	Literacy and numeracy skills	Technical training/ experience
Line Worker	No formal education required	Training

Table 11.2 (Continued)

Position	Formal Education Requirements	Training/Experience	Skill Level
Institutional Support			
Regulator	Bachelor's degree or higher	Training and experience	●
Environmental Specialist	Bachelor's degree or higher	Training and experience	●
Sanitary and Phytosanitary@@@@ (SPS) Certifier	Bachelor's degree or higher	Training and experience	◑

Skill Level	**Low**	**Low-Medium**	**Medium**	**Medium-High**	**High**
	●	◕	◐	◔	◔
	No formal education; experience	Literacy and numeracy skills; experience	Technical education/ certific ation	Technical education / undergraduate degree	University degree and higher
	No Schooling or Incomplete Primary	**Basic Education**	**Secondary Level**	**Tertiary**	**Tertiary**

Source: Bamber et al. (2014).

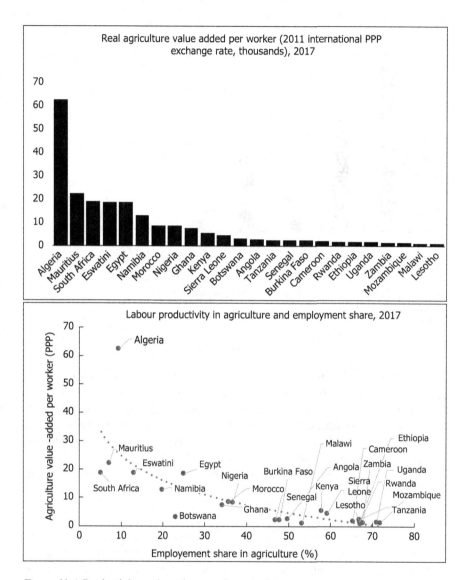

Figure 11.4 Productivity and employment in agriculture sector.

Source: World Bank (2020b), *Global Productivity: Trends, Drivers, and Policies*, database www.worldbank.org/en/research/publication/global-productivity

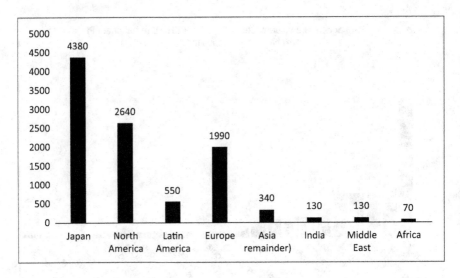

Figure 11.5 Agriculture researchers per million population, 2013.

Source: African Capacity Building Foundation (2016).

Several countries in the continent need to upgrade medium and high skills for the agriculture to be transformative and to meet expected skills demand to integrate the high end of agri-food value chains. In 2013, the continent was estimated to have only about 2.32 veterinaries per million population against an international norm of about 300 veterinaries and 70 agricultural researchers per million population against 130 for India or about 4,500 for Japan (Figure 11.5).

This small number of researchers and veterinaries reflects a lower rate of students enrolled and graduates from the agriculture field. In 2014 for instance, only 6.2 students per 100,000 population graduated in agriculture for an average of 18 countries in Africa, about less than half of graduates in the European Union (EU) for instance. Meanwhile, 33 students per 100,000 were enrolled against 75 in the EU. However, while some countries are substantially lagging behind the continent's average on those two indicators, other countries especially in the eastern and northern parts of the continent are closer to the EU average or are largely above the continent's average (Figure 11.6). Many countries in the continent therefore need an upgrading and development of new skills to integrate into the downstream stage of the agri-food value chains.

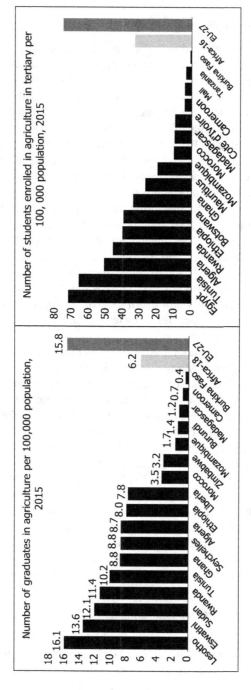

Figure 11.6 Number of graduates and enrollments per population in tertiary education in agriculture field.

Source: World Economic Forum: Human capital report (2015), Eurostat, authors' calculation.

11.4 Skills for the manufacturing value chains

11.4.1 Rationale: why manufacturing GVCs?

Industrialization has been a key driver of structural economic transformation, jobs creation and poverty reduction in many regions of the world. During the recent decades, a strong and dynamic manufacturing sector contributed to the strong economic growth episodes experienced by China and other southeast Asian economies. According to data from the Economic Transformation Database (EDT), the share of value added of the manufacturing sector in Africa declined from 13.2% to 11.6% between 1990 and 2018 whereas it increased from 16.3% to 17.6% on average in the other developing countries. During the same period, the share of employment in the sector increased from 8.4% to 9.1% in Africa and from 11.8% to 12.8% in the other developing countries.

The contribution of the manufacturing sector in terms of value added and employment is even lower in SSA countries with respectively 10.9% and 8.4% in 2018. At the country level, the manufacturing sector contributes more to the total value added in Senegal (19.7%), Lesotho (18.7%), Morocco (17.8%), Egypt (15.9%) and Cameroon (15.7%) and to employment in Mauritius (15.9%), Ghana (15.8%), Tunisia (15.7%), Kenya (14.3%). There is scope to improve the GDP contribution of the manufacturing sector in Africa given the opportunities offered on the continent such as a large stock of raw materials, low labor cost, and increasing demand for manufactured goods.

The AfCFTA aims at promoting African economic and social development through economic integration. Removing tariffs and non-tariffs barriers to allow the free movement of goods and services across the continent represents a tremendous opportunity for the African manufacturing sector to generate continental or regional value chains and to improve countries' participation in global value chains. Despite a low share of intra-continental trade in comparison to other regions, African countries trade between them more diversified and sophisticated products than those exchanged with the rest of the world (41.9% compared to 14.8% in 2014 according to the UNECA, 2018). The full implementation of the AfCFTA is expected to boost intra-African trade by 15% to 25% (UNECA, 2018) by 2040, to double the size of the African manufacturing sector between 2015 and 2025 and create an additional 14 million stable well-paid jobs (Signé, 2018) (the rationale of manufacturing GVCs is well aligned with the second "D", Diversification, of the 3Ds organizing framework—see also Chapters 9 and 11 with more developments on the opportunity offered by the AfCFTA for Africa's industrialization).

11.4.2 Skills requirements in the manufacturing GVCs

A common feature of developing countries is a higher concentration of their firms being at the low level of the manufacturing GVCs. Upgrading in the more value-added segments requires more advanced and specialized professional skills, as illustrated in Figure 11.7. Whereas the lower levels of the value chain concentrate

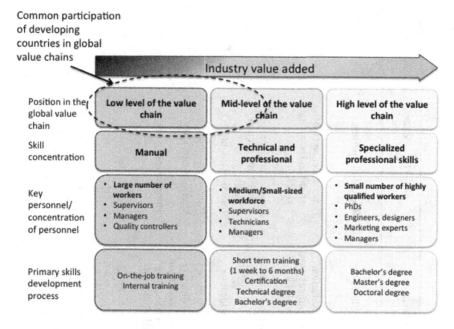

Figure 11.7 Global values chains and skills in industry.

Source: Fernandez-Stark at al. (2012).

on manual skills, the medium levels require technical and professional skills such as supervisors, technicians, and managers. The higher levels of the value chain require more specialized professional skills such as PhDs, engineers, designers, marketing experts, and managers.

In a study on the skills needed for upgrading in the global value chains in developing countries, Gereffi et al. (2011) provides the job profiles in different segments of the apparel value chains. Apparel manufacturing represents an important and growing share of exports in sub-Saharan countries such as Ethiopia, Lesotho, and Kenya. It also provides a good illustration of the participation in the manufacturing value chains of African countries with low value-added segments, such as assembly or production-related segments, and recruiting low-skilled workers including young, female workers with limited education. As illustrated in Table 11.3, the higher value segments in the value chains require more experience, a higher formal education (high school, bachelor, master), as well as more specific skills including management, marketing, finance, and clothing design.

According to the OECD (2017) report, four levels of GVCs can be classified in manufacturing: (i) low-tech manufacturing, which includes among other industries, processing of food products and therefore a continuum (or an extension) of the agribusiness GVCs, apparels, wood and products of wood; (ii) medium/low-tech

Table 11.3 Jobs and skills profile in the Apparel Global Value Chain

Position	Job Description	Formal Education Requirements	Training/Experience	Skill Level
CMT/Assembly/Production				
Hand Sewers	Sew, join, reinforce, or finish usually with needle and thread–a variety of manufactured items. Includes weavers and stitchers.	No formal education required	Required Experience	◑
Sewing Machine Operators	Operate sewing machines to join, reinforce, decorate, or perform related sewing operations in the manufacture of garment or nongarment products.	No formal education required, literacy and numeracy skills	Experience: Need of speed and accuracy skills	◑
Garment Pressers	Clothing pressers use steam irons and vacuum presses to shape garments and remove creases.	No formal education required	Experience: Need of speed and accuracy skills	◑
Cutting Machine Operators	In automated facilities, cutters electronically send the layout to a computer-controlled cutting machine.	Technical education	Technical training	◑
Line Leaders	Supervisory roles, ensure work flows expeditiously along the line.	High school diploma/technical education	Management skills	◕
Production Flow Supervisors	Supervisory roles; oversee the pace of the work and ensure stoppages are minimized, monitor production levels, train new workers, and manage constant problem solving.	Technical education/Bachelor's degree	Management skills	●
OEM/Full Package				
Quality Control	Maintain final quality prior to distribution of product, monitored by buyers	High school diploma/technical education	Knowledge of quality systems	◑
Sourcing, Purchasing, and Supply Chain Management	Capabilities related to OEM production: Workers must have financial skills related to purchasing inputs and coordinating production schedules	Technical education/Bachelor's degree in finance/management	Industry experience	◕

Category	Role / Skill	Description	Education / Qualification	Additional
ODM	Fabric and Apparel Patternmakers	Create the blueprint or pattern pieces for a particular apparel design. This often involves grading, or adjusting the pieces for different sized garments	Technical education in apparel	Experience
	Tailors. Dressmakers. Custom Sewers	Design, make, alter, repair, or fit garments.	Technical education in apparel	Experience
	Designers	Workers must have training in the "aesthetics" of product development, some market and consumer knowledge, and technical skills required to translate ideas into samples	Technical education/ Bachelor's degree in clothing design	Experience
	Senior Designers	Creative talent within the industry that can develop new design lines for production.	Bachelors/Master's degree in clothing design	Experience
OBM	General Business Skills	Responsible for financial management supply chain optimization, quality control and/or strategy, and new business development.	Bachelor's/Master's degree in business/engineering	Experience
	Branding and Marketing Capabilities	Responsible for market research, marketing/advertising, networking, and positioning brands in the market	Bachelor's/Master's degree in business	Marketing specialization and experience

Skill Level	Low	Low-Medium	Medium	Medium—High	High
	No formal education, experience	Literacy and numeracy skills, experience	Technical education/ certification	Technical education / undergraduate degree	University degree and higher

Source: Gereffi et al. (2011).

manufacturing comprising among other industries, refined petroleum, rubber and plastic products, basic metals and fabricated metal products; (iii) medium/high-tech manufacturing consisting of industries producing machinery and equipment, electrical machinery, motor vehicle and trailer/semi-trailers, and (iv) high-tech manufacturing, which includes industries producing chemical and chemical products, computer, electronic and optical products, and other transport equipment. While low-tech and medium/low-tech manufacturing require low to medium skill levels acquired from training, especially from Technical and Vocational Education and Training (TVET) and from experience, medium/high-tech and high-tech manufacturing require more advanced skills from tertiary education in STEM fields.

11.4.3 Current skills supply and gaps

Human capital is a major determinant of a country's participation in manufacturing global value chains. According to the 2016 survey from the Global Manufacturing Competitiveness Index, human capital (talent and productivity) is the first driver of growth and investment in manufacturing followed by other drivers such as cost, suppliers, networks, and domestic demand. However, one of the constraints for investment decisions in manufacturing in Africa is the limited availability of a skilled labor force (ACET, 2014). For instance, the African Capacity Building Foundation (2016) report estimated that in 2015 countries like Kenya, Tanzania, Malawi, and Rwanda had 154.4, 50, 17.3, and 14 engineers per million population respectively against 3,750 for Brazil. The same report estimated that the number of researchers in STEM-related areas in the continent was 79 per million population against an international norm of 1,081 per million population. The report pointed out that while in SSA research in the physical sciences and STEM makes up only 29% of all research output, STEM makes up the largest share of Malaysia's and Vietnam's total research output, with an average of 68%.

The extent of the deficit in manufacturing skills on the continent is further illustrated in Figure 11.8, which displays the number of graduates and the number of students enrolled in engineering, manufacturing, and construction. In 2015, there were seven times fewer graduates per 100,000 inhabitants (20.6 against 145.6) and more than five times the students enrolled (109.1 against 600.9) in this field on average in 18 countries in Africa than in the EU-27 countries. However, if the values of these two indicators are higher than these continental averages in some countries, especially in Northern African countries, they are extremely low in some other countries.

11.5 Skills for the digital economy[6]

11.5.1 Rationale: why digital economy matters for GVCs?

Fueled by disruptive technologies that are transforming markets, the digital economy and the new industrial revolution (Industry 4.0) are fundamentally changing the way firms operate internationally. Advances in technology and associated

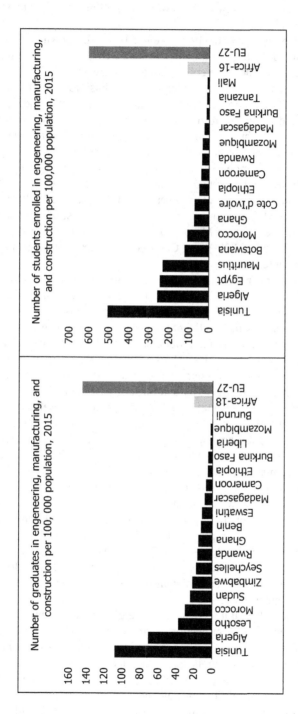

Figure 11.8 Number of graduates and enrollments per population in tertiary education in engineering, manufacturing, and construction field.

Source: World Economic Forum: Human capital report (2015), Eurostat, authors' calculation.

services have created opportunities for a wide range of new services in a variety of GVCs (Bamber et al., 2018).

The outbreak of the COVID-19 pandemic has also shown the tremendous opportunities offered by digitalization to facilitate work, business, and public governance. Across the continent, several digital tools were used to mitigate the health and socio-economic impact of the pandemic, ensure business activity, and provide public services. Mobile money transfers, remote learning, online trade, and drones delivering food and medicines to remote areas are examples of the application of digital technologies in finance, education, trade, and health. The increasing digitalization in the continent is driven by the fast-growing access to connectivity. Indeed, between 2000 and 2016, mobile cellular subscriptions increased 32-fold in Africa (from 2.6% to 83%) far larger than the 6-fold increase in the rest of the world (20.7% to 115.9%). Moreover, internet penetration increased 27-fold (from 0.8% to 21.5%) in Africa whereas it increased by 5-fold in the rest of the world (11.7% to 62.1%). In countries such as Morocco (58.3%), the Seychelles (56.5%), South Africa (54%), Mauritius (52.2%), and Cabo Verde (50.3%), more than half of the population use the internet.

Digitalization offers opportunities to address important challenges to successful implementation of the AfCFTA. In the agriculture sector, digital technologies are easing access to market information, crop monitoring, disease prevention, and disaster mitigation across the continent. Hence, companies such as Ghana-based Farmerline and Agrocenta provide mobile services for agricultural advice, weather information, and financial tips. The Nigerian startup Zenvus helps farmers select the correct fertilizer and optimally irrigate their farms by analyzing soil data. Through improvement in productivity and further access to local, continental, and global value chains, digital technologies have the potential to help Africa tap into its agricultural potential.

Digitalization is also fast advancing in the African financial sector, driven by the expansion of mobile money transactions. Africa is the leading region for mobile money services as money transactions average at close to 25% of GDP in Africa against 5% in the rest of the world (IMF, 2020). Moreover, African cities such as Johannesburg and Cape Town in South Africa, Nairobi in Kenya, and Lagos in Nigeria rank among the top 100 cities for fintech ecosystems worldwide. Across the continent, fintech services provide large financial services to people usually excluded from the financial system including youth, women, and informal workers. By solving the information asymmetry problem in financial systems, digitalization is a powerful tool to improve financial inclusion and access to credit for local small and medium-sized enterprises.

Governments are also taking advantage of digitalization to improve access to public services. Hence, social protection programs such as Novissi in Togo rely on the expansion of mobile money services to provide cash transfers to the poorest and most vulnerable populations. Mobile money services are also used in an increasing number of countries for tax payments (Mobile Tax platform in Benin, eSINTAX in Burkina for example), utility bill payments and registration fees for universities. Examples of digitalization in access to public services include university applications (CampusFaso in Burkina Faso), the ePassport agency in Cote d'Ivoire, the eCitizen portal in Kenya, the eVisa platform in Benin, etc. These digital technologies offer opportunities to efficiently fight corruption and improve trust in public officials.

To accelerate digital transformation and materialize the strategic vision of many African leaders in this domain, the AU Commission developed a comprehensive Digital Transformation Strategy for Africa in collaboration with its strategic partners including the World Bank. The AfCFTA presents an immense opportunity for the materialization of this strategy.

11.5.2 Skills requirements for digital technology

Digital skills are needed not only for Information Technology (IT) but for all sectors of the economy. The digital economy and the adoption of new technologies are changing manufacturing industries. The digital economy includes the software and services that make up the IT global value chain and the increasing incorporation of these activities in industry-specific GVCs (or digital transformation) (Bamber et al., 2018). The increasing digitalization of economic sectors is already reshaping skills demand in Africa. According to a survey from IFC & LEK (2019), about half of jobs require some digital skills in Sub-Saharan Africa. According to data from LinkedIn, digital jobs such as IT workers, software and app developers, 3D designers, data center workers, and care are among the trending professions on the continent.

The digital economy is composed of three primary segments: software; IT services; and internet software and services (ISS) platforms, supported by telecommunications and internet service providers that provide the infrastructure that enables digital firms to operate (Bamber et al., 2018). Table 11.4 provides a summary of the three segments of the digital economy along with the type of services for each segment and the required workforce.

Digital skills range from basic skills such as the simple use of computers and smartphones, and web research to more advanced skills such as computer programming, cloud computing, data sciences, Artificial Intelligence, etc. (Figure 11.9). Building inclusive digital skills and competences, both technical and vocational, to steer digital transformation will be critical to harnessing the opportunities offered by the AfCFTA.

11.5.3 Current skills supply and gaps

It is estimated that 230 million digital jobs will be created in Sub-Saharan Africa by 2030 (IFC & LEK, 2019). Benefiting from these employment opportunities requires the demanded digital skills to be available. However, the report finds that there is a significant gap in supply across all levels of digital skills in the region, with lower availability of skills than in other markets and significant gaps in the supply of intermediate and advanced skills.

Using self-reported information from LinkedIn users to assess digital skills in SSA, the World Bank (2020c) report found that Sub-Saharan African workers

Table 11.4 Digital economy segments and associated workforce

Segment	Type of services	Workforce
Software	Application (including software as a service (SaaS)) Operating	Software App Developers, Computer User Support Specialists
IT Services	IT consulting, Business process services, Data analysis (software users)	Programmers, Computer Systems Analysts, Data Analysts
Internet Software & Services (ISS) Platforms	Search engines, Social networks, Cloud (infrastructure as a service (IaaS), platform as a service (PaaS)), E-commerce	Software Developers; Architects, Programmers, Customer, Service Representatives. Sales Representatives
Infrastructure services (Telecom, Internet Service Providers)	Internet service (home & wireless), mobile	

Source: Bamber P. et al., 2018.

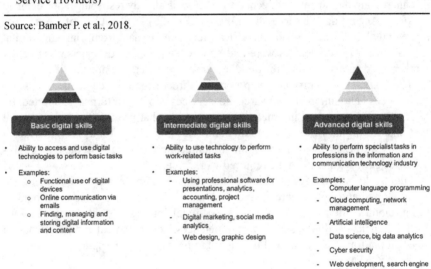

Basic digital skills

- Ability to access and use digital technologies to perform basic tasks
- Examples:
  - Functional use of digital devices
  - Online communication via emails
  - Finding, managing and storing digital information and content

Intermediate digital skills

- Ability to use technology to perform work-related tasks
- Examples:
  - Using professional software for presentations, analytics, accounting, project management
  - Digital marketing, social media analytics
  - Web design, graphic design

Advanced digital skills

- Ability to perform specialist tasks in professions in the information and communication technology industry
- Examples:
  - Computer language programming
  - Cloud computing, network management
  - Artificial intelligence
  - Data science, big data analytics
  - Cyber security
  - Web development, search engine optimization

Figure 11.9 A panorama of digital skills.

Source: International Finance Corporation & LEK Consulting (2019).

have a lower level of digital skills than workers in other regions, even among the small portion of the labor force that uses LinkedIn, which constitutes, on average, 4% of the labor force among the 27 Sub-Saharan African countries for which LinkedIn data are available (Figure 11.10-A). African countries are also heterogenous in terms of the availability of different types of digital skills. Apart from

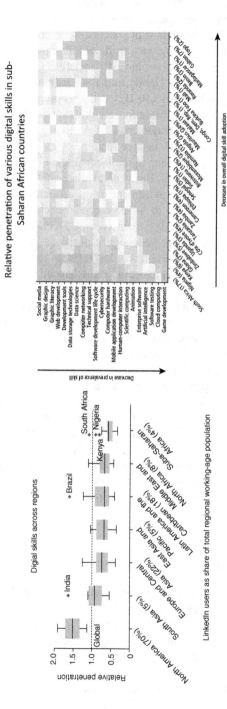

Figure 11.10 Digital skills prevalence among Sub-Saharan African workers using LinkedIn.

Note: Parentheses show the share of LinkedIn users in the total working-age population of each country. Relative penetration scaled by row for comparison across countries. The different shades of green and the white correspond to the degree of relative penetration. The darker the color, the higher the relative penetration of that specific skill in that country compared with others. Gray boxes indicate a relative skill penetration of zero.

Source: Digital skills across regions relative penetration of various digital skills in Sub-Saharan African countries The World Bank (2020c).

Mauritius (24%), South Africa (17%), Botswana (14%), and Namibia (12%), the share of the labor force using the LinkedIn platform is less than 10% among the 27 countries. South Africa has the highest prevalence in several digital skills such as game development, software testing, and artificial intelligence. Countries such as Nigeria, Kenya, Ghana, and Zimbabwe have also relatively higher digital skills adoption whereas Benin, Madagascar, Gabon, and Togo are at the bottom of digital skills prevalence distribution (Figure 11.10-B). As the report acknowledges, these results, while providing valuable information on the supply of digital skills in Africa, represent a small and non-random part of African workers: those using LinkedIn and working in technology-intensive sectors.

The extent of digital skills prevalence in the labor market in some countries in Africa can be driven by several factors. Based on available data, we looked at two indicators. The first indicator is the investment in infrastructure for pedagogical purposes, captured by the proportion of lower secondary schools with access to the internet for pedagogical purposes. While on average 57.1% of lower secondary schools have access to the internet for pedagogical purposes in developing countries and 98% in the EU-27, this proportion is only 41.2% for the sample average of African countries (Figure 11.11-A), which could be associated with the basic skills deficit in the labor market.

However, in some African countries, including Cabo Verde (100%), Mauritius (100%), Seychelles (100%), Tunisia (99.5%), Egypt (91%) or Morocco (86.8%), the proportion of lower secondary schools with the internet for pedagogical purposes is substantial, far above the sample average compared to countries like Burkina Faso, Burundi, DRC and Guinea. The second indicator that reflects more advanced digital skills is the share of youth and adults able to write a computer program using a specialized programming language. In a few countries with available data, interestingly, in countries such as Tunisia (16.1%), Morocco (9.3%), Egypt (8.8%), Algeria (6.9%) and Zambia (6.6%), this share is higher than the EU-27 average (6.0%) (Figure 11.11-B). Meanwhile, countries like Sudan (1.6%), Togo (0.5%), and Niger (0.3%) are lagging, explaining their bottom ranking in the prevalence of digital skills (Figure 11.10-B). Several countries in the continent, especially those lagging in digital skills, urgently need to upgrade their population's digital skills.

11.6 Skills for logistics

11.6.1 Rationale: Why logistics matter for GVCs?

A performant logistics sector is vital to a country's participation and position in the global value chains. Logistics refers to organizing and coordinating the movement of material inputs, final goods, and their distribution. Efficient logistics services reduce transportation costs and delays, enhancing a firm's productivity and GVC participation. Memedovic et al. (2008) argue that the benefits emerging from GVCs' spreading could not be achieved without co-developments in modern logistics services, underpinned by innovations in containerization, intermodal transport, and the application of IT in physical distribution and materials management.

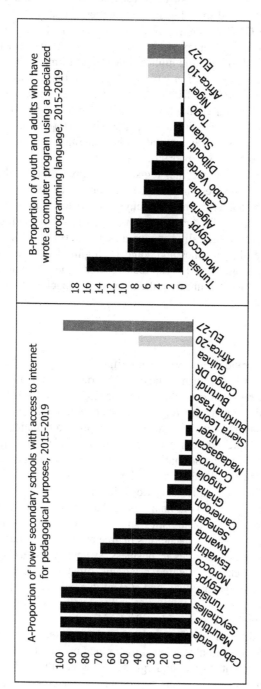

Figure 11.11 Lower secondary schools with access to internet and youth and adults with advanced digital skills.

Note: The chart displays for each country the most recent data point available between 2015 and 2019.

Source: Author's calculations based on World Development Indicators.

The WDR (2020) suggests a positive correlation between countries' participation in backward GVCs and their logistics capacities. Countries involved at the lowest stages of the GVCs (commodities traders) tend to have a lower World Bank Logistics Performance Index (LPI),[7] whereas those involved in the most sophisticated stage tend to have the highest logistic performance index score. In 2018, the average score of the LPI in Africa was 2.5 whereas it was 3.6 in EU-27 countries. However, the quality of logistics services is very heterogenous across countries as in several countries like South Africa, Cote d'Ivoire and Rwanda the index score was far above the continental average. The performance of the logistics and transportation sector in African countries is constrained by significant infrastructure gaps documented in Chapter 9 of this book.

McKinnon et al. (2017) argue that logistics strongly influence the economic performance of other industries and the countries in which they are located and must be adequately resourced both in the physical sense and in terms of human resources. Indeed, in spite of extensive mechanization and automation, logistics at the operational level intrinsically remains a people business which makes the logistics performance of companies and countries highly dependent on the quantity and quality of the workforce. To reap the expected benefits from the AfCFTA, African countries will need to improve their logistics capacities both in physical and human resources.

11.6.2 Skills requirements for logistics

The role of logistics providers in GVCs is multifaceted. They coordinate and integrate various logistics tasks within manufacturing, marketing, distribution, and sales. They possess a wide range of competences and come from various backgrounds, including transportation managers, freight forwarders, intermodal freight handling, warehousing, IT managers, software makers and supply chain managers. Logistics employees must therefore possess a cross-functional understanding of various business fields, strategic decision-making, communication, leadership and intercultural skills, and well-developed analytical and IT skills in order to manage the manifold tasks they face on a daily basis. Logistics employees on all levels need to acquire the ability to think and work on a process basis (McKinnon et al., 2017).

Because of the complexity of logistics and supply chains, companies usually hire workers who have at least a bachelor's degree at the managerial level. These logisticians have bachelor's degrees in business, systems engineering, or supply chain management. Bachelor's degree programs often include coursework in operations and database management, and system dynamics. Most programs also offer courses that train students on software and technologies commonly used by logisticians, such as radio-frequency identification.

Skills demand in logistics therefore varies from low-skilled blue-collar workers that require basic literacy and numeracy skills to medium and high-skilled white-collar positions requiring at least an undergraduate degree in formal education and or vocational training degrees such as certificates. The increasing use of digital technologies in logistics and transportation services also raises the demand for workers with a STEM background, especially those with medium and advanced digital skills.

Table 11.5 provides an illustration of categories of broad logistics occupations following McKinnon et al. (2017): (i) operational logistics or blue-collar staff who carry out basic operational tasks and do not have any staff responsibility; (ii) administrative staff who generally perform information processing tasks and have limited supervisory or managerial responsibilities; (iii) logistics supervisors who have frontline responsibilities, controlling logistics operations on the ground, and (iv) supply chain manager(logistics managers) who are managerial staff, with higher-level decision-making responsibility.

11.6.3 Current skills supply and gaps

Because of a lack of data, this discussion on skills supply will draw extensively on McKinnon et al.'s (2017) report. They carried out an online survey of logistics companies worldwide and conducted interviews with experts in logistics education and training to assess logistics employees' skills, competences and training. Their report complemented the World Bank's 2016 LPI report that carried out a first assessment of logistics skills and training. Both reports found that logistics faces a global shortage of qualified staff. Qualified staff are scarce to varying degrees at all four occupational levels (blue collar, administrative staff, supervisors, and managers) in all countries, especially in the countries that form the bottom quintile in the LPI. Shortages range from a lack of truck drivers to problems in filling senior supply chain management positions. Respondents in emerging and developing countries especially pointed to the supervisory and managerial level as the most severe perceived skills shortage (Figure 11.12-B).

At a regional level, while Latin America and the Caribbean was the region with the highest perceived skills shortage across all employee groups, SSA-perceived skills deficits vary between 20% and 30% of respondents across all job levels but with a higher degree of skills gap perceived at supervisor and managerial levels. The Middle East and North Africa (MENA) has the lowest perceived level of staff shortage at the managerial level with only about 11% of respondents against about 20% for each of the other occupations (Figure 11.12-A). This result for the MENA is attributable to education programs (B.Sc. and M.Sc.) in logistics and SCM that were introduced in the region over the past decade, like in Morocco where a severe shortage of managerial staff does not exist although the opposite applies for lower skill levels like truck drivers and warehouse pickers.

According to interviews with experts, several factors are behind these skills shortages. In all countries, the logistics sector suffers from low prestige and status of operational logistics workers in many cultures and societies. This might not necessarily be the primary factor for many countries in Africa where unemployment is high across all levels of skills. However, a limited supply of high-skilled labor, in the context of high levels of unemployment results primarily from the education system and lack of technical skills. Logistics developments, particularly

Table 11.5 Jobs and skills profiles for logistics

Position	Formal Education Requirements	Training/Experience	Skill Level
Operative logistics/blue-collar staff			
Truck drivers	Not formal education required, licenses, insurance	Training and experience	○
Transporter	Literacy and numeracy skills	Training and experience	◑
Forklift drivers	Not formal education required, licenses, insurance	On–the–job training	○
Warehouse pickers	Technical education / undergraduate degree	On the training	◐
Packer	Literacy and numeracy skills preferable	Training and experience	◑
Administrative logistics staff			
Traffic planners	Technical education / undergraduate degree	Training and experience	◐
Warehouse clerks	Technical education / undergraduate degree	Training and experience	◐
Costums clearance officer	Technical education / undergraduate degree	Training and experience	◐
Costumer service employee	Technical education / undergraduate degree	Training and experience	◐
Expediters	Technical education / undergraduate degree	Training and experience	◐
Logistics supervisors			
Shift leaders/ Traffic controllers	Technical education / undergraduate degree	Training and experience	◐
Logistics managers			
Storage unit manager	Technical education/ undergraduate degree	Training and experience	◐
Mechanics/Machine operator	Technical education	Technical training	◐
Warehouse manager	Technical education/ Certification	Training and experience	◐
Business manager	Bachelor's degree	Technical training/ experience	◕
Supply chain manager	Tehcnical education/ Bachelor's degree in finance/management	Industry experience	◕

Source: Authors building on McKinnon et al. (2017).

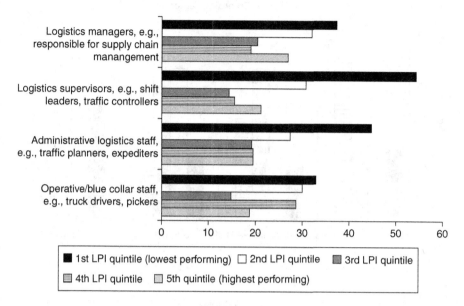

Figure 11.12 Availability of logistic qualified staff. A–Percentage of respondents who responded availability of skills staff was "low" or "very low". B–Percentage of respondents who responded availability of skills staff was from "very low" to "very high".

Source: Logistics performance Index 2016; McKinnon et al. (2017), *Logistics Competencies, Skills, and Training.*

in IT, demand new competencies that the existing workforce does not possess. Still, many countries in Africa disproportionately produce graduates in business and accounting relative to STEM, including ICT fields (see Sections 11.4 and 11.5). Also, according to the survey, higher educational programs across all regions have not been producing enough young logistics professionals to meet market demand. In addition to the quantity, in developing regions the quality of the academic logistics education is sub-optimal. In some countries, the number of people holding a logistics degree is adequate on paper, but unfortunately, graduates do not possess the skills or the knowledge required in practice. As a consequence, positions are held by unqualified staff or left vacant despite the large number of applicants. In some cases, the content taught in colleges and universities is often outdated, according to the interviews.

11.7 Policy recommendations

A series of interrelated policy interventions can help countries in Africa to upgrade the skills of their labor force to reap the opportunities offered by the AfCFTA. This will require a strong determination as business as usual will not move the continent

228 *Vincent Belinga and Kolobadia Ada Nayihouba*

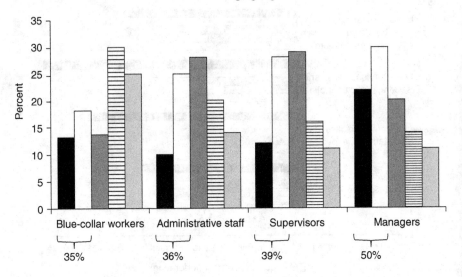

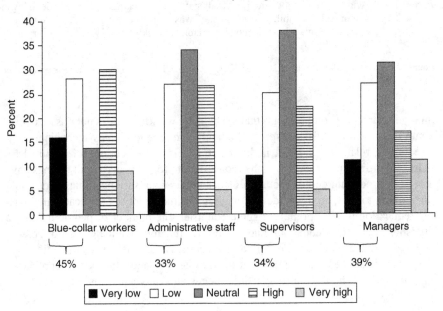

Figure 11.12 (Continued)

in the direction it wishes to. This requires commitment and collaboration between policymakers at the country and continental levels and private sector actors, educational institutions, and multinational and foreign partners. Policies should aim to improve access and outcomes of education and training systems, harmonize education systems, ensure recognition of academic credentials, and ease skilled workforce mobility across the continent. These objectives are critical conditions to align demand (and expected demand) and supply of skills on the continent. Areas of intervention are discussed below.

- *Equip graduates with reliable qualifications and a strong mix of relevant skills*. While the chapter has mostly focused on critical technical skills, a strong mix of core foundational skills remains critical with the changing nature of work and to be fully performant in the context of GVCs. From early childhood to adult learning, education and training systems need to equip all learners with a strong mix of skills. This requires maintaining a strong focus on cognitive and socio-emotional skills while developing innovative teaching strategies, flexibility in the curriculum choice and well-designed entrepreneurship education.
- *Promote STEM and ICT fields in education systems to provide the workforce with the technical skills required to accelerate the economic transformation of the continent*. Several countries in Africa do not produce enough graduates from STEM fields including ICT that are critical to transforming manufacturing and the digital economy. The demand for these skills is expected to continue growing with changing technology and opportunities offered by the AfCFTA. Interventions to increase students including young girls' interest and motivation in STEM studies are critical. At country and educational institutional levels, some policy interventions include relating science to students' daily lives, employing hands-on tasks and group activities, and ensuring STEM curricula focus on the most important topics in each discipline. Business leaders and educators also need to build bridges. Educational institutions that offer STEM programs can share their curricula with the business community to get their feedback. Collaboration between scientific colleges and polytechnic universities can be enhanced along with scholarship programs to motivate students toward these fields and increase enrolment rates in scientific programs. Universities in Africa could partner with well-established institutions in developed countries to initiate a knowledge transfer and obtain advice on how to adopt up-to-date teaching methods. The African Union Commission, through its Division of Education, should play a critical role in facilitating such partnerships.
- *Promote TVET and Continued Vocational Training (CVT) to match labor market needs and on–the–job training to upgrade workers' skills*. TVET programs play a key role in preparing staff for operational and supervisory jobs, provide specific technical skills and ease insertion in the labor market as their training programs typically have more practical content and give students more hands-on experience through internships and work assignments. Yet, these programs are still underused in Africa because of high enrolment fees and low wages in comparison to general education graduates. Only 3.7% of

15–24-year-olds were enrolled in vocational education in Africa over the period 2015–2019. This is less than half the average in the developing countries. Promotion of TVET programs by national policymakers through more facilities and strong partnerships between vocational institutions and the private sector could help match the labor market's needs and labor force skills. European and Scandinavian countries, where enrolments in TVET programs are high, provide examples of dual education systems combining the general education system and TVET programs in secondary education. Companies should also play their role by investing in the CVT of their staff to allow their workers to upgrade their skills. The share of African firms providing formal training to their employees is lower (29%) in comparison to those in Latin America (48%). According to World Bank Enterprise survey data, firms providing training to their workers tend to be more productive.

- *Boost R&D through partnerships between governments, academia and the private sector*. Strong partnerships between governments, universities and research centers could help mobilize co-financing in order to increase investments in research and development and compensate for low public expenditure in R&D. According to AfDB (2020), between 2012 and 2016, the average R&D gross expenditure was about 0.23%of GDP in Africa, only one-third of the level in Latin America of 0.68%.
- *Partner with multinational companies for skills development*. Large multinational corporations seek to improve local innovation, knowledge-based capital, and competencies. This offers an opportunity for governments to improve business environments to attract these corporations and scale up existing initiatives. For instance, to address shortages of technical and engineering skills in Africa and how these shortages could affect its global production network the Samsung group launched, in 2011, Samsung Electronics Engineering Academies in Kenya, Nigeria, and South Africa. Outstanding performers are sent to annual Leadership Programs in Seoul as part of Samsung's program for young leaders. Other corporations such as Nike, Microsoft, and Nokia are building skills interventions in the developing world including in Africa (Taglioni & Winkler, 2016).
- *Ease the free movement of labor across the continent and tap into the important African diaspora*. In addition to structural policies of human capital promotion, effective free circulation of labor across the continent can solve the skills shortages in some sectors. Implementing the project of the African single passport would significantly ease the movement of talents, skills, and labor across African countries. According to the Africa Visa Openness Report 2020, 46% of Africans still need visas to travel to other African countries. The African Union Commission should therefore accelerate the establishment of the African single passport. Meanwhile, the Division of Education of the Commission should enhance its collaboration with governments to harmonize education systems, promote collaboration between universities in Africa, and ensure recognition of academic credentials. Moreover, governments in Africa can tap into its large diaspora to increase the skills supply. It is estimated that

over 30 million Africans live outside of their home countries and a significant share of them are highly skilled in areas such as math, sciences, technology, engineering, and mining where the skills shortage is severe in African countries. Linking the highly skilled workers of the diaspora with the job opportunities in their home countries along with incentives to attract them could help African countries fully take advantage of their diaspora.

11.8 Conclusion

This chapter analyses the skills needed by African countries for the economic transformation of the continent and to fully reap the benefits of the AfCFTA. The removal of tariffs and non-tariffs barriers across the continent is expected to boost significantly the intracontinental trade, improve participation of firms in Africa into backward global value chains within the continent or globally, and deepen existing and/or generate new regional or continental value chains. Trade through GVC participation has proven to have higher economic outcomes than traditional trade. Skills are determinant in a country's participation and positioning in the high-end of the value chains. The chapter analyses the labor market implications of these economic opportunities through a discussion of the potential demand of skills (or skills requirements) and existing skills supply and gaps in two economic sectors: agribusiness, and manufacturing; and two key services sectors, the digital economy and logistics both critical for GVC participation and therefore economic transformation.

It first documents the stylized facts on the crucial role of skills in GVC participation. Countries that make the most of economic and social benefits from participating in GVCs are those where investments in skills are in line with their comparative advantages. Skills enhance productivity gains as they make it easier for knowledge transfer and adoption of new technologies. They also determine workers' jobs, incomes and their vulnerability to economic shocks.

Based on available data and existing studies, the analysis documents important gaps in the current supply of critical technical and advanced skills including STEM and ICT-related skills and skills requirements for backward participation in GVCs in the four areas of interest in several countries. The analysis also shows a high heterogeneity in the skills supply among the countries with significant differences between the leaders and laggers.

Going forward, a series of interrelated policy interventions that can help African countries to upgrade the skills of their labor force would be critical. This will require a strong determination as business as usual will not move the continent in the direction it wishes to head. Policies should aim to improve access and outcomes of education and training systems to align demand (and expected demand) and supply of skills on the continent. These policies should also include the acceleration of the establishment of the African passport, the harmonization of education systems and the recognition of academic credentials across the continent to ease mobility of skilled workforce. Incentives to attract skilled African diaspora and to achieve free movement for skilled workers within the continent can be part of the solution. Importantly, more structural reforms are needed in the educational and training systems to equip students with the right skills. Close partnerships between governments, educational institutions including TVET, domestic private sector, multinational companies, and foreign universities will improve education and training curriculums, attract youth in STEM and ICT-related fields, improve workers' access to skills upgrading, and the research agenda. Both countries' authorities and the Africa Union Commission should play their parts to achieve these objectives.

Notes

1 The views and opinions expressed in this paper are those of the authors and do not necessarily reflect the views or positions of their employers or institutions.
2 Backward GVC is measured as imports content in a country manufacturing exports.
3 www.brookings.edu/blog/africa-in-focus/2020/12/14/unpacking-the-misconceptions-about-africas-food-imports/
4 For the full description of each job position, see Bamber et al. (2014).
5 Because of lack of data, we are not able map each position and skills requirement with the supply side. Instead, we provide a broad assessment on major advanced technical skills acquired at tertiary education based on available information. The same applies for the rest of the chapter.
6 Skills for the digital economy is consistent with the third "D", Digital, of the 3Ds organizing framework.
7 Logistics Performance Index overall score reflects perceptions of a country's logistics based on efficiency of customs clearance process, quality of trade–and transport-related infrastructure, ease of arranging competitively priced shipments, quality of logistics services, ability to track and trace consignments, and frequency with which shipments reach the consignee within the scheduled time. The index ranges from 1 to 5, with a higher score representing better performance.

References

ACET (African Center for Economic Transformation). 2014. African Transformation Report 2014: Growth with Depth. Accra, Ghana: ACET.

AfDB (African Development Bank). 2020. African Economic Outlook 2020: Developing Africa's workforce for the future, Abidjan, Cote d'Ivoire.

AfDB, OECD, UNDP. 2014. African Economic Outlook,2014–Global Value Chains and Africa's Industrialisation.

AfDB/OECD/UNDP. 2017. African Economic Outlook 2017: Entrepreneurship and Industrialization, OECD Publishing, Paris.

African Capacity Building Foundation. 2016. African Union Agenda 2063: African Critical Technical Skills: Key Capacity Dimensions Needed for the First 10 Years of Agenda 2063, Harare: African Capacity Building Foundation.

Bamber P., Frederick S., and Cho J. 2018. The Digital Economy, Global Value Chains and Asia, Duke University Global Value Chains Center.

Bamber P., Gereffi G., and Abdulsamand A., Burundi in the Agribusiness Global Value Chain: Skills for Private Sector Development, 2014, Duke Center on Globalization, Governance and Competitiveness (CGGC).

Fernández-Stark K., Bamber, P. and Gereffi, G., 2012. *Upgrading in global value chains: Addressing the skills challenge in developing countries.* Duke Center on Globalization, Governance & Competitiveness at the Social Science Research Institute, Duke University.

Gereffi G., Fernandez-Stark K., and Psilos, P. 2011. "Skills for Upgrading: Workforce Development and Global Value Chains in Developing Countries" November, 2011.

International Finance Corporation & LEK Consulting. 2019 Digital skills in Sub-Saharan Africa: spotlight on Ghana, International Finance Corporation, Washington, viewed 1 Jun 2021,

International Monetary Fund. 2020. Regional Economic Outlook, April 2020, Sub-Saharan Africa. USA: International Monetary Fund.

Landry S. 2018. "The potential of manufacturing and industrialization in Africa: Trends, opportunities, and strategies", The Brookings Institution (Washington, D.C., 20 September 2018).

McKinnon A., Flöthmann C., Hoberg K., and Busch C. 2017. Logistics Competencies, Skills, and Training: A Global Overview. World Bank Studies. Washington, DC: World Bank. doi:10.1596/978-1-4648-1140-1

Memedovic, O., Ojala, L., Rodrigue, J.-P., and Naula, T. 2008. Fuelling the global value chains: what role for logistics capabilities? *International Journal of Technological Learning, Innovation and Development,* 1(3), pp. 353–374.

OECD (2013), Interconnected Economies: Benefiting from Global Value Chains, OECD Publishing, Paris, https://doi.org/10.1787/9789264189560-en

OECD Skills Outlook 2017: Skills and Global Value Chains, OECD Publishing, Paris. http://dx.doi.org/10.1787/9789264273351-en

Taglioni D. and Winkler D. 2016. Making Global Value Chains Work for Development. Trade and Development series. Washington, DC: World Bank. doi:10.1596/978-1-4648-0157-0

UNCTAD. 2015. The Economic Development in Africa Report, Unlocking the potential of Africa's services trade for growth and development, United Nations publication. New York and Geneva.

United Nations Economic Commission for Africa. 2018. An Empirical assessment of AfCFTA Modalities on Goods. UNECA.

World Bank. 2020. World Development Report 2020, World Bank Publications, The World Bank, number 32437, June.

World Bank. 2020a. The African Continental Free Trade Area: Economic and Distributional Effects. Washington, DC: World Bank. © World Bank.

World Bank. 2020b. Global Productivity: Trends, Drivers, and Policies, database.

World Bank. 2020c. The Future of Work in Africa: Harnessing the Potential of Digital Technologies for All. Africa Development Forum. Washington, DC: World Bank. © World Bank.

12 Realizing the promise of the AfCFTA

The role of industrial and competition policies[1]

Witness Simbanegavi and Tendai Gwatidzo

12.1 Introduction

Africa is the richest continent in terms of natural resources and boasts 60% of the world's arable land and perhaps the best agro-climatic conditions globally, as well as a large array of minerals.[2] While gains have been realized with respect to the reduction of extreme poverty, Africa has yet to fully exploit its wealth for the benefit of its citizens. A characteristic feature of most African economies is that they are under-diversified, being dependent on few economic activities, mostly in the primary sector (agriculture and mining), for export receipts and growth, making economic outcomes susceptible to the vagaries of the weather or volatility in global markets (AfDB 2017). Africa is also highly dependent on trade with the rest of the world for its growth. Between 2000 and 2017, Africa's exports to the rest of the world ranged between 80% and 90% of its total exports, showing a high export dependence for the region (UNCTAD 2018), and the bulk of this trade was in commodities, reflecting the low value-added nature of Africa's exports and the constrained trade among African countries. For a detailed analysis of Africa's trade patterns see Chapter 2.[3]

Intra-African trade, defined as the average of intra-African exports and imports, averaged about 15.2% between 2015 and 2017. To put this in perspective, intra-African exports were about 17% of total exports in 2017, compared with 68.1% in Europe, 59.4% in Asia, 55.0% in America and 7.0% in Oceania (UNCTAD 2018). Unlike Africa's trade with the rest of the world, which is dominated by commodities, trade within Africa is dominated by manufactured goods, foodstuffs, and services (Songwe 2019), and typically involves small to medium enterprises (SMEs). Intra-African trade favors increased value addition within the continent, which should support higher growth in the region.[4]

The absence of major regional value chains in the continent reflects the underdeveloped manufacturing/processing sectors and a trade regime that is not supportive of intra-Africa trade. Similarly, the incentive structures at the global level do not favor value addition on African soil. For instance, the World Trade Organisation (WTO) rules that push for unfettered free trade mean that newly emerging African industries must compete on equal footing with the experienced and highly competitive firms from the industrialized countries, many of whom

DOI: 10.4324/9781003456568-12

grew under trade protection or have accumulated knowledge and network externalities over decades. This, according to Altenburg and Rodrik (2017), undermines industrialization efforts in the continent. In addition, developed economies often apply tariff escalation on value-added goods from developing economies, while encouraging exports of unprocessed goods through favorable tariff dispensations.[5]

This chapter explores two issues, namely: (i) the role of industrialization in the realization of the AfCFTA; and (ii) what it would take to industrialize Africa. In addressing these issues, the chapter explores the constraints to intra-African trade; the role of regional industrial policy; the industrial policy lessons for Africa from other regions; and the role of competition and competition policy in industrial development. Increasing value addition on African soil requires the strategic deployment of trade and competition policies, with the goods originating in the AfCFTA getting preferential treatment and unfettered access to the continental free trade area. The AfCFTA came into effect at an opportune time for the continent, as countries are beginning to rebuild their economies after the devastation caused by the COVID-19 pandemic.

The remainder of the chapter is organized as follows. Section 12.2, which assesses the investment and industrial development imperatives for Africa, is followed by Section 12.3, which analyses the instruments of industrial policy in the AfCFTA. Section 12.4 focuses on regional industrial policy and the AfCFTA. In Section 12.5, industrial policy experiences and lessons learnt from Asia and the EU are documented. Section 12.6. shows potential challenges to implementing/coordinating industrial policy at the continental level. Finally, Section 12.7 concludes.

12.2 The investment and industrial development imperatives for Africa

The COVID-19 pandemic serves as a wake-up call for Africa to strengthen industrial capabilities and intra-Africa trade. First, Africa is perhaps the only large continent with no home-grown COVID-19 vaccine, and for this reason, Africa will likely be the last continent to achieve herd immunity (at least through the vaccination route). Second, global trade is unlikely to fully recover to pre-COVID-19 levels.[6] This is worrying on several levels. Over 80% of Africa's exports are to the rest of the world, hence weaker global growth and trade bode ill for the continent. Furthermore, Africa was increasingly getting integrated into global value chains (GVCs) (agribusiness and apparel—Ethiopia and Kenya; manufacturing goods—Tanzania; auto industry—South Africa, Morocco, Rwanda; and minerals—the Democratic Republic of Congo and Zambia),[7] and thus reorganization of GVCs could scuttle Africa's participation in them (though it is also possible that this could enhance Africa's participation in the new structures). Therefore, as much as Africa should remain pro-globalization, these developments point to the need to strengthen the internal market and production structures to engender resilience to global shocks.

African economies are among the least complex and least diversified economies in the world (Observatory of Economic Complexity 2016), confirming their susceptibility to adverse economic shocks and inability to appropriate much share of global value added (high ubiquity).[8] Again, the slow progress towards COVID-19 vaccine development or production in the continent demonstrates well the weak production complexity across Africa.[9] Ubiquity implies that the goods produced by African countries are sold in highly competitive and thus low-margin (global) markets. Manufactured goods, on the other hand, are typically characterized by monopolistic competition or oligopoly more generally, allowing the producers some degree of market power.

Africa also faces a huge employment challenge, especially among the youth. As of 2015, only 15% of Africa's youth were in wage employment, 35% were in vulnerable employment, and the rest (50%) were unemployed or discouraged (AfDB 2016). While industrialization may not provide all the answers to this policy challenge, the strong linkages between industry and other sectors of the economy mean a more vibrant industrial sector should, through the multiplier effects, support increased job creation in the rest of the economy. As noted by Simbanegavi (2019), the long-term solution to Africa's youth employment challenge will turn on the diversification of African economies, closing of the infrastructure gap and development of productive capabilities in manufacturing and services.

Industrial development has delivered high growth and high living standards for East Asian countries in record time (Chang 2006) and it can deliver similar outcomes for Africa.[10] Africa needs to structurally transform its economy with an emphasis on value addition, leveraging the internal market. The processes of structural transformation and economic diversification are never market driven nor naturally occurring, but rather policy induced, with the state either taking concrete steps or providing clear signals that they want to see the private sector moving into that space. This is so since these processes require mastering specific capabilities across many areas, as well as having well-developed supporting institutions and infrastructures (Felipe 2015). In other words, market failures preclude market-led structural transformation.

12.3 Instruments of industrial policy in the AfCFTA

In implementing industrial policy, two instruments stand out as candidates, namely, trade policy and competition policy.

12.3.1 Trade and competition policies

By definition, the AfCFTA is a trade instrument that favors goods originating from within the continental free trade area against non-originating goods. For effectiveness, therefore, Africa will have to have a common or coordinated trade policy with non-AfCFTA members (see Chapter 7 in this volume for details). In addition, trade frictions ought to be minimized within the AfCFTA, with the goal being the promotion of free and unimpeded circulation of goods originating from within the continent.

One of the major challenges in intra-REC trade has been contestations around the rules of origin issues. The AfCFTA magnifies this challenge multiple-fold as it involves more countries. Thus, policy needs to address rules of origin issues and develop the necessary monitoring upfront to avoid interfering with free trade, and thus creating trade uncertainty.[11] Trade uncertainty could also arise from the delayed implementation of key tenets of the agreement. Therefore, African governments should stick to the AfCFTA schedule with respect to the removal of tariff and non-tariff barriers.

The second instrument is competition policy. A common market requires free and fair competition. While countries are likely to conform to the dictates of the AfCFTA with respect to the removal of tariff barriers, the real test will be whether countries will move swiftly to remove non-tariff barriers to ensure the unfettered movement of goods across borders.[12] In addition, policies geared at enhancing market competition should be prioritized as weak competition stifles innovation and investment, while rewarding inefficiencies (Aghion et al. 2005). African governments should harmonize competition policies across the continent, beginning perhaps with harmonization among the eight regional economic communities, and then later pushing for harmonization at the continental level.

Several policy instruments could be deployed by African governments in their quest to spur industrial development. Over and above the development of core infrastructures (energy, transport, communications, etc.), governments can use tax, grants/subsidies, public procurement, local content rules and other incentives to encourage private sector investment. These policies are meant to risk-share with the private sector, and thus reduce investment or production costs. While these generally work well at the national level, in a common market these policies can be abused to give artificial competitive advantage to domestic firms or to attract foreign direct investment.[13] Rules will need to be developed, agreed upon and implemented to help mitigate risks of counterproductive competition, and thus market distortions that undermine the AfCFTA. Without that reciprocity or countervailing measures could easily lead to a 'race to the bottom'.

12.3.2 *AfCFTA to shape the continental merchandise trade landscape*

The AfCFTA commits countries to remove tariffs on 90% of goods, progressively liberalize trade in services and address several other non-tariff barriers. The agreement seeks to build on the level of integration attained in the existing regional economic communities (RECs), which form its institutional foundation (see Chapter 6 for a detailed discussion on RECs). Karinigi and Mevel (2012) evaluate the potential impact of the AfCFTA and conclude that its implementation could increase intra-Africa trade by almost 130% within five years. Meeting this level of trade would require substantial investments in productive capacity.

African policy makers are searching for answers on how to "transform, restructure and diversify their economies, and move up the value ladder" (Felipe 2015). The AfCFTA can be viewed as an African-level industrial policy intervention. It fulfils the role of an infant industry protection mechanism. The AfCFTA creates an enlarged, more integrated and harmonized market, promoting the production and exchange of goods within Africa, and enabling the exploitation of scale economies and 'learning by doing' opportunities associated with producing progressively more sophisticated goods while being shielded (at least to some degree) from outside competition. By harmonizing the trading environment, the AfCFTA reduces uncertainty on trading relations within the continent which, together with complementary measures such as infrastructure, skills development and trade facilitation, should foster both domestic and foreign direct investment. It must however be noted that some major advanced countries may seek to circumvent the AfCFTA, using their economic and political muscle to push for bilateral agreements with individual African countries instead. Unfortunately, failure to abide by or enforce a common external trade position could unravel the AfCFTA.

Manufacturing, which is at the center of intra-African trade, has strong gross domestic product (GDP) and employment multipliers due to its strong forward and backward linkages with the other economic sectors, particularly agriculture, mining and services. Manufacturing is also associated with R&D and the attendant spillovers which benefit other economic sectors. The AfCFTA will also enable African countries to leverage regional integration to enhance economic governance and regulatory frameworks through agreements on enforceable rules and the creation of common institutions. This should help reduce protectionist tendencies at the national level. The question is whether African policy makers will be resolute enough to resist short-term national political imperatives that go against the prescripts of the AfCFTA. Indeed, the costs and benefits of AfCFTA should be equitably shared.

12.4 Regional industrial policy and the AfCFTA

Industrial policy can be characterized as any policy intervention(s) aimed at positively influencing one or more of the following: restructuring and diversification of the economy with a bias towards manufacturing; enhancing competitiveness; engendering resilience of industry to shocks; enhancing innovation and skills development.[14] Africa's low manufacturing value-added means the continent could easily substantially raise manufacturing productivity (off of a low base).[15] Industrial policy could be deployed to address the externalities or market failures that inhibit the development of industrial competitiveness in Africa.[16]

12.4.1 Market failures inhibiting industrialization in Africa

Market failures in relation to industrial development can take several forms—information and coordination externalities (Rodrik 2004; Stiglitz 2015; Aghion et al. 2011), principal-agent problems facing investors investing in learning-by-doing processes and externality problems affecting investments in improving workforce skills (Khan 2015).[17] These market failures are ubiquitous both at the national and regional levels. Their presence constrains investment in productive capital.

Given Africa's distance from the frontier, addressing self-discovery externalities could unleash significant productivity growth in manufacturing through imitative investments. Self-discovery externalities are said to exist when entrepreneurs must invest to experiment with 'new products' and/or new ways of producing available products using domestic resources, yet the risks they carry are not directly rewarded as the discoveries are non-patentable. In this case, the entrepreneur bears all the risk but cannot fully appropriate the benefits in the event of success.

Of particular interest in the context of the AfCFTA are the coordination and learning by doing externalities. Coordination externalities arise when there is a failure to properly coordinate and/or sequence investments in a way that makes private investments profitable. This often is the case with high fixed-cost investments which can be subject to hold-up problems. Under these circumstances, entrepreneurs may not be able to coordinate their investments in a way that is socially efficient. Coordination externalities are arguably the most binding in Africa, particularly given the huge infrastructure deficit in the region (AfDB 2018), and hence should perhaps attract the most urgent attention.

In the context of the AfCFTA, coordination externalities get magnified as this not only requires government-private sector coordination but rather coordination across different governments and private sectors. Poor coordination on infrastructure development can hamper development of regional value chains, for instance. Equally, disharmony in policies and regulations can scuttle potential cross-border investments or the development of regional value chains. Presently, many African countries still do not have a 'one-stop border post' system, which raises the cost of trading and makes 'just in time' manufacturing near impossible for regional chains given the border delays.

Khan (2015) argues that building a factory and equipping it does not in and of itself generate competitiveness gains. Firms need to learn by doing, and this often takes time and money.[18] Consequently, learning by doing can become a constraint to industrial development, and thus ought to be an object of industrial policy.[19] Indeed, as noted by Altenburg and Rodrik (2017), it is inconceivable that Africa could develop a viable manufacturing base while exposed to highly competitive global corporations that have accumulated knowledge and network externalities over decades. The AfCFTA is potentially a game changer, as it allows for the realization of scale and scope economies and thus learning by doing within Africa. However, industrial policies to support learning by doing could easily be abused by national governments resulting in unfair competition. These considerations around externalities point to the need for an African industrial policy, to better harmonize policy and reduce trade disputes.

Another source of market failure is imperfections in credit markets, which hamper industrial financing as market-based financing fails to socialize the risks of investing in high-risk new activities with high social value (Stiglitz 2015). In Africa, a case can be made for the deployment of properly mandated national development banks, perhaps with (technical) support from the African Development Bank, to support investment in the industrial sectors. In fact, given its positioning with respect to the African development agenda, the AfDB could spearhead the development and implementation of an African industrial policy.

Industrial development in Africa should account for environmental externalities to engender global competitiveness (see for instance, Gwatidzo and Simbanegavi 2021). African countries, like many other countries, made commitments during COP 21 to reduce their carbon footprint. Thus, as African countries look to industrialize, they will have to do so in a sustainable manner, i.e., develop greener industries.[20] Greening of African economies has competitiveness implications for at least two reasons. First, consumers are becoming increasingly environmentally conscious and thus will vote with their wallets. Second, given the growing global awareness and country commitments around sustainability, it is likely that there will soon be changes to global trading regimes to explicitly account for carbon content in trade, with the possibility of penal codes directed at the non-conformers.[21] Africa should therefore avoid the carbon lock-in effect, whereby investing in carbon-intensive production processes now will generate path dependence going forward, thereby raising transition costs.

To address the existing market failures, African countries could deploy both horizontal and vertical industrial policies. *Horizontal* industrial policies are those policies that do not directly target any sector, but rather provide support across a large swathe of sectors, for example, investment tax incentives or skills development. *Vertical* industrial policies are typically targeted at specific sectors. While some scholars and policy makers have argued against vertical industrial policies arguing that they tend to be distortionary, or susceptible to capture, the fight between vertical and horizontal industrial policy is misplaced (Chang 2006; Khan 2015; and UNECA 2016). All industrial policy interventions are, to a degree, selective. Equally, policy, by its very nature, is always open to capture, and industrial policy is no exception (Rodrik 2008). In the language of Evans (1995), policy makers should practice *embedded autonomy* (arm's length consultations with industry) in order to get to grips with the real challenges that industry face, and thus be able to formulate appropriate policies. Given the information asymmetry between policy makers and industrialists, the industrialists will always be guaranteed some informational rents.[22]

12.4.2 *Infrastructure: A barrier to industrialization in Africa*

To fully realize the potential of the AfCFTA, African countries will need to address several challenges that have contributed to the current state of affairs, including infrastructure development, closing the technology gap, and trade facilitation (see Chapter 8 on the current state of transport infrastructure in Africa).

Part of the market failures highlighted above relate to the inadequacy of economic infrastructure—key to investment, productivity, and thus economic growth. Infrastructure (electricity, road, rail and air logistics, border and customs administration, etc.) facilitates the production and movement of goods from one point to the other, supporting investment, economic activity and economic growth.[23]

As shown in Table 12.1, it takes about 11 days to clear exports through customs in SSA (the world average is about 8 days); and about 17 days to clear imports (the world average is 12 days). Consequently, SSA has the highest proportion of firms

Table 12.1 Trade-related indicators for manufacturing firms Africa versus the world

Economy	Days to clear direct exports through customs	% of firms exporting directly (at least 10% of sales)	Days to clear imports from customs	% of firms identifying customs and trade regulations as a major constraint
All Countries	7.8	10.9	12.1	18.1
East Asia & Pacific	8	9.4	9.9	12.1
Europe & Central Asia	4	15.8	5.8	9.1
High income: OECD	13.7	9.5	12.8	5.5
Latin America & Caribbean	8.3	9.9	15.4	20.4
Middle East & North Africa	7.6	15.1	10.8	21.2
South Asia	8.7	7.3	8.9	17
Sub-Saharan Africa	10.6	8	16.6	26.1

Source: World Bank Enterprise Survey Online Database.

that consider customs and trade regulations to be major constraints. These factors increase the cost of participating in international trade, including regional trade, and thus reduce the benefits of doing so, and ultimately investment. It is therefore not surprising that SSA has the smallest proportion of firms that participate in international trade.

Energy is perhaps the biggest infrastructure gap in Africa (AfDB 2018). Without readily available and competitively priced electricity, industrial development, in particular, manufacturing, is a difficult proposition for the continent. Equally, Africa is an expansive continent, with many landlocked countries and therefore, in the absence of good transport infrastructure and efficient logistics to facilitate the movement of goods (and people), the AfCFTA cannot achieve much as producers will be unable to fully exploit economies of scale. Intra-African trade would remain regionalized on account of trade costs, restricting the potential benefits of learning by doing. Table 12.2 provides a regional comparison of infrastructural problems faced by manufacturing sector firms. SSA had the largest proportion of firms that consider transportation as a major constraint (26% versus a world average of 20%) and that experienced electricity outages (about 76%), resulting in about 42% of SSA firms owning generators. Water insufficiency is also rife (22%).

The AfCFTA provides an opportunity for Africa to close the *technology and productivity gaps*. While hitting the frontier will likely take time for most product categories, and thus may not be the immediate objective, Africa should leverage the AfCFTA to invest towards the realization of the Agenda 2063 goals. For instance, a large share of Africa's import bill could easily be replaced by home-produced goods, particularly light manufactures or processed foods. On the back of the AfCFTA, Africa should support targeted import substitution to develop

Table 12.2 Regional comparisons of infrastructural problems facing firms

Economy	% of firms experiencing electrical outages	% of firms owning or sharing a generator	% of firms identifying electricity as a major constraint	Percent of firms experiencing water insufficiencies	% of firms identifying transportation as a major constraint
All Countries	57.8	35.1	33.6	13.3	20.3
East Asia & Pacific	56.8	35	18.2	10	14.4
Europe & Central Asia	33.1	20.5	24	4.3	12.5
High income: OECD	22.2	7.9	43.8	4.7	9.6
Latin America & Caribbean	64.8	26	36.6	12.8	23
Middle East & North Africa	42.2	37.8	38.9	15	23.5
South Asia	66.2	45.4	46.1	11.3	21.1
Sub-Saharan Africa	75.6	51.5	41.7	22.3	26.3

Source: World Bank Enterprise Survey Online Database (Several years).

or strengthen manufacturing capabilities. This can be aided through incentivizing self-discovery by local 'innovators'. To ensure long-term competitiveness, governments should, among other interventions, raise R&D spending (both public and private) and human capital development.[24] African countries should also leverage trade agreements such as AGOA and EBA to climb the technology ladder.

While regional infrastructure is central to regional trade, and thus the efficacy of the AfCFTA, *trade facilitation* plays an important role in reducing trade costs. As noted by the World Bank (2015), intraregional trade, which boasts of a larger share of manufactured and processed goods, is sensitive to border delays, logistics disruptions and corruption. Administrative red tape, logistics deficiencies and non-harmonized regulations and customs processes make it too risky or too costly to invest in regional value chains—the type of supply chain trade that has been the growth engine in East Asia (Hoekman et al. 2017). With trade facilitation, and thus unimpeded flow of goods, people and services, the AfCFTA has the potential to unlock investment, including inward FDI to the region, and enhance the viability of regional value chains. Trade facilitation measures should be accompanied by reductions in tariff barriers which remain high in the region.[25]

12.5 Industrial policy experiences and lessons from Asia and the EU

East Asian countries in general and the Asian Tigers (South Korea, Taiwan, Singapore and Hong Kong) and China in particular, have successfully diversified their economies through deliberate industrial policies. These countries adopted a 'directed development' model whereby the government identified the desired development trajectory for the country (e.g., heavy industries in South Korea, Japan, Malaysia or electronics in Singapore) and then incentivized the private sector (and to a lesser extent state-owned enterprises) to invest and produce. The countries adopted different models with respect to investment: Japan and South Korea relied on investment by domestic firms, whereas Malaysia and Singapore leveraged FDI for manufacturing sector development (Chang 2006; Yean 2015), while China relied on both. Equally, Asian countries have used a wide range of incentives to promote industrialization (see Chang 2006; Yean 2015). Asian countries also made extensive use of subsidies (export, investment, R&D, and infrastructure). However, this was largely during the 1970s and 1980s, prior to these countries joining the WTO (Chang 2006; Yean 2015). The use of subsidies has since been scaled down as per WTO rules.

Another characteristic feature of industrial policy in East Asia is government-private sector engagement in policy development and implementation (Chang 2006; Yean 2015). This model (often termed 'deliberation councils') was widely used across East Asia but with very little capture of policy—the principle of *embedded autonomy* (see Evans 1995). There were instances of failure of industrial policy in these countries, which should not be surprising. As noted by Chang (2006), "in assessing industrial policies in East Asia, the real question is not whether governments make mistakes, but whether there are more successes than failures and how quickly and effectively mistakes are corrected".[26] In addition, one needs to assess broad spillovers (including the development of productive capabilities across the economy) associated with industry to correctly evaluate the impact of industrial policy.

Farla et al. (2015) divide the EU industrial policy into three broad categories, namely, the general market framework (workings of markets, including competition policy), horizontal policy interventions (e.g., subsidies and tax incentives aimed at nurturing investment) and lastly, vertical industrial policies (e.g., technology policies).[27] A guiding principle for the EU common market is that firms from all EU countries should have unfettered access to the national markets of member states (Farla et al. 2015; Landesmann and Stöllinger 2020).[28] The EU industrial policy is two-tiered, namely, at the EU level and also at the national level. The EU industrial policy has focused on bolstering competition, improving antitrust policy and regulation, and also has a geographic focus, allowing for both sectoral and regional targeting (Farla et al. 2015).

Lately, the EU has adopted a more forward-looking active industrial policy geared towards facilitating structural change and global competitiveness, though some countries (e.g., France) adopt a more interventionist approach (more vertical industrial policies) while others (e.g., Germany) emphasize horizontal industrial policies. In general, vertical industrial policies in the EU are not defensive (or protective) in nature, but rather are aimed at engendering structural transformation. Vertical policies are targeted at the sectors (particularly knowledge and innovation) that are expected to drive structural change and are meant to incentivize firms to invest in these sectors. On average, the EU spent about 1.1% of the EU GDP funding industrial policy (broadly defined) between 2014 and 2017, a decrease from 3% of GDP in the 1970s and around 2% of GDP during the 1980s (Landesmann and Stöllinger 2020).

There are lessons to be learned from the industrial policy approaches of the EU and Asia.

First, industrial policy is a viable means to drive structural transformation and diversification of the African economy.

Second, a suite of interventions is necessary—both horizontal and vertical type interventions—as each of these addresses different, though sometimes related, market failures. The key among the horizontal industrial policies should be infrastructure (e.g., roads, ports, rail, airports and information and communications technology), so as to lower trade costs and human capital investment to enhance capabilities.

Third, industrial policy should seek to strengthen the relationship between knowledge-generating institutions, private enterprises and public institutions, engendering synergies.[29]

Fourth, industrial policy at the African or sub-regional level should be deployed in such a way as to reduce the concentration of industrial activity in one region or country and thus diffuse the potential tension due to the uneven distribution of benefits from the implementation of the AfCFTA.

Fifth, while the infant industry argument may be applicable to some manufacturing activities in some African countries, policy makers should take cognizance of the following (i) applying such against peer African competitors could invite countervailing measures, and (ii) defensive industrial policies are generally ineffective as they tend to slow adjustment and adaptation by the protected firms. Where infant industry protection measures are necessary, transparency would be key to minimizing suspicion about breaking the free trade area rules.

Sixth, African countries should seek to promote industrial clusters to strengthen agglomeration economies. This could take the form of EPZs (Ethiopia and Kenya are good examples).

Last, but not least, there should be no conflict between industrial and competition policies. In particular, 'firms from all African countries should have unfettered access to the national markets of member states'.

12.6 Potential challenges to implementing/coordinating industrial policy at continental level

12.6.1 Winner takes all and the race to the bottom

Perhaps the biggest challenge to the success of the AfCFTA is the 'race to the bottom' phenomenon, where failure to harmonize rules and regulations around competition and use of incentives could see countries competing through conferring incentives either to attract FDI or to give a competitive edge to national firms. A zero-sum game mentality is a likely outcome where there are strong short-term national interest considerations or perceived inequities from the AfCFTA (see Chapter 7 in this volume). Unlike the EU, which is a political union, with a properly constituted EU supranational government that generates binding EU-wide policies, the AfCFTA is not an outcome of a political union, but rather a political agreement. As such, there is no apex regional body in Africa that is mandated to formulate regional industrial policy and adequately resourced to oversee its implementation. The AU Commission and the AfCFTA Secretariat could serve as, respectively, the policy arm and the implementing agency for the AfCFTA. However, presently the AU Commission does not have the political muscle that the EU wields. Another challenge is that the benefits of free trade are seldom equitably distributed, with initial endowments often determining the winners (and losers). African leaders need to develop a framework or mechanisms for inter-country transfers to address any distributional injustice questions (some countries benefiting or being perceived to benefit disproportionately from the AfCFTA). To ensure countries fully implement the AfCFTA, the benefits have to be seen to be equitably distributed (see Chapter 6 on challenges likely to be faced by RECs as they transition into AfCFTA).

12.6.2 Competition, competition policy and enforcement

One of the key arguments for the AfCFTA is that it will increase competition across the region, driving investment and productivity, and providing variety and competitive prices for the African consumer. This thesis supposes that there are no impediments, exogenous or endogenous, to competition. This however is unlikely to be the case. As we show below, African markets are mostly uncompetitive, and the AfCFTA on its own is unlikely to change that fact. There is a need for deliberate policy to enhance competition in the region, which requires empowering existing competition authorities and constituting competition authorities where they are currently non-existent. To ensure coherence of policy across countries, and in particular, the application of policy, African policy makers should constitute an African Competition Authority—a supranational competition authority.

We briefly look at the competitiveness of Africa's manufacturing and banking sectors—the two sectors that are key to the realization of the objectives of the AfCFTA. The banking sector facilitates trade and investment, while the manufacturing sector invests and produces. Stronger competition in the banking sector can improve the flow of goods from one country to another. Figure 12.1 shows the average annual 5-bank concentration ratios in SSA. Ghana, with a 5-bank concentration ratio of 53%, is the least concentrated while countries like Namibia, Malawi and Guyana had concentration ratios close to 100%. Figure 12.2 shows the average Lerner indices for several countries in SSA. Countries like South Africa, Egypt and Togo, with Lerner indices close to 0.2, have the most competitive banking sectors while countries like Algeria and Ethiopia have Lerner Indices that are close to 0.5, indicating weak competition.

Stronger competition in the manufacturing sector will ensure that some of the benefits emanating from the AfCFTA accrue to consumers. Open trade should increase competition, and thus stimulate productivity (including labor productivity)

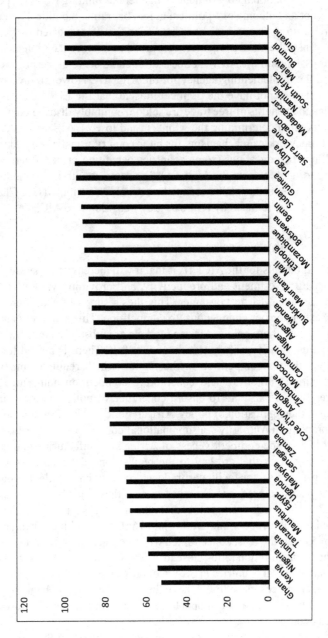

Figure 12.1 Average annual 5-Bank concentration (2010–2017).

Source: Global Financial Development Indicators Database.

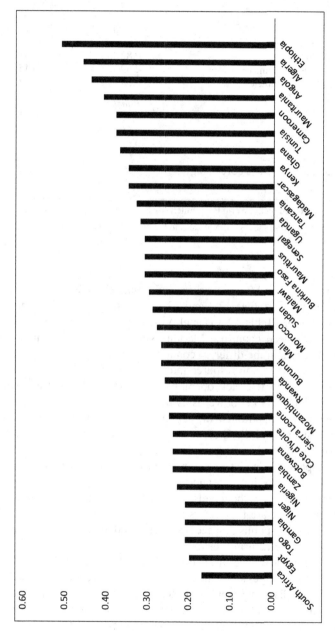

Figure 12.2 Lerner Index for African countries (2000–2014 annual average).

Source: Global Financial Development Indicators Database.

Table 12.3 Firm markup and profitability for Sub-Saharan Africa by resource intensity and region

Country Grouping	Panel A: By Resource Intensity	
	Markup	Profitability
Oil exporting countries	0,82	0,51
Other resource-intensive countries	0,69	0,45
Non-resource-intensive countries	0,64	0,42
	Panel B: By Region	
Central Africa	0,82	0,51
East Africa	0,66	0,44
Southern Africa	0,62	0,43
West Africa	0,65	0,42
Emerging market economies and developing countries[30]	0,57	0,39

Source: IMF estimates based on the World Bank Enterprise Surveys (various years).

Notes: Markup is calculated as the log ratio of sales to the cost of inputs; profitability is calculated as the difference between revenue and the cost of inputs relative to revenue.

and increase incomes for African workers and ultimately reduce poverty (Global Agenda Council 2015). Tables 12.3 and 12.4 show the levels of competition in the SSA Africa region. Table 12.3 (Panel A) shows the markup and profitability for resource-rich African countries. Markup, which indicates the market power possessed by the firms in the different countries, is highest in oil-exporting countries (0.82) and lowest in non-resource-intensive countries (0.64). This suggests that perhaps there are some cartels operating in resource-rich countries. The table also shows that higher market power is associated with higher profits. Table 12.4 (Panel B) shows that competition in the manufacturing sector is highest in Southern Africa and lowest in Central Africa. It also shows that competition in Africa is lower than that found in other emerging economies.

To further unpack the extent of competition in Africa's manufacturing sector we looked at average profitability and markup indicators for the continent (see Table 12.4). The table shows that hotels, wholesale trade and retail trade, with very high markup indicators, are the sectors with low competition levels. Textiles as well as paper and paper publishing sectors were found to be the most competitive sub-sectors of the manufacturing sector.

As international trade evolves in shape and form African countries must identify their comparative advantages along the global value chains (Global Agenda Council 2015). For example, diamonds from the DRC can be beneficiated in Botswana and marketed in South Africa while Ivory Coast's cocoa can be used to make the right chocolate for the African continent. Indeed, African countries do not have to wait for entire industries in their countries to develop as they can easily connect to lucrative parts of the production processes (Global Agenda Council 2015). African

Table 12.4 Average sector markup and profitability for Sub-Saharan Africa

Manufacturing Sub-sector	Profitability	Markup
Manufacturing of food products and beverages	0.48	0.77
Manufacturing of motor vehicles and trailers	0.48	0.76
Manufacturing of electrical machinery and apparatus	0.48	0.76
Manufacturing basic metals	0.47	0.75
Manufacturing of other non-metallic mineral products	0.47	0.74
Manufacturing chemicals and other chemical products	0.47	0.73
Manufacturing of rubber and plastic products	0.46	0.72
Publishing and printing	0.46	0.71
Manufacturing of wood and wood products	0.46	0.71
Manufacturing of furniture: manufacturing n.e.c	0.44	0.67
Manufacturing of fabricated metal products	0.44	0.66
Manufacturing of wearing apparel. Dressing	0.44	0.66
Manufacturing of machinery and equipment	0.43	0.64
Manufacturing of leather products	0.42	0.63
Manufacturing of textiles	0.41	0.59
Manufacturing of papers and paper products	0.39	0.57
Average	**0.45**	**0.69**

Source: IMF estimates based on the World Bank Enterprise Surveys.

Notes: Markup is calculated as the log ratio of sales to the cost of inputs; profitability is calculated as the difference between sales and cost of labor, raw material and intermediate inputs of sales.

countries should also identify potential competitive advantages and invest in those to move up the value-added ladder.

12.7 Conclusion

This chapter examined two important policy issues. First, it looked at the role of industrialization in the realization of the AfCFTA. Second, it looked at what it would take to industrialize Africa. It argues that industrial policy and competition policy are important instruments required to support the AfCFTA. These policies incentivize investment and drive productivity growth, thereby supporting learning-by-doing and the unfettered movement of goods on the African continent. The continent needs to structurally transform its economy with an emphasis on value addition.

The process of structural transformation is, however, neither market driven nor naturally occurring, but rather policy induced, with the government taking concrete steps through (industrial) policy. For example, to encourage private investment in industry, Africa must invest in infrastructure, particularly energy and logistics, and ensure that policies to support investment (e.g., tax and other investment incentives) are in place. Such incentives must however be carefully structured so that short-term national interests do not drive individual countries to hand out incentives to attract FDI or to give national firms a competitive edge.

Africa does not have to reinvent the wheel when it comes to industrial policy. It can, for example, learn from the EU and Asian experiences. Many of these countries have successfully diversified their economies through deliberate industrial policies. The lessons for Africa include the fact that industrial policy is a viable means to drive structural transformation and diversification of the African economy; that African countries should seek to promote industrial clusters to strengthen agglomeration economies; and that firms from all African countries should have unfettered access to the national markets of member countries.

Regarding competition, we show that African markets mostly exhibit weak competition, and the AfCFTA on its own is unlikely to change that. Given that weak competition stifles innovation and investment, policy makers should deliberately intervene to enhance competition in the region. This involves empowering existing competition authorities and constituting competition authorities where they are currently non-existent. To ensure policy coherence a supranational competition authority, akin to the European Competition Commission, will be necessary.

Coordinating industrial policy at the continental level brings about several challenges (World Bank 2016). First, Africa does not have an apex and adequately resourced regional body that is mandated to formulate and oversee the implementation of regional industrial policy. Second, the benefits of free trade are seldom equitably distributed. This may affect the willingness of other member states (especially the losers) to remove non-tariff barriers to trade. African leaders therefore need to develop a framework for inter-country transfers to address possible concerns about inequitable outcomes. Third, there is a possibility that short-term national interests could induce some countries to deviate from the AfCFTA protocols. A system of sanctions may therefore be required to minimize countervailing measures by the aggrieved party.

This chapter therefore proposes the following policy recommendations:

- The African Heads of State and Government should move to empower the AU Commission by giving it political muscle to drive the AfCFTA agenda, including the power to enforce the implementation of agreed-upon protocols.
- Harmonise competition laws and policies. Start with harmonizing policies in RECs and then harmonize across the RECs.
- Ensure competition commissions (or equivalents) are independent. The AfCFTA could develop a harmonized framework for an 'independent' national competition authority. Where there are no existing competition institutions, there is a need to constitute such institutions.
- The AfCFTA Secretariat should lead the development of a common trade policy framework, in partnership with the AU Commission.
- The AfCFTA Secretariat to develop and implement the framework for trade facilitation across African countries.
- The AU Commission to develop a framework for a system of transfers to ensure equitable sharing of the benefits accruing from the AfCFTA.

Notes

1 The views and opinions expressed in this paper are those of the authors and do not neces-sarily reflect the views or positions of their employers or institutions.

2 See Simbanegavi (2019: 1–2) and references therein.

3 For more information on regional value chains and the relevant skills see Chapters 7 and 10, respectively.

4 Intraregional trade also affects economies indirectly through growth spillovers propagated by trade linkages. Evidence suggests a spillover of 0.11% to a country's GDP growth for every percentage point increase in the growth of trading partners (Arizala et al. 2018).

5 There are a few exceptions however, such as the AGOA and the EU's everything but arms dispensation.

6 There are real risks of de-globalisation post COVID-19. Already, some countries, par-ticularly the USA and Japan, are moving to incentivise reshoring of their key suppliers out of China, with Japan setting aside USD2.2 billion for this purpose. See the following link from Bloomberg for more details: www.bloomberg.com/news/articles/2020-04-08/japan-to-fund-firms-to-shift-production-out-of-china

7 The World Bank Africa's Pulse, April 2020, Volume 21.

8 Economic Complexity Index (ECI) assesses the complexity of a country's productive structure by considering (i) the number of products in the export basket and (ii) the quality or "ubiquity" of products in the export basket (Hausmann et al. 2013). The lower the ECI score the higher the ranking (or the greater the complexity of the productive cap-acity) of that country.

9 South Africa has made notable progress in COVID-19 vaccine production underpinned by a strong private health/ science sector .

10 Of course, Africa and other regions, e.g., Latin America, have dabbled with industrial policies in the past, with little, if any, sustained structural transformation. As noted by Rodrik (2004) and Stiglitz (2015), East Asian policy makers, unlike their Latin American counterparts, applied stick (penalties) and carrot (rents) measures in equal proportions, thus better aligning incentives. See also Chang (2006) and Khan (2015). Also, given the passage of time and changes in the international trading architecture, some of the policy options that were available to the East Asian policy makers back then (e.g., export sub-sidies) are no longer available.

11 See Chapter 12 on non-tariff measures in the AfCFTA, which also looks at rules of origin.

12 Non-tariff barriers include customs clearance delays, restrictive licensing processes, cer-tification challenges, uncoordinated transport related regulations, corruption, sanitary and phytosanitary measures, specific limitations, and charges on imports (Tralac 2017). These non-tariff barriers raise trade costs and can significantly impair trade and compe-tition, to the detriment of African consumers.

13 The AfCFTA, by creating an enlarged market, is likely to attract significant FDI to the continent as firms chose to locate within the AfCFTA in order to take advantage of the opportunities. There is a risk that competition to attract FDI could see countries offering overly generous tax incentives and tax holidays—the so-called 'tax competition'.

14 Chang (2006) defines industrial policy as "a policy aimed at affecting particular indus-tries (and firms as their components) to achieve the outcomes that are perceived by the state to be efficient for the economy as a whole". However, since we are considering industrial policy at a regional level, we believe a broader definition is more appropriate.

Industrial policy is also applicable to policies directed at the development of service-oriented industries/ sectors such as business process outsourcing or tourism.

15 Manufacturing value added per capita in 2017 was a measly USD136.5, less than half the value for second worst performer, South Asia, and about one-fiftieth the value for North America, the best performer (Ibrahim et al. 2019).

16 Industrial policy has gained new traction post the global financial crisis of 2008/09. As noted by Aghion et al. (2011), China's success with industrial policy has all but "wiped out the stains from previous economic failures and has made industrial policy legitimate again". Stiglitz (2015) quips: "industrial policy is back in fashion, and rightly so" (see also UNCTAD 2018); UNECA 2014, 2016; and Aiginger 2014).

17 Inefficiencies of markets are not restricted to developing economies, however. Aghion et al. (2011) lament how, pre global financial crisis, laissez-faire policies had led several countries, in particular Southern European countries, to allow the unfettered development of non-tradable sectors at the expense of tradable sectors that are more conducive to sustainable growth and competitiveness.

18 "Owners, managers, and supervisors often do not know how best to set up the factory, align the machinery, set up systems for quality control, reduce input wastage and product rejection, manage inventories, match order flows with production cycles, maintain after sales services, and approach a host of other internal team coordination and management issues that are essential for achieving competitiveness" (Khan, 2015).

19 Indeed, the infant industry argument was developed precisely for this purpose—to protect 'young' enterprises as they experiment and learn the ropes up to a point where they can compete with the established competitors.

20 According to UNIDO (2011), "Greening of Industry is a method to attain sustainable economic growth and promote sustainable economies. It includes policymaking, improved industrial production processes and resource-efficient productivity".

21 The EU's carbon border adjustment mechanism, currently under development, is a case in point.

22 In discussing the EU industrial policy, Farla et al. (2015: 372) state: "The inclusion of some sectors, the recurrence of others, and the practice of establishing priorities after consultations with industry stakeholders suggest a lobbying process in the workings of industrial policy that is more evident in some contexts than others".

23 Poor infrastructure reduces Africa's economic growth by at least 2% per annum, and private sector productivity by up to 40% (Kaberuka 2013).

24 Countries could for instance commit at the African Union level to ratchet up R&D spending to at least 1% of GDP by, say, 2025. In addition, investments in infrastructure (energy, water, ICT, logistics, etc.) and reduction of regulatory burden, particularly for SMEs are important complementary measures to support the development of a vibrant industrial sector.

25 For example, in 2016, the applied average most-favored-nation tariff for African countries, at 14.5%, was about twice that of the European Union.

26 As noted by UNECA (2016: 51) 'ideological' flexibility is key to the success of industrial policy. Absence of mistakes imply that the industrial policy is not ambitious enough.

27 Post WWII, European countries adopted interventionist industrial policy to achieve structural transformation of their economies, targeting certain sectors such as heavy capital and scale-intensive manufacturing (e.g., steel production) with success. Later on, defensive industrial policies became untenable, and the EU shifted to more selective interventions related to technology development (Farla et al. 2015).

28 This feature will be the test case for the AfCFTA. Countries would need to let go of some of their protective policies and to harmonize policies for universal access of the African markets by firms from the region.

29 National systems of innovation are generally underdeveloped on the continent, partly due to the failure to incorporate them in policy discussions and developments and also due to inadequate funding.

30 Excluding SSA.

References

AfDB. 2016. "Jobs for Youth in Africa: Catalysing Youth Opportunity Across Africa". African Development Bank Group.

AfDB. 2018. African Economic Outlook. African Development Bank 2018.

African Development Bank. 2017. The Africa Visa Openness Report 2017.

Aghion, P., Bloom, N., Blundell, R., Griffith, R. and Howitt. P. 2005. Competition and innovation: an inverted-U relationship. *The Quarterly Journal of Economics*, 120(2): 701–728.

Aghion, P., Boulanger, J., Cohen, E., Rethinking Industrial Policy, *Bruegel Policy Brief*, 04/2011.

Aiginger, K. 2014. "Industrial Policy for a sustainable growth path". Policy Paper No. 13, OECD.

Altenburg, Tilman and Rodrik, Dani. 2017. Green industrial policy: Accelerating structural change towards wealthy green economies. *In* Altenburg, T., & Assmann, C. (Eds.). 2017. *Green Industrial Policy. Concept, Policies, Country Experiences*. Geneva, Bonn: UN Environment; German Development Institute / Deutsches Institut für Entwicklungspolitk (DIE), pp. 1–20.

Arizala, F., Bellon, M. and MacDonald, M. 2019. Regional Growth Spillovers in Sub-Saharan Africa. IMF Working Paper, WP/19/160.

Calderon, C., Kambou, G., Cantu Canales, C., Korman, V. and Kubota, M. 2019. Africa's Pulse, No. 20, October 2019: An Analysis of Issues Shaping Africa's Economic Future. © Washington, DC: World Bank. http://hdl.handle.net/10986/32480 License: CC BY 3.0 IGO.

Chang, H-J. 2006. "Industrial policy in East Asia: Lessons for Europe", EIB Papers, ISSN 0257-7755, *European Investment Bank (EIB)*, Luxembourg, Vol. 11, Iss. 2, pp. 106–132.

De Vries. G. Mensah. E. Kruse H. and Sen. K. 2021. Sub-Saharan Africa had a manufacturing renaissance in 2010s–it's a promising sign for the years ahead. www.wider.unu.edu/publication/sub-saharan-africa-had-manufacturing-renaissance-2010s-%E2%80%93-it%E2%80%99s-promising-sign-years-ahead#:~:text.

Evans, P. 1995. *Embedded Autonomy: States and Industrial Transformation*. Princeton University Press.

Farla, K., Guadagno. F., and Verspagen, B. 2015. "Industrial policy in the European Union". In Jesus Felipe (ed.). 2015. *Development and Modern Industrial Policy in Practice: Issues and Country Experiences*. Asian Development Bank.

Felipe, J. (ed.). 2015. *Development and Modern Industrial Policy in Practice: Issues and Country Experiences*. Asian Development Bank.

Global Agenda Council. 2015. *Outlook on the Global Agenda 2015*. World Economic Forum, Geneva.

Hausmann, R., et al. 2013. "The Atlas of Economic Complexity: Mapping Paths to Prosperity".

Hoekman, B. and Njinkeu, D. 2017. "Integrating Africa: Some Trade Policy Research Priorities and Challenges". *Journal of African Economies*, Volume 26, Issue suppl_2, November 2017, Pages ii12–ii39, https://doi.org/10.1093/jae/ejx031.

Hoekman, B., Senbet, L. W., and Simbanegavi, W. 2017. "Integrating African Markets: The Way Forward". *Journal of African Economies*, Volume 26, Issue suppl_2, November 2017, Pages ii3–ii11, https://doi.org/10.1093/jae/ejx033

Ibrahim, G., Simbanegavi, W., Prakash, A., Davis, W., Wasike, W., and Patel, A. 2019. Industrial Development and ICT in Africa: Opportunities, Challenges and Way Forward. T20 Japan.

Kaberuka, D. 2013. "Sustaining Africa's Economic Growth: The Challenges of Inclusion and Financing Infrastructure". (Speech by the President of the African Development Bank at the AACB Symposium on Financial Inclusion. AfDB, October).

Karingi, S., and Mevel, S. 2012. Deepening Regional Integration in Africa: A Computable General Equilibrium Assessment of the Establishment of a Continental Free Trade Area Followed by a Continental Customs Union. Paper presented at the 15th Global Trade Analysis Project Conference, Geneva, June 27–29.

Khan, M. H. 2015. "Industrial policy design and implementation challenges". In Felipe. J (ed.), *Development and Modern Industrial Policy in Practice: Issues and Country Experiences*. Asian Development Bank, pp. 94–126.

Landesmann, M. and Stöllinger, R. 2020. The European Union's Industrial Policy: What are the Main Challenges? Policy Notes and Reports 36. The Vienna Institute for International Economic Studies.

Observatory of Economic Complexity. 2016. MIT's Observatory of Economic Complexity: Country Ranking. (n.d.). Retrieved June 15, 2016, from https://atlas.media.mit.edu/rankings.

Rodrik, D. 2004. Industrial policy for the twenty-first century, Paper prepared for UNIDO.

Rodrik, D. 2008. *Industrial policy: Don't ask why, ask how*. Asian Development Bank, Manila, Philippines.

Simbanegavi, W. 2019. Expediting Growth and Development: Policy Challenges Confronting Africa. *Journal of Development Perspectives* 3(1–2): 46–79.

Stiglitz, J. E. 2015. Industrial Policy, Learning, and Development. WIDER Working Paper 2015/149.

Tralac. 2017. Intra-African trade profile 2017. www.tralac.org/resources/infographic/13964-intra-africa-trade-profile-2017.html

UNCTAD. 2018. World Investment Report 2018: Investment and new industrial policies. Geneva.

UNECA. 2014. Dynamic Industrial Policy in Africa: Innovative Institutions, Effective Processes and Flexible Mechanisms. Economic Commission for Africa.

UNECA. 2016. Transformative industrial policy for Africa. Economic Commission for Africa

United Nations Industrial Development Organisation (UNIDO). 2011. "Policies for Supporting Green Industry". www.unido.org/fileadmin/user_media/Services/Green_Industry/web_policies_green_industry.pdf.

Vera Songwe. 2019. "Intra-African trade: A path to economic diversification and inclusion". Africa Growth Initiative, Brookings Institution.

World Bank. 2015. Trade facilitation for global and regional value chains in SACU. World Bank. Washington, DC.

World Bank. 2016. *Breaking down barriers: Unlocking Africa's potential through vigorous competition policy*. Washington DC, World Bank Group.

Yean, T. S. 2015. "Diversification and industrial policies in Malaysia". In Felipe. J (ed.), *Development and Modern Industrial Policy in Practice: Issues and Country Experiences*. Asian Development Bank, Manila, Philippines, pp 320–345.

13 Intellectual property and the African Continental Free Trade Area

A public health perspective[1]

Amal Nagah Elbeshbishi

13.1 Introduction

This chapter discusses intellectual property (IP) currently under negotiation in phase II of the African Continental Free Trade Area (AfCFTA) from a public health perspective to come out with solutions to protect African countries. IP is pertinent because of its cross-cutting nature ranging from agriculture, chemistry, biotechnology, and information technology to creative industries and public health. IP laws may hinder or promote economic growth within the AfCFTA.

According to the World Health Organization (WHO), the continent has 25.7 million people living with HIV/AIDS, and the region will experience a 27% increase in deaths from non-communicable diseases (NCDs). The continent accounts for 24% of the global disease burden (Ahen and Salo-Ahen, 2018). This is primarily because the region is undergoing a demographic transition, leading to increasing demand for safe, effective, and affordable health commodities (Gouda et al., 2019). The Business and Sustainable Development Commission (2017) and the United Nations Economic Commission for Africa (ECA) report on Health Care and Economic Growth in Africa (2019) estimates Africa's health and wellness markets at US$ 259 billion, which will be the second-largest market after the United States by 2030 (United Nations Economic Commission for Africa (ECA), 2019).

Based on reports from WHO, Africa shows that there is a 20.7% chance of a person aged between 30 and 70 years dying of NCDs (WHO, 2018). With the chronic nature of NCDs, affected persons may have to rely on life-sustaining medicines for their lifetime. However, most African countries' continued reliance on China and India for drug importation has been threatened in recent times by the obligation imposed on these countries by the TRIPS Agreement to enforce protectionist IP frameworks (Owoeye, 2013). Consequently, a balanced IP framework incorporating the TRIPS flexibilities such as compulsory licensing to facilitate access to medicines is crucial and contributes to achieving Sustainable Development Goal 3. The full use of TRIPS flexibilities will legally allow the production of generic medicines (Ombaka, 2002). It may encourage significant pharmaceutical investment in the form of foreign generic firms investing in a country's domestic pharmaceutical sector.

DOI: 10.4324/9781003456568-13

The chapter documents that trade in pharmaceutical products between African countries is relatively small, which is mainly due to differences in the regulations of these countries relating to the manufacturing, import, export, and distribution of pharmaceutical products. This finding indicates that enhanced integration on the continent represents a huge opportunity for Africa's pharmaceutical industry. The chapter also documents that despite a public health crisis of enormous proportions for a compulsory license for HIV/AIDS for example, apparently no African country has issued a compulsory license for any medicine.

The remainder of the chapter is organized as follows: Section 13.2 presents the international pharmaceutical market and Africa's situation. Section 13.3 analyses the TRIPS Agreement and patents on drugs. Section 13.4 analyses the arguments for and against IP protection. Section 13.5 answers the question 'what should African countries do'. And Section 13.6 concludes and provides policy recommendations.

13.2 The international pharmaceutical market and Africa's situation

The international pharmaceutical market is comprised of two sectors: Patented drugs and generic drugs. The market for patented drugs is the most important economically. This market is dominated by large conglomerates from developed countries, which are responsible for the development of new therapies. The other fast-growing sector of the international pharmaceutical industry is that of generic medications, which began to be developed in industrialized countries in the 1970s as the most profitable patented medications were released into the public domain and manufacturers of generics began a price war amongst themselves and against developers whose drugs were in the public domain. Generic drugs currently make up half the pharmaceuticals market.

Most African countries lack research, administrative and resource capacities to negotiate in international fora, and lack production capacity in the modern pharmaceutical industry. However, the pharmaceutical industry in some of these countries has evolved considerably. Often motivated by the industrial politics of the 1950s, some African countries such as Egypt, Morocco, Kenya and South Africa began to create national pharmaceutical industries to replace imports as well as to guarantee themselves autonomy in a domain considered strategic; to reduce expenditures in foreign currencies by limiting imports of materials, and to supply the countries' needs at the lowest prices for social and public health reasons.

At first glance, it should be possible to produce medication cheaply in African countries because of reduced production costs (most significantly, labor costs). However, it is not so simple in countries without industrial or environmental expertise. It is also difficult for countries with limited internal markets (those with small and/ or impoverished populations), which cannot benefit from the economies of scale larger countries' multinational companies enjoy.

Africa's tropical climate makes the continent the largest reservoir of infectious diseases, particularly malaria, tuberculosis (TB), and AIDS, besides frequent outbreaks of polio, meningitis, cholera, pandemic influenza, yellow fever, measles, hepatitis, and tetanus. With the increasing adoption of the Western lifestyle in

Africa, there has been a paradigm shift in illness burden towards NCDs, driving the demand for chronic prescription drugs. While continuing to suffer from infectious and parasitic illness, lifestyle diseases such as cardiovascular diseases, diabetes, and cancer witnessed high growth rates. WHO predicts that NCDs' proportional contribution to the healthcare burden in Africa will rise by 21% through 2030.[2]

ECA estimates that 94% of Africa's pharmaceuticals are imported (United Nations Economic Commission for Africa, ECA, OECD, 2020). One of the obstacles to the development of trade in pharmaceutical products within African countries arises from differences in these countries' regulations relating to the manufacture, import, export and distribution of pharmaceutical products (Karingi, 2020). Therefore, there is a need for regional trading blocks to collaborate in harmonizing such regulations, because in Africa, even though the proposals for restoring pooled tenders for obtaining drugs appear to have been discussed for a long time, no significant progress has been made in their practical implementation.

Despite the prospects of the regional mechanism for tackling the conundrum of access to medicines in Africa, some factors may inhibit its effective use. *First,* it has been argued that the challenge of access to medicine in Africa is not only caused by the TRIPS Agreement (Soyeju and Wabwire, 2018). The challenges posed by non-TRIPS factors such as lack of good roads, inadequate power supply, poor logistics, inadequate medical personnel, etc. will render the regional mechanism of little or no effect, if left unsolved. *Second,* there is a lack of coherence in the IP domestic laws of African countries. For the regional mechanism to be effectively used, some specific provisions must be uniformly incorporated in individual countries' domestic legislation. To achieve this, legal expertise and a strong political willpower, which is not readily available in most African countries, will be needed. *Third,* developed countries' trend to incorporate higher standards of IP protection (TRIPS-plus) into bilateral and free trade agreements could reduce the potency of the regional mechanism. TRIPS-plus provisions elongate the life span of patented drugs beyond the statutory period. The fact that some African countries are signatories to TRIPS-plus Agreements will have a distressing effect on the regional collective drive for access to life-saving drugs in Africa.

13.3 The TRIPS Agreement and patents on drugs

The TRIPS Agreement establishes minimum standards in the field of IP. All member countries must comply with these standards by modifying their national regulations to accord with the rules of the agreement. The main change with respect to pharmaceuticals is the obligation to grant patent protection to pharmaceutical products and process inventions (Subramanian and Watal, 2000).

Under the TRIPS Agreement, member countries must grant patents for a minimum of 20 years to any inventions of a pharmaceutical product or process that fulfills the established criteria of novelty, inventiveness, and usefulness. As soon as the agreement comes into force in a member country, unauthorized copies of patented drugs are prohibited. Countries that break this rule will incur trade sanctions authorized by the World Trade Organization (WTO).

For the AfCFTA State parties that are also members of the WTO, the TRIPS Agreement serves as a useful international benchmark and a tool for harmonizing IP laws since it establishes minimum standards for intellectual property rights (IPRs) protection. Hence, the AfCFTA is entirely consistent with the letter and spirit of the WTO agreements. Therefore, implementing the AfCFTA will not interfere with or diminish any WTO obligations or commitments for those African countries that are members of the WTO. In fact, the AfCFTA will extend WTO discipline to non-members, which may help them better prepare for accession eventually while benefiting from the predictability offered by a rules-based system.

The AfCFTA is an unprecedented opportunity to allow African countries to enhance regional and international cooperation, improve countries' enforcement standards and move towards a harmonized, predictable, and reliable regional IPRs enforcement system building from TRIPS and other treaties (ECA, AU, AfDB and UNCTAD, 2019).

The AfCFTA needs to be compatible with the TRIPS Agreement (with careful attention to ensure it preserves TRIPS flexibilities). Member states should be encouraged and supported to pass domestic TRIPS-compatible patent legislation. By supporting the African continent to negotiate as a coherent bloc, the AfCFTA should be harnessed as a vehicle to strengthen Africa's ability to ensure TRIPS flexibilities are fully utilized to enable local production and access to essential medicines (UNDP, 2016). Over the longer term, African countries must use the AfCFTA to create regional value chains (RVCs) for Africa to better serve its own health market, estimated at $259 billion annually (UNECA, 2020).

13.4 The arguments for and against IP protection

The issues surrounding IP protection are a double-edged sword. Such protections contribute to world welfare by creating market incentives to reward those who generate new knowledge. The rewards are provided by granting monopoly power to the owners of knowledge, enabling them to charge prices above costs for the goods and services containing that knowledge. If such monopoly power were not granted, the incentives for discovery and the volume of resources devoted to research and development would be smaller (Peukert, 2017).

On the other hand, monopoly power is typically granted to owners of knowledge for a long period of time during which competitors are significantly restricted. The market for knowledge goods and services is distorted, with smaller volumes being produced for consumers and prices being higher. Fewer competitors at the point of market entry provide less competition in the discovery of small innovations and improvements. These factors lessen world welfare (Oh and Khor, 2001).

African countries will be disadvantaged in many ways. Firms in these countries that wish to produce and sell products covered by patents will be forced into a licensing agreement which likely will involve royalty payments to the patents' owners. Consumers will be charged higher prices (Oh, 2000). In some cases, the patent's foreign owner will choose to serve African countries' markets through exports rather than local production; employment opportunities will be lost and the foreign exchange cost of imports will rise. Similar consequences would apply in the case of local firms producing counterfeit goods in violation of trademark provisions. Finally, African countries will also be burdened with the costs of legislating laws for IP protection and the administrative costs of enforcing those laws.

13.4.1 The arguments for IP protection

The arguments for IP protection can be summarized as follows:

- Strong IP protection not only benefits research-based pharmaceutical companies and the patients they serve. It also helps African countries by improving the conditions for investment, encouraging local industry development, creating jobs, transferring technology, and enabling more goods to be produced. If such a regime is not in place, investors will shy away from investing, research and licensing in these countries.
- Multinational companies (MNCs) would like to see the immediate adoption of patents instead of benefiting from the grace period. They argue that the development of new and improved compounds is becoming costly and more difficult. Multinationals argue that high profits are the reward for success in the risky business of pharmaceutical research and development.
- Innovative drugs often originate in countries where prices are free. Thus, the industry sets the price, not based on cost, which adds a profit margin, but at a far higher level, that the market can bear. So, if for example, a drug permits savings on hospital costs, it can be sold at a far higher price.
- Due to fear of piracy and low product prices in many African countries, most multinational companies are reluctant to introduce their top-of-the-line products in these places. Therefore, patients in these countries compulsorily lose out on better treatment options.
- Strengthened patent protection is expected to encourage foreign direct investment (FDI) in African countries. An environment hospitable to innovative foreign technology sets in motion a range of other dynamics such as licensing, co-marketing and joint ventures, generating multiplier effects that benefit local drug manufacturers.

13.4.2 The arguments against IP protection

The arguments against IP protection can be summarized as follows:

- A major issue of concern is the incentives for creating and maintaining research and development (R&D) capabilities in African countries. In the absence of IP protection, firms in these countries have incentives to copy (reverse engineer) products patented in developed countries to produce them locally for sale in the domestic market. African countries benefit from the provision of jobs. Local production provides competition with imports that might otherwise be sold at very high monopoly prices, reducing the volume of imports and thereby saving on foreign exchange. Moreover, it creates R&D capability and mentality. In the early stages, this activity may have been limited to rather unsophisticated reverse engineering. However, over time, these capabilities may become more sophisticated and result in product innovations and improvements aimed at developing products more suitable to local consumers' demands. In some cases, the result may be R&D capabilities that are truly competitive worldwide.[3]

- The indigenous capability of the local drug industry in African countries will be hit hard. Consumers will have to pay higher prices. The infrastructure created by local industry will remain unutilized. Local production will be confined to making age-old drugs, denying the benefits of new drugs and innovation. Local producers will have to wait 20 years for the patent to expire on a new drug before they can start to manufacture it, by which time a new drug in the market will probably undermine its value.
- Many African countries are careless about patency issues for cost reduction purposes. African countries should either have the financial capabilities to buy patented drugs from MNCs or develop the technological and research capacities that produce their own pharmaceutical products. Unfortunately, most African countries lack both (De Beer et al., 2017).

13.5 What should African countries do?

The answer is simple: take advantage of the good aspects and introduce policies to minimize the adverse effects of IP protection's bad aspects. Active government policy intervention is needed to design national legislation that addresses human development needs in terms of access to health care and ensures that products are priced to market and, irrespective of their patent status, are affordable to consumers (Adekola, 2019). The following discussion will present some solutions for African countries.

13.5.1 Compulsory licenses

Compulsory licenses are essential to protect public health. Countries should take the view that the TRIPS and the AfCFTA Agreements in no way stand in the way of public health protection. Therefore, it should provide the broadest flexibility for the use of compulsory licenses in a systematic and efficient way.

Compulsory licenses can represent a significant tool for governments to ensure access to pharmaceuticals. In general, patent owners are expected to provide access to their patented medicines to the market. In specific circumstances, however, governments may deem it necessary to grant compulsory licenses to allow interested third persons to produce medicines, to ensure that it will be more affordable to the public (Correa, 2000, 2001).

Some of the most relevant provisions of the TRIPS Agreement with respect to compulsory licenses are Articles 7, 8, 31 and 40 of TRIPS and Article 5 of the Paris Convention. When read together, such provisions allow members to ensure that governments can exercise regulatory policies to promote public health policies.

Based on Article 5 A of the Paris Convention and 31 of TRIPS, governments may issue compulsory licenses as a way of ensuring that medicines will be available at more affordable prices.

Reference should also be made to the provisions of the Paris Convention related to compulsory licenses, which have been incorporated into the TRIPS Agreement and could be added to the AfCFTA Agreement. The Paris Convention allows countries wide discretion to issue compulsory licenses "to prevent the abuse, which might result from the exercise of exclusive rights, conferred by the patent".

In many cases, African countries—particularly Least Developed and smaller economies—have limited industrial capacities and very small domestic markets to manufacture medicines locally to ensure adequate access to drugs. In this regard, it should be noted that nothing in the TRIPS Agreement prevents members from granting compulsory licenses for foreign suppliers to provide medicines in the domestic market.

The WTO decision on access to medicines adopted on August 30, 2003, requires a country importing pharmaceutical products produced by the exporting country under a compulsory license granted in accordance with its terms, to use them exclusively for the treatment of a disease prevailing in its territory. Re-exports of such products to other countries are prohibited. However, the decision makes an exception in the case of countries that are members of certain types of regional economic groupings; these countries could re-export the imported product to the countries belonging to the region. This WTO decision provides that its provisions could be used by countries belonging to regional economic groupings [of which at least half of the members are Least Developed countries (LDCs)] for developing imports and production on a regional basis. At the same time, it calls on these countries to develop "systems for the grant of regional patents".

The development of such systems avoids the need on the part of the companies or inventors of having to apply for the registration of patents in each of the countries belonging to the region; acceptance of the application by the regional patent organization could result in the patent being registered in all countries in the region. The practices in this regard could however vary. For instance, while the rules of the African Regional Intellectual Property Organization (ARIPO) provide its members with the right to reject the patent provisionally approved by it, the Organization of the African Intellectual Property [Organisation Africaine de la Propriété (OAPI)], imposes a binding obligation on its member countries to accept and register the regional patents approved by it.[4] The adoption of such regional patents may enable regional IP organizations to issue compulsory licenses for imports (on a regional basis) in pursuance of the provisions of the decision, instead of each member country having to issue separate licenses.

The decision envisages that the countries' flexibility could be used with no or insufficient manufacturing capacities for developing gradual production under compulsory licenses. However, one of the major difficulties these countries are facing is that because of the small size of the market, there is reluctance from the entrepreneurs to invest in the production of pharmaceutical products. To overcome these difficulties, the decision provides that products produced under compulsory licenses by a country belonging to certain types of regional economic groupings could be exported to other countries belonging to such a grouping.

The objective of these provisions is to enable countries with no manufacturing capacities "to enhance their purchasing power" by pooling orders on a regional basis when products produced under compulsory licenses are to be imported and to provide an advantage of "economies of scale" to manufacturers producing under compulsory licenses by providing them a regional market. The flexibility available under the decision could be used to grant compulsory licenses to foreign companies, which are willing to establish plants in their territories or enter into a collaboration arrangement with local companies to establish these plants.

The measures described above, which could be taken for the development of imports, and production are subject to the following conditions:

- Countries belonging to the regional economic groupings of which at least half of the current members are Least Developed can take advantage of these provisions. Most of the regional economic groupings in Africa [Common Market for Eastern and Southern Africa (COMESA), Economic Community of West African States (ECOWAS) and Southern African Development Community (SADC)] would satisfy these conditions. The flexibility provided by the decision that would enable a country to re-export imported pharmaceutical products under compulsory licenses or export products produced under such licenses can be available only if the importing country shares the same health problems.
- The territorial nature of the patent must be respected. This condition implies that where the patent relating to the product to be exported is registered in the concerned country, imports would be permitted only if a compulsory license to import has been issued.

The term "compulsory licensing" does not appear in the TRIPS Agreement. Instead, the practice falls under "other use without authorization of the right holder" (Article 31), of which compulsory licensing is only part, since "other use" also includes use by governments for their own purposes (Love, 2001). The option to grant a compulsory license under Article 31 for the purpose of manufacturing or import is available to all members. While there has been particular attention paid to the use of compulsory licensing for pharmaceuticals, it applies to patents in any field. All members may grant such licenses for health technologies, such as medicines, vaccines and diagnostics, as well as any other product or technology needed to combat COVID-19 (WTO, 2020). In response to the COVID-19 pandemic, Canada, Germany and Hungary amended their national laws, further empowering the governments to authorize government use and compulsory licenses. In Ecuador and Chile, the governments have been urged by legislative bodies to declare the COVID-19 pandemic to be a national public health crisis and then to issue compulsory licenses (Wu and Khazin, 2020).

The TRIPS Agreement does not limit the reasons for which governments may grant compulsory licenses. However, compulsory licensing or government use of a patent without the right holder's authorization can only be done under many conditions aimed at protecting the legitimate interests of the patent holder. Article 31 lists many provisions that should be respected in such cases. For example, the person or company applying for a license must have first attempted unsuccessfully to obtain a voluntary license from the right holder on reasonable commercial terms. However, for "national emergencies", "other circumstances of extreme urgency", "public non-commercial use" or remedying anti-competitive practices, there is no need to try for a voluntary license. If a compulsory license is issued, adequate remuneration must still be paid to the patent holder, considering the authorization's economic value (Article 31 h). Compulsory licensing must meet other requirements listed in the same Article. It cannot take the form of an exclusive license, and "shall be authorized predominantly for the supply of the domestic market of the Member authorizing such use" (Article 31 f). This condition need not be applied where such use is permitted to remedy a practice determined after judicial or administrative process to be anti-competitive (Article 31 k).

An amendment was made to the TRIPS Agreement which came into force on 23 January 2017. In its Article 31bis (4), the amendment creates a policy space for a regional collective effort, which allows less-developed countries to harness their economies of scale and purchasing power for collective procurement of medicines and joint effective use of TRIPS flexibilities. The regional mechanism's essence is to ensure that low-income countries stand strong together to tackle their shared public health concerns as opposed to when an individual country makes a seemingly futile effort to do the same alone. For the regional agreement to be effective, however, a free trade or single market policy is required within the regional alliance to facilitate the free flow of pharmaceuticals.

Article 31bis (4) of the TRIPS Agreement stipulates three conditions that must be satisfied before a regional trade agreement can use the regional mechanism:

1. Half of the current membership of the regional agreement must be ranked as LDCs.
2. Members of the regional trade agreement must share similarities in disease burden.
3. The regional agreement must comply with the requirements of the WTO.

A critical look at the regional mechanism shows that African regional groupings are the targeted beneficiaries. This is because the continent has the highest concentration of LDCs in the world. The AfCFTA matches the regional model envisaged in Article 31bis (4) of the TRIPS Agreement for the following reasons: first, of the 54 African countries, 33 are ranked LDCs by the United Nations; second, the continent shares similarities in disease burden, particularly malaria, tuberculosis, HIV/AIDS, and other NCDs; and third, the AfCFTA provides that the WTO shall be duly notified of the regional trade agreement.

The signing of the AfCFTA is indeed a commendable feat for African countries. The regional drive will provide the platform to jointly tackle the manifold socio-economic challenges of the regions, particularly that of access to medicines. The African continent can leverage the regional mechanism by combining its economies of scale and purchasing power for the bulk importation of patented drugs under compulsory licensing. The creation of a single economic space under the AfCFTA allows more secure logistics and a controlled environment for procurement and distribution. It is important to note that the regional mechanism expands pharmaceuticals' scope under the system to include active ingredients and diagnostic kits. The regional mechanism can also utilize the benefits of regional patents, patent pools, voluntary licensing, collective price negotiation with patent holders, and collective production and/or procurement of generic drugs to make medicines more affordable and accessible to its poor population.

Furthermore, the TRIPS amendment stresses the imperative of building jointly owned local manufacturing capacity for the regional alliance as an enduring solution to the access to medicine conundrum (Annex to the TRIPS Agreement Paragraphs 5 and 6). To achieve this, the TRIPS amendment emphasizes the undertaking of developed countries under the TRIPS Agreement to assist in technical cooperation and technology transfer. In addition, LDCs are to enjoy a transition period until July 2021 and January 2033 for the substantive provision of the TRIPS Agreement and pharmaceutical patents, respectively (See WTO document Nos IP/C/64 and IP/C/73).[5] These transitional waivers' rationale is to afford LDCs sufficient time to build a viable technological base and local pharmaceutical manufacturing capacity before full compliance with TRIPS obligations. The implication of these flexibilities on the regional mechanism under TRIPS reforms is that members of the 'qualified' regional alliance can collectively appropriate the gains of the transitional waivers enjoyed by its LDC members to facilitate the combined local production and onward distribution of generic versions of patented pharmaceuticals within the economic coalition without fear of falling foul of TRIPS obligations. Suppose the waivers are fully harnessed by Africa's continental and regional economic blocs. In that case, LDC members can become the 'pharmacy shop' where generic drugs can be legally sourced for the collective utilization of all.

Enhanced integration on the continent represents a huge opportunity for Africa's pharmaceutical industry. The pharmaceutical sector in the name of public health should occupy the center stage of the AfCFTA and should be prioritized in the initial implementation stages. The AfCFTA needs to be TRIPS-compatible (with careful attention to ensure it preserves TRIPS flexibilities). Member states should be encouraged and supported to pass domestic TRIPS-compatible patent legislation. By supporting the African continent to negotiate as a coherent bloc, the AfCFTA should be harnessed as a vehicle to strengthen Africa's ability to ensure TRIPS flexibilities are fully utilized to enable local production and access to essential medicines. African institutions such as the African Union (AU), the AfCFTA Secretariat and ECA can play an important role in coordinating efforts and guiding appropriate specialization strategies based on comparative advantage.

Compulsory licenses have been used extensively in Canada, Japan, and Europe for a variety of purposes. Canada has the most extensive experience with the use of compulsory licenses for pharmaceutical drugs. Until pressured by the United States (US), as a condition to join the North American Free Trade Agreement (NAFTA), to abandon a compulsory licensing approach that was nearly automatic, Canada routinely granted compulsory licenses on pharmaceuticals, with compensation based upon royalties, typically set a 4%of the competitor's sales price. Such evidence indicates that arguments—voiced by developed countries governments and industry—against compulsory licenses as a deviation from acceptable standards for IPRs are not reflected in the policies applied in such countries.

Despite a public health crisis of enormous proportions for a compulsory license for HIV/AIDS for example, apparently no African country has issued a compulsory license for any medicine. Given the permissive global trade framework for compulsory licensing, one must wonder why.

Government use of provisions should be strong. The TRIPS rules give governments very broad powers to authorize the use of patents for public non-commercial use, and this is one area where there are many good state practice models to consider. No African country should have weaker statutory public use provisions than the US, German, Irish, or United Kingdom (UK) provisions. There is a high variance in national provisions for government or public use of patents. Some are quite permissive, while others are not. The US for example has very broad rights to use patents for public purposes, the government can use patents for any government purpose, and it is not obligated to negotiate for licenses, and does not authorize any injunctive relief to the patent owner, the patent owner is granted compensation, as a government taking under eminent domain laws. In Germany, "a patent shall have no effect where the Federal Government orders that the invention be exploited in the interest of public welfare".

13.5.2 Generic drugs

The term "generic" is used to denote versions of products, which are under patents produced based on a license granted voluntarily by the patent holder, a compulsory license granted by the government, or after the expiry of the duration of the patent period. The generic versions produced and marketed must be interchangeable with the patented product and generic versions of such patented products as doctors often substitute generic versions for a patented drug. The patients may also change over to using a generic version, instead of the patented product, particularly where they are substantially cheaper than the patented products. The government can ban the practice of manufacturers offering economic incentives to doctors who prescribe their products.[6]

As the definition of the term "generic version" differs considerably under different countries' national laws, WHO refers to such products as Multisource Products. In relation to such multisource products, the producers are required to submit evidence that the multisource product is "therapeutically equivalent" to the innovative product and has the same standards of quality, efficacy and safety as the innovative product (WHO, 2001).

Countries must devote the proper resources to improve the number and rate of generic drugs approved. These are the products that can bring the most financial relief to the drug bill. The potential for generic drugs to bring even greater cost savings depends in large measure on government policy and practice. The more quickly a generic is added to drug formularies, the more savings can accrue to the drug program and all consumers.

Generic drugs are priced 40–50% lower than their brand–name counterparts. Competition from generics ensures the availability of affordable, high-quality substitutes for expensive brand–name prescription drugs, thereby reducing overall drug costs. When a generic substitute for a brand–name drug enters the market, it does so at a substantially lower price and, as more generic versions of the same drug enter the market, the price drops even further.

During the AIDS pandemic, for example, the world benefitted from the absence of product patent protection in pharmaceuticals in India. After supplies from India started, the prices of an effective patented AIDS drug combination crashed leading to a significant scaling up of treatment. India became the dominant source of AIDS drugs for the majority of the people in low–and medium-income countries (LMICs). India could do this because India succeeded in developing the industry from the basic stages. Indian generic firms developed manufacturing capacities to manufacture and supply the drugs in large volumes for HIV/AIDS patients around the world (Waning et al., 2010).

African countries under the coordination of the AU should pool their resources and strengthen their capacity to manufacture the needed generic pharmaceutical products. The regional trading blocs such as COMESA, ECOWAS and SADC should share the manufacturing of generic drugs based on their comparative advantages and trade among themselves. The AU should also network with its members to negotiate bulk procurement of raw materials for generic production since the costs will be lower than what countries can negotiate individually.

13.5.3 Parallel imports

Parallel imports (or gray-market imports) involve the import and resale in a country, without the patent holder's consent, of a patented product that was put on the market of the exporting country by the patent holder. The practice of parallel importation is driven by the disparity between prices for goods between markets. Parallel imports are generally exported from a low-price market for resale at a higher price in the importing country. The underlying concept for parallel imports is based on the principle of exhaustion of rights. This principle is premised on the fact that where the patent holder has been rewarded through the first sale or distribution of the product, he/she no longer has the right to control the use or resale of the product.

Parallel imports are of importance for public health interests, since the pharmaceutical industry generally sets prices differently throughout the world for the same medicines. Parallel imports would prevent market segmentation and price discrimination by patent holders on a regional or international scale. Parallel importation of a patented medicine from a country where it is sold at a lower price will enable more patients in the importing country to gain access to the medicines. Such a measure would also not prevent the patent owner from receiving remuneration for the patented invention in the country where the product is first sold. In this regard, parallel importation must be regarded as a legitimate measure, which WTO members are permitted to adopt to protect public health and nutrition as is provided for in Article 8 of the TRIPS Agreement.

In the TRIPS Agreement, parallel importation is regulated by the concept of the "exhaustion" of IPRs. The TRIPS Agreement simply says (Article 6) that none of its provisions, except those dealing with non-discrimination based on nationality (National Treatment and Most-Favored-Nation treatment), can be used to address the issue of exhaustion of IPRs in a WTO dispute. In other words, even if a country allows parallel imports in a way that might violate the TRIPS Agreement, this cannot be raised as a dispute in the WTO unless fundamental principles of non-discrimination are involved. To avoid a possible discrimination complaint under Article 27.1 and benefit all sectors of the economy, it is recommended that parallel importing should be permitted within national legislation, for patented goods in all fields of technology, and not only for health-related inventions.

Article 6 of the TRIPS Agreement is extremely relevant for member countries, particularly LDCs and smaller economies. Article 6 provides that members are free to incorporate the principle of international exhaustion of rights in national legislation. Consequently, any member can determine the extent to which the principle of exhaustion of rights is applied in its own jurisdiction, without breaching any obligation under the TRIPS Agreement.

Whenever governments deem it appropriate, the adoption of the principle of international exhaustion of rights can be a useful tool for health policies. Where the prices of pharmaceutical products are lower in a foreign market, for instance, a government may decide to allow the importation of such products into the national market, to allow the offer of drugs at more affordable prices. Such measures may be beneficial to prevent anti-competitive practices on behalf of patent owners who offer their patented products at unreasonably high prices in the domestic market. In this case, patent owners would compete with other legitimate products, and given their exclusive rights would be exhausted, the interests of the patent owner would not be damaged.

For African countries, in particular, LDCs and smaller economies, "parallel importation" can be a significant way of increasing access to medications, where the prices charged by patent holders for their products are unaffordable. Moreover, in situations where the local manufacture of the product is not feasible, and therefore compulsory licenses may be ineffective, parallel importation may be a relevant tool to ensure access to drugs.

Considering the importance of Article 6 as an instrument for health policies, we consider that Article 6 should be implemented in such a way as to ensure the broadest flexibility for members to resort to parallel imports. Members should therefore confirm their rights to apply regimes of exhaustion of rights in their jurisdiction.

13.6 Conclusions and recommendations

This chapter shows that trade in pharmaceutical products between African countries at present is relatively small. One of the obstacles to the development of such trade arises from differences in the regulations of these countries relating to the manufacture, import, export and distribution of pharmaceutical products. There is therefore a need for regional trading blocks to collaborate in harmonizing such regulations. The signing of the AfCFTA presents a great opportunity for the continent to take advantage of the policy space made available for parties to regional trade agreements under the amended TRIPS Agreement. Even though several challenges threaten the effective use of the system, African countries' pooled effort holds a lot of promises in surmounting the challenges. For instance, if an African country within the regional alliance has shortcomings, other countries possessing a complementary condition could help alleviate the inadequacies. Hence, regional collective effort is indeed the way to go.

The chapter emphasizes the fact that enhanced integration on the continent represents a huge opportunity for Africa's pharmaceutical industry. The pharmaceutical sector in the name of public health should occupy the center stage of the AfCFTA Agreement and should be prioritized in the initial stages of implementation. The AfCFTA needs to be TRIPS-compatible (with careful attention to ensure it preserves TRIPS flexibilities), and member states should be encouraged and supported to pass domestic TRIPS-compatible patent legislation. By supporting the African continent to negotiate as a coherent bloc, the AfCFTA should be harnessed as a vehicle to strengthen Africa's ability to ensure TRIPS flexibilities are fully utilized to enable local production and access to essential medicines. African institutions such as the AU, the AfCFTA Secretariat and ECA can play an important role in coordinating efforts and guiding appropriate specialization strategies based on comparative advantage.

The chapter suggests compulsory licensing as a solution, and it highlights that despite a public health crisis of enormous proportions for a compulsory license for HIV/AIDS, apparently no African country has issued a compulsory license for any medicine. Given the permissive global trade framework for compulsory licensing, one must wonder why this is so. The chapter recommends the use of generic drugs. African countries under the coordination of the AU should pool their resources and strengthen their capacity to manufacture the needed generic pharmaceutical products. Regional trading blocs such as COMESA, ECOWAS and SADC should share the manufacturing of generic drugs based on their comparative advantages and trade among themselves. The AU should also network with its members to negotiate bulk procurement of raw materials for generic production since the costs will be lower than what countries can negotiate individually. Finally, it recommends using "parallel importation" as well; it suggests that for African countries, in particular, LDCs and smaller economies, parallel importation can be a significant way of increasing access to medications, where the prices charged by patent holders for their products are unaffordable. Moreover, in situations where the product's local manufacture is not feasible, and therefore compulsory licenses may be ineffective, parallel importation may be a relevant tool to ensure access to drugs.

Notes

1 The views and opinions expressed in this paper are those of the authors and do not necessarily reflect the views or positions of their employers or institutions.
2 https://news.africa-business.com/post/the-changing-face-of-the-pharmaceuticals-market-in-africa
3 India and Bangladesh are very good examples of the positive impact of abolition of product patents. Before TRIPS, India was known for its ability to manufacture and sell patented products at low prices. But after product patent protection, entry of generic firms in the market has been prevented and the MNCs taking advantage of the monopoly patented markets in India are charging exorbitant prices particularly for anti-cancer drugs. But because of the absence of such entry barriers in Bangladesh for example, markets are competitive and local firms there can supply some of these medicines at much cheaper prices. For example, medicines such as Ibrutinib, Osimertinib, Crizotinib, Palbociclib and Tofacitinib are sold in Bangladesh at a fraction of the cost in India (Chaudhuri, 2020).
4 There are many IP frameworks in Africa at continental, regional and national levels. These include for example, the proposed Pan-African Intellectual Property Office, ARIPO, OAPI, and the East African Community Regional Intellectual Property Policy on the Utilization of Public Health-Related WTO-TRIPS Flexibilities and the Approximation of National Intellectual Property Legislation. The plethora of institutions is an indication of the potential overlapping jurisdiction and the inevitable confusion it causes in the trading environment. The AfCFTA IPR Protocol affords AU member states the opportunity to reflect on how best to achieve policy coherence within and among these initiatives. This could harmonize the fragmented IP landscape of today while safeguarding national policy space on key issues, strengthen the hands of African negotiators in international forums and even help propel currently deadlocked international negotiations towards the finish line (Wendland, 2020).
5 The TRIPS Agreement also makes provision for the possibility of further extension upon satisfactory request by LDCs (see Article 66 of TRIPS).
6 There is a need to find a solution to the tendency of some doctors to push patients into buying expensive imported medicines.

References

Adekola, T.A. (2019). Public health oriented intellectual property and trade policies in Africa and the regional mechanism under Trade-Related Aspects of Intellectual Property Rights amendment, The Royal Society for Public Health. Published by Elsevier Ltd.

Ahen, F. and Salo-Ahen, O.M.H. (2018). 'Governing Pharmaceutical Innovations in Africa: Inclusive Models for Accelerating Access to Quality Medicines', Cogent Medicine 5: 1500196.

Chaudhuri, S. (2019). 'Are Medicines High-priced and Unaffordable after TRIPS?: Evidence from Pharmaceutical Industry in India,' Commentary on India's Economy and Society Series, Centre for Development Studies, Trivandrum.

Chaudhuri, S. (2020). *Evolution of the Pharmaceutical Industry in Bangladesh, 1982 to 2020*. Centre for Development Studies, Thiruvananthapuram, Kerala, India, July 2020.

Correa, C. (2000). *Integrating Public Health Concerns into Patent Legislation in Developing Countries. South Center*, Geneva, Switzerland.

Correa, C. (2001). The TRIPS Agreement: How Much Room for Maneuver? Background paper for Human Development Report 2001. United Nations Development Programme, New York.

De Beer, J., J. Baarbé, and C. Ncube (2017). "The Intellectual Property Treaty Landscape in Africa, 1885 to 2015". OpenAIR Working Paper 4.

ECA, AU, AfDB and UNCTAD (2019). Assessing Regional Integration in Africa IX: Next Steps for the African Continental Free Trade Area. Addis Ababa.

Gouda, H.N. et al. (2019) Burden of non-communicable diseases in sub-Saharan Africa, 1990–2017: results from the Global Burden of Disease Study 2017. *Lancet Global Health* 7: e1375–1387.

Karingi, S. (2020). "COVID-19 in Africa: Building resilience through boosting pharmaceutical production and trade", Regional Integration and Trade Division, ECA, presentation at the Peer Learning Group Meeting of the PTPR of Egypt, held virtually on 21 April 2020.

Love, J. (2001). 'Compulsory Licensing Models for State Practice in Developing Countries, Access to Medicine and Compliance with the WTO TRIPS Accord'. Background Paper for Human Development Report 2001. United Nations Development Program, New York.

Oh, C. (2000). TRIPS and Pharmaceuticals: A Case of Corporate Profits over Public Health, *Third World Network*, August–September 2000, pp.1–7.

Oh, C. and Khor, M. (2001). TRIPS, Patents and Access to Medicines: Proposals for Clarification and Reform. *Third World Network Briefing Paper*, June 2001, p.8.

Ombaka, E. (2002). Trade–Related Aspects of Intellectual Property Rights (TRIPS) And Pharmaceuticals, *The Pharmaceutical Program*, Nairobi, Kenya, April 2002.

Owoeye OA. (2014). Compulsory patent licensing and local drug manufacturing capacity in Africa. Bull World Health Organ; 2014. p. 92 (November 2013):214e9. Available from: https://doi.org/10.2471/BLT.13.128413

Peukert, A. (2017). Intellectual property and development–narratives and their empirical validity. *The Journal of World Intellectual Property* 2–23.

Soyeju O. Wabwire J. (2018). The WTO-TRIPS flexibilities on public health: a critical Appraisal of the East African community regional framework, *World Trade Review*, 17(01):145e68.

Subramanian, A. and Watal, J. (2000). 'Can TRIPS Serve as an Enforcement Device for Developing Countries in the WTO?' *Journal of International Economic Law* 3 (3): 403–16.

United Nations Development Programme (UNDP). (2016). How Local Production of Pharmaceuticals Can Be Promoted in Africa: The Case of the United Republic of Tanzania, New York: UNDP.

United Nations Economic Commission for Africa (ECA), OECD. (2020). Africa's Response to COVID-19: What roles for trade, manufacturing and intellectual property? www.oecd.org/coronavirus/policy-responses/africa-s-response-to-covid-19-what-roles-for-trade-manufacturing-and-intellectual-property-73d0dfaf

United Nations Economic Commission for Africa (ECA). (2019). Third Africa Business Forum "Investing in People, Planet and Prosperity", African Continental Free Trade Area: An opportunity to accelerate towards implementation of the 2030 Agenda and Agenda 2063 through pooled procurement of essential safe and quality drugs and products and local pharmaceutical production for the continent, Addis Ababa, Ethiopia.

United Nations Economic Commission for Africa (ECA). (2020). Trade Policies for Africa to Tackle Covid-19, 27 March 2020, Addis Ababa, Ethiopia.

Waning, B., Diedrichsen, E. and Moon, S. 2010. 'A Lifeline to Treatment: The Role of Indian Generic Manufacturers in Supplying Antiretroviral Medicines to Developing Countries,' *Journal of the International AIDS Society*, 13:35.

Wendland. (2020). The Draft Protocol on Intellectual Property Rights to The African Continental Free Trade Agreement (AfCFTA): Annotations on Genetic Resources, Traditional Knowledge and Cultural Expressions.

WHO. (2001). Globalization, TRIPS and Access to Pharmaceuticals. WHO Policy Perspectives on Medicines 3. Geneva.

WHO. (2018). Addressing the global shortage of, and access to, medicines and vaccines. Report by the Director general, World Health Assembly 2018; EB142/13:50.

WTO. (2020). The TRIPS Agreement and COVID-19, information note, 15 October 2020.

Wu, X. and Khazin, B. P. (2020). Patent–Related Actions Taken in WTO Members in Response to the COVID-19 Pandemic, WTO, 21 October 2020.

Index

Printed in the United States
by Baker & Taylor Publisher Services